WARRIORS OF THE WORLD

The
Ancient
Warrior

WARRIORS OF THE WORLD

The Ancient Warrior

3000 BCE–500 CE

MARTIN J. DOUGHERTY

THOMAS DUNNE BOOKS
ST. MARTIN'S PRESS ✿ NEW YORK

Thomas Dunne Books
An imprint of St. Martin's Press

WARRIORS OF THE WORLD
THE ANCIENT WARRIOR 3000 BCE–500 CE

For information, address
St. Martin's Press, 175 Fifth Avenue,
New York, N.Y. 10010.

www.thomasdunnebooks.com
www.stmartins.com

Library of Congress Cataloging-in-Publication Data
on file at the Library of Congress

ISBN-13: 978-0-312-59688-0

Editorial and design by
Amber Books Ltd
Bradley's Close
74–77 White Lion Street
London N1 9PF
United Kingdom
www.amberbooks.co.uk

Project editor: Michael Spilling
Design: Joe Conneally
Picture research: Natascha Spargo
Maps and illustrations: JB Illustrations

Printed in China

First U.S. Edition: March 2010

10 9 8 7 6 5 4 3 2 1

PICTURE CREDITS:

AKG Images: 36bl & 38 (Erich Lessing), 48tr (John Hios), 57 & 86 (Erich Lessing), 156 (Peter Connolly), 191, 209, 212
Art Archive: 23br (Kharbine-Tapabor/Larrieu-Licorne), 51tr (Gianni Dagli Orti/British Museum), 59 (Alfredo Dagli Orti/British Museum), 98/99 (Gianni Dagli Orti/Musée Archéologique, Naples), 100 (Gianni Dagli Orti/Heraklion Museum), 107 (H.M Hergct/NGS Image Collection), 168 (Gianni Dagli Orti/Musée Municipal Sémur en Auxois), 186 (Alfredo Dagli Orti/National Museum, Bucharest), 188/189 (Gianni Dagli Orti/Museo Nazionale Palazzo Altemps, Rome)
Bridgeman Art Library: 16 (Musée du Louvre, Paris), 18 (National Museum of Iran, Tehran), 21 (Iraq Museum, Baghdad), 35 & 113 (Look & Learn), 152 (Pushkin Museum, Moscow)
Corbis: 6/7 (Pierre Colombel), 12/13 (Gianni Dagli Orti), 14 (Gianni Dagli Orti), 15 (David Lees), 22 & 29 (Gianni Dagli Orti), 30 (Gianni Dagli Orti), 36/37 (Thorne Anderson), 44tl & 48l (Gianni Dagli Orti), 62/63 (Gianni Dagli Orti), 66 (Gianni Dagli Orti), 68 (Robert Harding World Imagery), 69 (Gianni Dagli Orti), 70 (Jose Fuste Raga), 82 (Gianni Dagli Orti), 116 & 119tr (Bettmann), 127 (Gianni Dagli Orti)
De Agostini Picture Library: 50 (G. Nimatallah), 54 (C. Sappa), 65 (M. Carrieri), 72, 103 & 117 (G. Dagli Orti), 119bl (G. Dagli Orti), 146 (A. Dagli Orti), 204
Dorling Kindersley: 89 (Max Alexander), 128 & 193 (De Agostini Picture Library)
Dreamstime: 144/145 (Verity Johnson)
Getty Images: 9 (Bridgeman Art Library), 102 (National Geographic), 129 (Bridgeman Art Library), 135 (National Geographic), 163 & 199 (Bridgeman Art Library)
Photos 12: 171 (ARJ), 197tr (Oronoz), 201 (ARJ)
Photos.com: 17, 25, 64, 84, 169
Photoshot: 8 (World Illustrated)
Public Domain: 49

CONTENTS

Introduction

Human history, whether recorded or not, has always been filled with conflict. At the time of the Last Glacial Maximum 20,000 years ago, when the ice sheets reached their greatest extent, humanity was mainly contending against its environment in order to survive. Human populations were small enough that, while conflict between people was certain to occur, there was no need for a specialist social class dedicated to combating fellow humans.

As the ice age came to an end and the glaciers retreated, human numbers expanded in the more hospitable conditions that began to prevail. The availability of food sources also increased, so for a time there was little change in the social order. Hunting was of paramount importance, and both the tools and the techniques of the hunt could be applied to humans as well as animals.

Indeed, as conflict between groups of humans fighting over resources such as good hunting grounds became more common, the methods used were much the same as those of the hunt. Men armed with throwing spears or bows sent projectiles at human targets, perhaps from ambush. Hand-to-hand combat was fought with spears or primitive maces fashioned from a rock and a wooden haft.

◀ **These North African rock paintings showing a battle between two forces of archers date from the fourth millennium BC. It is quite possible the painting depicts a battle between two hunting or war parties, fighting over resources or territory.**

Cave paintings show people fighting with weapons of this sort, and even using defensive technologies. Some images seem to depict men equipped with what amounts to body armour fashioned from bark or hides, and using what appear to be shields.

These defensive technologies are of great interest to us, as they are specific to war-making as opposed to hunting. A spear, club, knife or bow might be obtained or fashioned with hunting in mind and then turned to personal combat, but there are few threats in nature that can be countered by a shield or primitive body armour. Therefore, these items must have been intended to protect against weapons wielded by war parties from other tribes. People do not expend time and effort to create things they are unlikely to need. It is thus reasonable to assume that conflict between humans was common enough to require specialist tools by the time of these paintings, i.e. roughly 10,000 to 5000 years ago.

However, a tribe of hunter-gatherers cannot support individuals whose sole function is the making of war on other humans. Hunters provide food for themselves and others, but for warriors to exist there must be a suitable excess of food to support them. It is unlikely that this could be obtained by raiding other tribes. Thus these primitive warriors must have been hunters who occasionally went to war against other humans.

FROM HUNTER TO WARRIOR

As people began to settle and turned to agriculture to support themselves, a suitable surplus of food gradually became available. This also made settlements a target for raids, as it was easier to steal what was needed than to grow it. Ironically, as people turned to farming rather than hunting, the skills with bow and spear that allowed any hunter to fight other humans were no longer practised by most of the community. As the need to defend what they had grew, most people were too busy farming or crafting to practise the skills they needed to do so.

The typical late Stone Age or early Bronze Age farmer had no need to learn to throw a spear or shoot a bow, and had too many other demands on his time to do it just in case the need arose. Several solutions presented themselves. One was to protect the

▼ **A Neolithic rock painting from the seventh millennium BC shows two groups of warriors fighting with spears and shields.**

settlement with some form of fortifications, making it harder for an attacker. Methods ranged from ditches, stockades and barricades to building a settlement on piles driven into a lakebed.

These passive measures helped somewhat by giving advantages to the people within the settlement, but an obstacle that was not actively defended would not stop a determined attacker. Of course, anyone could grab or improvise a weapon of some kind and try to fight, especially if the alternative was a grisly death. However, most societies evolved a social class whose duties included (and in some cases were solely restricted to) defending their own community and harming those of others.

In many societies these individuals became the basis of a warrior aristocracy, perhaps simply due to their ability to impose their will on others by force. Although details varied considerably from one region to another, the usual military organization of these settlements was to have a small group of well-armed individuals who engaged in some kind of training for war, backed up by the rest of the population with lesser weapons and fighting as best they could.

Not all cultures adopted the model of warrior as protector and ruler, but it became the basis for many emerging states as the general population of humans increased and organizations larger than a single agricultural settlement began to emerge.

THE MAKING OF WAR

The role of the warrior is, of course, to fight and defeat other combatants. However, this must serve some greater purpose if it is to be more than self-indulgent mayhem. The most obvious and immediate purpose is to drive off raiders and other attackers. This probably should not be considered war-making as such; simply driving off raids as they occur is more self-defence than military activity.

However, once a measure of military capability became available, it was possible to use force for strategic purposes. This might include taking stockpiled resources from another settlement, gaining control over a key area, capturing slaves or eliminating a threat by destroying the military and/or economic capabilities of another group.

BRONZE AGE WEAPONRY
This collection of Neolithic to early Bronze Age weapon heads includes a Danish flint leaf-shaped dagger and black stone battle axe and a Scandinavian stone macehead dating from 2500–1000 BC.

There are two ends that can be served by the making of war – strengthening the community or weakening another. These usually overlap to some extent, not least because a society that cripples its rivals can turn its attention to other projects without having to worry so much about security.

War-making and diplomacy go hand-in-hand. A community that obviously has the capability to repel invaders or to send its forces to harm its neighbours is less likely to be troubled by raids, and may find that the words of its emissaries carry a great deal of weight. Similarly, a weak society is likely to be preyed upon by others, or at least subjected to onerous demands by stronger neighbours.

When military forces clashed, the defeat of one side or the other was a useful bargaining chip in any negotiations that might follow, but the goal of warfare, especially in the Ancient World, was rarely simply to defeat the enemy in battle. It was far more common to plunder whatever could be carried off and destroy what could not.

'Laying waste' in this manner was a common feature of ancient warfare. It was not mere spite; it was good strategy. If the economic base of the opposition was damaged by burning crops, killing people or destroying property, this directly impacted the ability of that society to make war. Punishing enemies in this manner made other potential foes think carefully about whether the conflict was worth what might happen.

If this sort of strategy seems primitive, it might be compared to a modern nation crippling another's industrial capabilities with air strikes and cruise missiles. The principle is no different; laying waste to an area reduced the enemy's capability to equip and support troops, and ensured that a victory won quickly in a fight had a long-term strategic benefit.

Of course, given that many leaders of ancient societies were warriors and had to expend resources to maintain their military forces, it was only natural that they sought some

◀ The Seleucid hoplite was trained to fight in a Macedonian-style phalanx. However, his equipment reflects both Greek and Roman influences: the traditional small shield of the phalangite has been replaced by a circular imitation of the Roman *scutum*.

additional return from their expenditure. This could be obtained by raiding, demanding tribute or gaining territory by conquest. Thus a state founded on the principle of the warrior élite tended to find ways to use its military strength. Success resulted in greater power, creating a cycle of increasing capability. However, nothing lasts forever and sooner or later these great military empires of the Ancient World met with a greater power or slid into decline and eclipse.

THE NATURE OF MILITARY FORCES

All military forces are the product of many influences; some social, some economic, some political and some technological. The weaponry available and the nature of the threat likely to be faced will dictate the general nature of a military force, with economic and social factors shaping its form.

Some societies preferred to keep military capability in the hands of a small group of professionals, who usually formed part of the ruling élite or at least had a vested interest in ensuring its continuation. Such societies tended to have a small group of trained warriors equipped to as high a standard as possible, often backed up by a larger number of ill-equipped troops of marginal capability.

In other areas, the concept of the citizen-soldier took root. This was advantageous in some ways, as it allowed large forces to be raised. If each man were responsible for providing his own equipment the drain on the general economy was slight. However, training levels for non-professionals can never be very high. Nor can citizen-soldiers afford to be long away from their workplaces and farms. Not only can a long campaign be personally ruinous, the effects on the national economy may be devastating.

The choice of weapons and equipment was often dictated by technological or economic factors. Axe-heads, for example, are easier to produce than sword blades. Other factors may also be involved. A group of ill-trained levies is more likely to stay and fight if packed into a dense mass than if the same number of individuals is scattered all across the battlefield. Spears are an excellent choice for troops intended to fight in close order. Therefore, the choice of the spear

▶ The Assyrians employed cavalry from the ninth century, primarily to act as scouts and skirmishers. Chariots were very much preferred by the Mesopotamians and Egyptians, and cavalry only became a significant force in Ancient warfare with the advent of Scythian horse archers from the fourth century BC.

or pike as a weapon for infantry may not be due to its all-conquering capabilities; it may be dictated by the nature of the troops involved. Or it may simply be that spears are cheap and easy to manufacture.

For example, the phalanx of hoplites used by the Greek city-states was not invented and implemented because a design committee thought it would be all-powerful. Hoplite warfare evolved out of social and economic factors prevailing at the time. Conflicts between city-states needed to be resolved quickly so that the citizen-soldiers could get back to their normal economic activities. In the terrain of Greece there was a limited number of routes an army could take, so it was possible to intercept invaders, fight a quick and decisive battle, and get home again with minimum disruption to the economy.

In order to field the requisite numbers, a system of citizen-soldiery was used which precluded intensive military training. Thus organization and tactics had to be simple. A phalanx of spearmen fulfilled all these requirements and in addition was quite capable of defeating another phalanx fighting in the same manner. Indeed, there was little that could stand up to the head-on charge of a phalanx except another phalanx of equivalent size.

So long as everyone was playing the same game, the conventional rules of phalanx warfare prevailed. The side that charged home most vigorously and kept pushing the other back would win. But a phalanx could be beaten by an enemy that fought differently.

Other Greek city-states would not do so; they were subject to the same factors that made phalanx warfare a first choice.

However, outsiders from beyond Greece had their own ways of fighting. A Roman legion that tried to stand and take the charge of a phalanx was doomed, but one whose commander played to his strengths could out-manoeuvre the phalanx, break it up and destroy it. Once the phalanx met the legion, it became apparent which was superior. The Greeks did not choose to adopt an inferior fighting system, however; they evolved a system that fitted their needs and was shaped by the various factors at play at the time.

And so it was with all ancient military systems. They evolved out of internal factors and were modified by external ones, i.e. the nature of the foes they faced. Those states whose military systems best fitted their needs became dominant, at least until internal factors caused a decline and they were eclipsed by the next ascendant power.

CHAPTER 1

Mesopotamia: Birthplace of the Warrior

Mesopotamia is rightly known as the Cradle of Civilization, but it was also the birthplace of the first organized military systems. This was not due to innate barbarism in humans; quite the opposite. An effective military system is an absolute necessity for the creation of a great civilization.

As humans moved from a nomadic existence based on subsistence to a settled way of life that produced a surplus of some items, larger social structures became possible. Not only could settlements grow to be much larger than a band of nomadic hunters, but those settlements could forge links with others.

Nomadic groups would of course meet up from time to time. There is evidence that primitive nomadic people arranged meetings annually or every so many years for ceremonial and social reasons as well as to trade items and to intermarry between the groups. However, formal trade was only really possible between settled groups.

A fixed settlement can be founded at any time, facilitating regular or irregular trade. More importantly, a fixed settlement has access only to resources found in its locality. Any item or

◀ **The Stele of Vultures (c. 2600 BC) is a Sumerian limestone bas-relief found in Ngirsu. A section of it shows a tight phalanx of Sumerian soldiers armed with long spears and protected by helmets and shields trampling their opponents.**

commodity that is lacking must be obtained elsewhere. Initially this allows settlements to survive, but those that have a surplus of something needed elsewhere, and who trade wisely, will begin to prosper and gain in power.

MILITARY CAPABILITY IN EARLY CIVILIZATIONS

Some early civilizations were based on trade, and even those that took a direct approach to obtaining what they needed — i.e. raiding and outright conquest —

needed to move goods around. Trade also took place even in the most aggressive society.

These trade routes needed protection against raiders and hostile societies, creating an increased need for some sort of military system even in states that had no interest in conquest and expansion.

Thus military capability tended to go hand-in-hand with the development of a culture. While agricultural surplus and the movement of necessary goods by means of trade made a society above the subsistence level possible, military force was necessary for it to survive. A body of warriors could repel hostile invasions, protect the trade routes and settlements, and enforce the will of the rulers.

Of course, warriors produce no direct economic benefit unless they are constantly employed in plundering resources from elsewhere. However, their contribution is very real. Military force and the will to use it helps in creating stability, which is vital to the economic business of agriculture, crafting and trade.

It is one thing, however, to have a group of armed men available to fight at need, and quite another to deploy an effective military force. One key advantage that an early civilization had over a collection of small settlements was the ability to concentrate force on a problem, and move on to something else when it was dealt with.

This required more than individual training and possession of decent weaponry. A force had to be organized, commanded, fed and supplied. This required the creation of a military system — an army and its supporting and administrative apparatus — rather than just a collection of armed individuals.

The progression is logical and obvious. As a society grew, it required not only more

◄ **This Hittite stele depicts a merchant, as denoted by the scales he holds. One critical task for early armies was keeping the trade routes open.**

▲ The art of fortification accompanied the rise of organized militaries, offering security to a settled community. These ruins form part of the ancient walls of Ur.

warriors but a more effective military system to deploy and support them. This in turn often led to new ideas and techniques that benefited society at large. Roads, storehouses and workshops built to support the military often had benefits for the populace in general. The benefits of a good military system thus went beyond the admittedly important advantage of not having fields and homes burned and people put to the sword by invaders.

Communities and states facing the threat of raids or military action would often protect themselves by constructing defences around the city or settlement. If it seemed that victory in a field battle was not likely, the defenders could retire inside the safety of their walls. Thus, increasing military capability on the part of early civilizations forced a move towards fortification as a counter.

Village Fortifications

Even a fairly small settlement was capable of creating some kind of fortifications, and larger cities were often defended by quite extensive walls and other defensive works. For a mere band of raiders, a fortified city was not worth the cost of mounting a raid, especially since the likely outcome was a large number of casualties for no gain. A good set of walls might deter raids for profit, but war between cities or states was another matter. Political necessity or the desire for conquest might force a state to mount an attack on a walled city.

An enemy that hid in its fortresses when attacked, sallying out to launch raids when the conditions were right, was a severe threat that could only be eliminated by attacking and conquering its fortified places. The capability to conduct siege warfare was essential if this were not to result in prohibitively high casualties.

It might be possible to starve a city into submission, or to gain entry by stealth or treachery. The only other option was assault. Techniques had to be developed to reduce the defences of a city or to get over, under or through them. Siege warfare became a vital part of early military capability, especially when dealing with enemies that refused to come out and be defeated in the field.

However, siege warfare required taking military organization and logistics to a whole new level. Military forces engaged in a siege would be required to remain in the field for extended periods and undertake large-scale engineering works whilst in the face of the enemy. This required a standard of organization far above that needed to fight a skirmish against a rival tribe or raiders from another town.

Thus the development of an effective military system was very much the hallmark of an emerging civilization, and is inextricably linked with the rise of even the most unaggressive of societies. The ancient warrior was not merely a political tool of these emerging

states; he was part of a large and organized fighting force that was utterly indispensable to any civilization that wanted to survive.

In many ways, the early civilizations were defined by their military system as much as by any other factor.

THE RISE OF SUMER

The greatest of the early civilizations arose on the fertile lands around three great rivers: the Tigris-Euphrates, the Indus and the Nile. Other river valleys were home to lesser societies. Most of the rivers of the region now occupied by Pakistan and Iraq had some kind of society that can be considered a minor civilization. However, these were not tied into a large economic or military system and remained of lesser importance during the gradual rise of the world's first great civilizations.

It is generally accepted that the first civilization arose in southern Mesopotamia. By 3500 BC there

▲ These Elamites are armed with slings, an effective missile weapon favoured by many tribal peoples. Slings were used for hunting and to protect herds, honing skills that could be used in war.

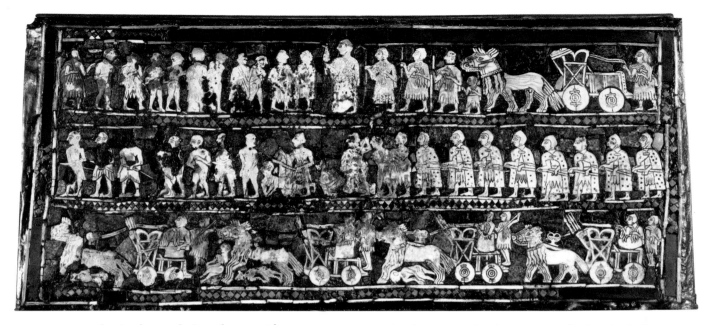

was an urbanized population there, with access to written script and sufficient resources to build large structures not connected to immediate subsistence needs. The people of this civilization were Sumerians, who had arrived in the area as nomads a few centuries earlier and supplanted the local population.

The Sumerians inherited a system of irrigation from the previous inhabitants, and improved upon it to not only enhance their agricultural capability but also to provide transportation for produce. This laid the foundations for a civilization based around a dozen or more large cities, each acting as the hub for an outlying region of smaller towns and villages.

For about 700 years from 3000 BC onwards, the cities of Sumer were in a state of near-constant warfare among themselves and with foreign enemies. Internal conflict was brought to an end by Sargon the Great, who united Sumer into what amounted to a military dictatorship.

Among the enemies of Sumer were the Elamites of what is now northern Iran. Conflict had probably been ongoing for centuries before the first recorded incidence, in 2700 BC. Constant warfare resulted in rapid progress in the technique and the technology of war-making. Records from 2600 BC

▲ **Dating from around 2600–2400 BC, the Standard of Ur depicts light troops, infantry protected by armoured cloaks and early chariots or war carts. Lighter, faster chariots were developed later in history.**

reveal that the kings of the Sumerian city-states maintained a standing force of a few hundred professional soldiers, and that their equipment was uniform. These men did not fight with what they had; they were issued standard equipment at the king's expense.

Equipment and Organization

Carvings dating from 2525 BC depict a conflict between the city-states of Lagash and Umma. The king of Lagash is depicted as riding in a chariot and being armed with an axe, but at that time the armies of Sumer were dominated by foot-soldiers. Chariots were a new invention and had not been developed to the point where they were an effective fighting platform. The main combat arm was the infantry.

The city-states of Sumer are recorded as maintaining a few hundred professional soldiers, but they were capable of raising much larger armies at need. However, the standard tactical formation was a tight phalanx, eight men across the front and six deep.

Fighting in a close-order formation of this sort required formal training, so it is likely that additional forces would be lightly equipped and used to support the professional soldiers rather than attempting to emulate them.

The professional infantry were equipped with spears or pikes as their main weapon. Personal protection took the form of bronze body

▼ A selection of sword and dagger blades used by the Elamites. A small bladed weapon made an ideal sidearm; easy to carry yet deadly at close quarters.

armour and a helmet of copper with leather padding. Early versions of the armour amounted to a cloak sewn with metal discs. Although poor by the standard of armour adopted later, this still provided good protection against the weapons of the period.

Indeed, this adoption of rather basic body armour caused a revolution in weapon design. In the Stone Age, a heavy weight in the form of a stone (possibly shaped to give some semblance of a point or edge) attached to a stick, was a basic and effective hand weapon. As metalworking became prevalent, the stone axe was replaced by either a mace with a head of metal, or an axe with a metal blade.

Types of Axes

The first metal axes simply used a haft tied to the head rather than passing into a socket on it. This was entirely sufficient for braining unarmoured men or smashing their bones, but once metal body armour and helmets became common these early axes became obsolete. They were incapable of penetrating armour; indeed the axe head was prone to come off the shaft upon contact with something solid.

Around 2500 BC the Sumerians developed the socket axe, which was something of a superweapon in its day. Rather than being tied on with thongs, the head was securely fixed onto a haft that ran through the stone itself. Alterations to the shape of the head created a weapon that reliably concentrated force behind a penetrating edge and did not fly apart upon striking armour.

Axes of this sort were effective against body armour and remained a standard close-combat weapon for millennia. The weapons wielded by Saxon house-carls or the knights of the Middle Ages were little different in terms of basic design. The development of protection to defeat the hand axe, and the modification of

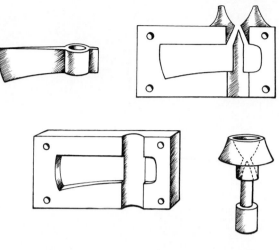

SUMERIAN AXEMAN AND AN AXE MOULD
Requiring a special mould to cast its head, the socket axe wielded by this Sumerian enables him to penetrate an opponent's armour. His head is protected from a mace or club attack while his shield defends against arrows or hand weapons.

the axe to penetrate the new armour, may represent the world's first example of the eternal race between offensive and defensive technologies.

Protected by their armour and armed with spear and socket axe, the armies of the Sumerian city-states made war upon one another and also upon outsiders. Captured enemies were enslaved, and it was not uncommon for the military forces of a city-state to launch raids specifically to gather slaves.

Many of the opponents of the Sumerian city-states were technologically unsophisticated. Sumer was the world's first civilization and enjoyed massive

advantages over outsiders. These included the obvious superiorities in weapons and military organization but also resources. Sumerian city-states could afford to support an organized campaign where less civilized groups were restricted to simple raiding and tribal warfare.

In this respect, Sumer was making a wholly new form of war. In Neolithic or uncivilized Bronze Age societies, conflict often involved the whole tribe or community, with large numbers of people fighting as best they could but not in a very coherent manner. Sumer instead sent small bodies of highly trained and well organized professionals out to fight. The rest of the population were still involved of course, but their involvement took the form of working at their normal occupations and contributing to the resources of the city-state, which then used those resources to support the army.

This meant, among other things, that each Sumerian warrior was vastly more capable than a tribesman who turned his hand to fighting. Sumerian

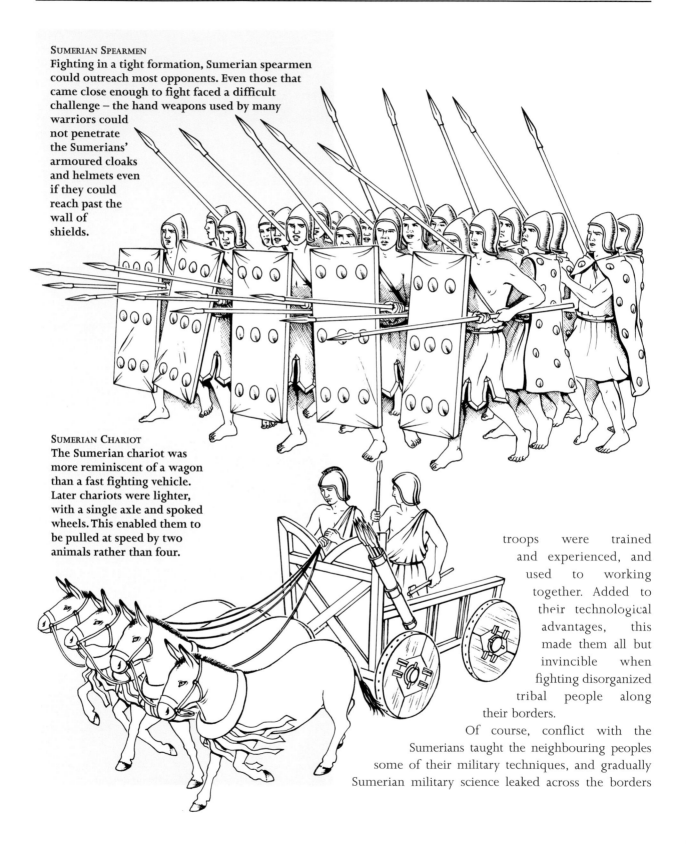

SUMERIAN SPEARMEN
Fighting in a tight formation, Sumerian spearmen could outreach most opponents. Even those that came close enough to fight faced a difficult challenge – the hand weapons used by many warriors could not penetrate the Sumerians' armoured cloaks and helmets even if they could reach past the wall of shields.

SUMERIAN CHARIOT
The Sumerian chariot was more reminiscent of a wagon than a fast fighting vehicle. Later chariots were lighter, with a single axle and spoked wheels. This enabled them to be pulled at speed by two animals rather than four.

troops were trained and experienced, and used to working together. Added to their technological advantages, this made them all but invincible when fighting disorganized tribal people along their borders.

Of course, conflict with the Sumerians taught the neighbouring peoples some of their military techniques, and gradually Sumerian military science leaked across the borders and out into the wider world. But most neighbouring states lacked the resources to make use of this knowledge, at least initially.

SARGON THE GREAT AND THE AKKADIANS

Historical sources, notably the Tablets of Shuruppak (records maintained on clay tablets in the city of Shuruppak, possibly the largest grain storage centre in Mesopotamia, which have survived thanks to being 'baked' hard by a huge fire in the city in around 2350 BC), suggest that the city-states of Sumer could support a population of around 30–35,000 people including outlying settlements and farms. This was more than enough to support a reasonably large army, but instead the city-states maintained a small standing force. They may have been able to raise much greater armies at need, and probably had a system in place for doing so.

By 2400 BC, the functions of king as civic ruler and the priesthood as spiritual leaders and advisors had been differentiated. Previously, kings had a major religious role which was gradually shifted to a formal priesthood. This left the ruler in charge of commerce, industry, construction and, of course, warfare.

In his capacity as ruler and war-leader, King Lugalzagesi of Umma established dominance over Sumer. His empire did not bring about any large-scale changes; the city-states retained their essential identity and way of life.

Around 2270 BC, a challenge arose to the rule of Lugalzagesi in the form of Sargon, whose origins are shrouded in mystery. It seems likely that he was the son of a priestess, and while his father is named in some sources, others specifically state that his identity was unknown. Sargon became an official at the court of Kish, eventually becoming its king by means that remain obscure. It was as King of Kish that Sargon began his campaign against the empire of Lugalzegesi. His first target was Uruk.

▲ The *electrum* helmet of King Mes-Kalem-Dug, dating from 2500–2400 BC. By this time, the king's religious role had been eroded, and his main function was as political and military leader.

Sargon is recorded as having dismantled the walls of Uruk after conquering the city. Sargon conquered a great many cities in a short time; too short to have starved the defenders into submission each time. He must therefore have possessed the means to breach their walls, i.e. some kind of siege train and knowledge of how to conduct a siege.

Sargon's campaign took him all the way to the Persian Gulf and won him dominance over all of Sumer. Some cities were laid waste; others were incorporated into the empire. He is also credited with the building of the city of Akkad (Agade), although other sources suggest that Akkad existed before the time of Sargon. If this is the case then presumably he undertook an expansion of the city, perhaps in preparation for making it his capital. In any case,

▶ **The stele of Naram-Sin depicts a successful siege. The attackers appear to have built ramps to attack the fortifications, a common practice throughout the ancient world.**

Sargon became known as Sargon of Akkad and his people as Akkadians.

Sargon expanded his empire by force, becoming the ruler of a united Mesopotamia. He pushed his empire out to the Mediterranean Sea and into Anatolia, and even as far south as modern Oman. The Akkadian empire was ruled directly by Sargon, with an efficient system of officials and bureaucrats to oversee his domains. The Akkadian army was Sargon's political instrument, making his empire a contender for the title of the world's first military dictatorship.

Sargon is recorded as fighting 34 wars in his 54-year reign. At first these were wars of conquest and expansion, though many later conflicts were fought to protect Akkadian holdings or trade routes.

Sargon's empire was founded on a sound economic base, with river, sea and land trade bringing in a large income. The importance of this economic base did not go unrecognized so the Akkadians built a chain of fortresses to protect their main grain-farming regions. This focus on trade and productive activity provided additional impetus to the creation of an imperial bureaucracy.

The Akkadian empire was culturally and linguistically diverse, incorporating several areas and city-states with a strong identity of their own. The Akkadian language became a *lingua franca* for trade and diplomacy while the system of bureaucracy and officials helped maintain order and stability.

The empire was thus sufficiently well organized to respond to any threat whilst keeping the majority of its people content, at least most of the time. Threats were not uncommon, ranging from external invasion to internal rebellion. In the last years of his life, Sargon was besieged in his capital by the forces of a large-scale revolt against him. He was able to defeat these forces and re-establish stability until his death, which is normally dated at 2215 BC.

Equipment and Organization

Sargon inherited a military system that was fairly typical for the time; a body of professional troops with armour and helmets, equipped with spears and trained to fight in a tight phalanx-like formation. These would have been backed up with levies or conscripts armed with weapons requiring less training.

In the course of Sargon's campaign of conquest, his troops would quickly gain experience, but their numbers would be insufficient to hold down an expanding empire. It is likely that Sargon recruited the forces of conquered city-states to augment his initial force. This practice was followed by later empires. It is likely that troops from one region would be sent to serve in or garrison another, to decrease the chances of a revolt.

Some sources suggest that Sargon the Great commanded a standing army of 5400 men. This was far more than any single city-state could maintain in the long term, though it would be possible to raise a similar army in the short term. Such a force would be no match for Sargon's veterans in terms of training, experience and equipment.

The Akkadian army was of necessity dispersed into regional forces, which could at need supply troops to a

AKKADIAN ARCHER
The professional core of the Akkadian army was supported by large numbers of lightly equipped irregulars, many of whom used bows or javelins. These men were scantily trained but brought the skills of the hunt to the battlefield as skirmishers.

▲ **This Akkadian axe is designed to concentrate the force of a blow behind the head, punching deep into the target despite any protection it may have.**

field army. The logistical effort involved in equipping, maintaining and manoeuvring these forces was considerable, but the Akkadians had the advantage of a well-established bureaucracy which could be expanded and amended to fit the needs of a military empire.

The Akkadians were forced to undertake a great many sieges of fortified cities. Indeed, writings of the period speak of sieges as the tools of statecraft, implying that warfare was a near-constant part of Akkadian foreign and internal policies.

At some point, the Akkadians introduced a revolutionary new weapon, the composite bow. This was probably during the reign of Naram-Sin, Sargon's grandson. Bows had been in use in warfare for centuries but the much more advanced composite bow was capable of shooting further and penetrating the armour of the time at ranges of up to 100m (91 yards) or more.

The Akkadians adopted a mobile style of combat, using their lightly equipped bowmen to shoot holes in the solid pike formations of their opponents, which could then be exploited by close-order infantry to defeat the enemy by shock action.

> "AFTERWARD IN HIS OLD AGE ALL THE LANDS REVOLTED AGAINST HIM, AND THEY BESIEGED HIM IN AKKAD, AND SARGON WENT FORTH TO BATTLE AND DEFEATED THEM; HE ACCOMPLISHED THEIR OVERTHROW, AND THEIR WIDESPREADING HOST HE DESTROYED."
>
> **CHRONICLE OF EARLY KINGS**

These tactics worked very well against the Sumerian style of combat, with its tight formations of close-packed infantry. Those formations had been a battle-winning innovation earlier, and for a time the only counter was to field similar bodies of close-order armoured infantry. The technological innovation of the composite bow allowed the Akkadians to implement a form of combined-arms warfare that gave them significant advantages on the battlefield.

This combination of firepower and shock action required a high degree of training to be fully effective, but the armies of Akkad were composed of highly experienced professionals. In terms of organization, logistics, tactics, weaponry and personal protection the armies of Akkad represented a high point in military development. Indeed, it was not until the invention of the musket and socket bayonet that the 'pike and bow' or 'pike and shot' model of infantry warfare became truly obsolete, over 3500 years later.

THE FALL OF AKKAD AND THE RISE OF THE BABYLONIAN EMPIRE

The Akkadian empire rose in a number of revolts upon Sargon's death, as various regions sought independence or to exploit the situation. However, his sons were able to put down the revolts and gradually restored the empire to stability. However, from around 2150 BC onwards the Gutians, probably originating in the Zagros mountains, began to overrun the Akkadian empire.

The Gutians did not invade and conquer Akkad, but launched a series of raids over many years. They avoided open battle with the superior forces of Akkad and instead caused economic damage by pillaging and 'laying waste'. This was a fairly common tactic in tribal warfare; a tribe whose lands were less able to support them was weakened in the long term and could be eventually conquered or driven off, or at least rendered a lesser threat for a generation or so.

It is likely that at this time the Akkadians were weakened by plague or famine. Even before the foundation of the Akkadian empire, the Sumerians had begun to suffer from salination of their farmlands; the Akkadians inherited this problem. Coupled with the disruption and economic damage caused by the raids and possible revolts within the empire, Akkad was gradually weakened until the Gutians were able to overrun most of its northern territory.

▶ **Sargon the Great stands before the tree of life. Kings in Mesopotamia were not just seen as powerful men but as superhuman figures backed up by the gods.**

Akkad itself was destroyed, and its former location has never been established by modern archaeologists. The Gutians conquered most of northern

AMORITE NOBLEMAN
Once they had come to dominate Babylon, the Amorites developed a highly organized, prosperous urban civilization under the world's first known formal system of laws. Among their other innovations was the concept of a kingdom containing several cities rather than a loose collection of city-states.

Mesopotamia, though some of the city-states remained independent. In the south, the city-states formerly of Sumeria were able to buy off the invaders with tribute and began to regain their power.

The Sumerians enjoyed a brief resurgence from around 2050 BC. They made war on the Gutians and drove them from northern Mesopotamia, but were then attacked by Amorites from the west and Elamites from the east. By 1950 BC the cities of Sumer were being sacked by the invaders, marking the end of the Sumerian era.

The Amorites were a nomadic people, but some settled on the banks of the Euphrates and became associated with the city of Babylon. By this time, the population of Mesopotamia was greatly diminished as a result of poorer agricultural conditions.

It has been claimed that Babylon was founded by Sargon the Great, but this seems unlikely. It is possible that these references are to Sargon II of the Neo-Assyrian empire, who undertook restoration of the city at a later date. Since Sargon's capital, Akkad, has never been found it is sometimes theorized that Babylon was essentially built on top of Akkad, and that its ruins lie underneath.

More probably, the city of Babylon grew gradually from humble beginnings on the fertile banks of the Euphrates River. By 2300 BC it was a major city, but like much of the region was overrun by the Amorites, some of whom settled there.

The Amorite kings of Babylon included Hammurabi (c.1792–1750 BC), famous for his code of laws. Hammurabi is known to have allied with Larsa to fend of an invasion by the Elamites. He then turned on his former ally and defeated Larsa. An alliance with Mari followed, leading to the defeat of Assur. Babylon immediately betrayed this ally too, adding to its empire. Campaigns against other city-states of Mesopotamia and the tribal lands beyond followed, resulting in a Babylonian empire stretching from the Persian Gulf to Harran.

These conquests brought with them new problems. A border with the Hittite empire in the north was created, resulting in more conflict. Meanwhile independent realms to the south of

Babylonia launched raids, as did the tribes of the Zagros Mountains. Babylonian military power was gradually eroded until, around 1595 BC, the Hittites were able to march along the Euphrates and sack Babylon itself.

Babylon then became the territory of the Kassites, a tribal people who adopted many aspects of Babylonian culture and gradually evolved into a new generation of Babylonians. Babylon spent the next few hundred years in eclipse, independent but of limited importance.

THE HITTITES

The Hittite people created an empire in Anatolia and Syria, and came into conflict with the Mesopotamian civilizations. They were a Bronze Age people, but were capable of manufacturing small quantities of iron goods as early as 2000 BC. Hittite warriors fought with bronze weapons like their opponents, as iron was too expensive.

The first period of Hittite history is normally known as the Old Kingdom (1750–1500 BC). Towards the end of this period, the Hittites were sufficiently powerful to be able to advance through Mesopotamia and sack Babylon, though they did not remain as conquerors. The second period, 1500–1430 BC, is known as the Middle Hittite Kingdom and was a time of relative weakness.

The New Hittite Kingdom (1430–1180 BC) saw a resurgence of Hittite power, leading to expansion into Syria and Canaan. This brought about conflict with Egypt, notably the battle of Kadesh in 1274 BC. During this period the Hittites were weakened by internal conflict and raided by the Sea Peoples. The Hittite Empire gradually collapsed, with only remnant states surviving long enough to be absorbed into the Assyrian Empire.

The Hittites also made good use of chariots. The horses of the time were not strong enough to bear a rider into combat, though they were sometimes used by messengers. However, even a pair of quite small ponies could pull a chariot.

HITTITE CHARIOT
The Hittite chariot was fast yet robust enough to carry two warriors in addition to the driver. The use of spoked wheels greatly lightened the vehicle. Experimentation over many years demonstrated that the centrally-mounted axle was less efficient than a rear-mounted one.

HITTITE INFANTRY
Although lightly equipped by some standards, these Hittite warriors are moving as an organized body rather than a collection of individuals. The sight of well-drilled formations could be very intimidating to an enemy who doubted his chances of success.

Chariots were primarily important for the mobility they afforded. A Hittite army could strike swiftly at a weak point, retreat from a bad situation, transfer reserves around the battlefield and take advantage of an opportunity much more readily than a force composed entirely of infantry.

It is possible that the Hittites may have been the first people to use chariots in warfare, but the concept was soon adopted by the armies of Egypt, Canaan and Mesopotamia. Chariots fell out of common use once cavalry emerged, since troops mounted on horses could provide all the advantages of chariotry without the extra logistics and maintenance drain associated with keeping chariots in good working order.

Equipment and Organization

The main striking force of the Hittite army was composed of charioteers. Before around 1380 BC and after 1180 BC, a light chariot was in use, normally crewed by a driver and an archer or javelinman. These chariots functioned much like the horse archers of later periods, advancing rapidly to within shooting range, delivering a missile attack, and then speeding off before the enemy could effectively respond.

Other chariots were crewed by a driver and a warrior equipped with a long spear. Their role was primarily one of harassment and skirmishing, making hit-and-run attacks. The mode of combat was often what amounted to a drive-by spearing, with the warrior exploiting the length of this weapon to strike from beyond his enemy's reach and the chariot carrying the crew to relative safety before any retaliation could be mounted.

Used in numbers, these chariot-mounted spearmen could cause great confusion, throwing up a cloud of dust out of which chariot teams darted to make an attack before vanishing again. This kind of swarm attack could be very confusing and demoralizing to an enemy, wearing down his troops without exposing the Hittites to great risk.

However, from around 1380 to 1180 BC, the Hittites switched to using their chariots for shock action. A heavier chariot was in use, crewed by a driver and either two spearmen or one spearman and a shield-bearer. These chariots were used for massed attacks, using their mass to smash a hole in the enemy line. Ideally each chariot would break through the enemy line, its crew striking around them, and then move clear before rallying for another charge, since a chariot that became stuck in the middle of an enemy formation could be swarmed by infantrymen.

Infantry were not always present in Hittite armies. When they were deployed, it was in support of the chariots in open country, or as a substitute in rougher terrain. Infantry were typical of Bronze Age soldiery; a mix of spearmen and javelinmen or archers, plus troops armed with the sickle-sword, which became a standard sidearm in the period.

The infantry could serve as protection for the chariots if they were repulsed, allowing the mobile chariots to pull back and regroup while the infantry held off the enemy, or could exploit a gap in the enemy line made by the heavy chariot charge.

THE HURRIANS

Like the Hittites, the Hurrians are sometimes credited with the introduction of the chariot into warfare. Some historians have stated that the Hittites developed their own chariot forces as a counter to those of the Hurrians. It is also possible that the Hurrians were responsible for the introduction of horses into the region, around 2000 BC.

The Hurrians arrived in northern Mesopotamia around 2500 BC, probably from the north. They were well established in the region by the time of the Akkadian empire, with a number of small kingdoms and city-states. Their fortunes rose and fell as they clashed with the Hittites, Amorites and other rivals.

Originally, the various Hurrian tribes and city-states of the region were disunited and warred upon one another frequently. However, after the sack of

▲ This Hittite archer is depicted with a helmet, a sword and a bow. He is thus more likely to be part of an organized force than an irregular.

Babylon and the general decline of the Sumerian city-states, the Hurrians became more unified and took advantage of the weakness of their neighbours.

The most important Hurrian kingdom was Mitanni, which ruled an area centred mainly in what is now Syria between 1500–1300 BC. Like many states of the period, the Mitanni used a feudal system whereby a warrior nobility ruled and led the armies in time of war. At the height of their power, the Mitanni controlled very important trade routes along the Tigris and Euphrates, extending their influence far south into Mesopotamia.

The Hittites to the north were able to contain the Mitanni advances, but elsewhere they became dominant. Assyria became a vassal state along with other neighbours. However, Egyptian advances into the region brought about a series of conflicts. The most notable of these was the battle of Megiddo in 1457 BC.

Although defeated at Megiddo, the Mitanni did not cede rulership to the Egyptians. Some regions became Egyptian territory, but Mitanni power was undiminished. Indeed, additional territories were gained by conquest. Eventually, the Mitanni made peace with Egypt and arranged dynastic marriages with the Pharaohs.

Like the Hittites, the Mitanni used chariots as their main striking arm. This gave them an advantage over the predominantly infantry armies of many local states and tribes, but against the sophisticated Egyptian and Hittite forces the contest was more equal.

Mitanni power was broken by a civil war over succession to the throne, which allowed the Hittites to overrun their northern vassals. Foreign influence, notably from Assyria and the Hittites, exacerbated internal conflicts until eventually the Mitanni capital was overrun by a Hittite army.

TRIBAL WARFARE

As humans moved from the Stone Age to the Bronze Age, it became possible to field forces supplied with efficient weapons and protective equipment. Even nomadic tribes were able to obtain or manufacture metal tools and weapons, though these were often limited in both quality and quantity.

The complex large-scale metalworking required to construct advanced armour and weapons required a large

◄ A Hittite king crushes his enemies beneath the wheels of his chariot. This was not just a figure of speech; rulers and great nobles led the chariot forces in person.

population to support the metalworkers as well as the infrastructure to transport raw materials. Many of the people of Mesopotamia and the lands to the north and west belonged to tribes that built small towns and villages and traded among them, but lacked the organization of a true state. Thus while the city-states and nations of the region could produce good armour and weapons, the tribal cultures could not. Nor could they, as a rule, trade for advanced weaponry except in the smallest quantities.

Weapons

Thus while a tribal leader and his immediate followers might have good weapons and some armour, the average villager or tribesman was simply armed. The commonest weapon was a short spear with a bronze head. Cheap and easy to make, a spear allowed the warrior to deliver a killing thrust from beyond the reach of most hand weapons.

Spears are very basic weapons in many ways, but they are no less effective for that. Impaling weapons are, on average, more lethal than slashing or crushing implements, though a thrust may miss completely where a swung weapon might make at least a glancing contact. At close quarters, however, spears are more awkward to use than a dagger or hand axe.

Daggers and knives were often carried as a tool that could also serve as a last-ditch personal weapon. Although lacking reach, a dagger thrust can be just as lethal as a spear, and may be easier to deliver at close quarters or in the press of combat.

Hand axes and sickle-swords were also common sidearms. The latter was an axe-like weapon with a metal blade. This was curved so as to belly out near the tip, then curve back. It could not be used to thrust but was effective when swung somewhat like an axe, though relied more on a sliding, slashing contact than the impact of an axe head, which punched into the target.

Sickle-swords required little training to use and were thus popular for arming the conscript forces raised by city-states as well as tribal warriors. They were ineffective against armour, but this was not much of a drawback when fighting other irregulars who were unlikely to be well protected.

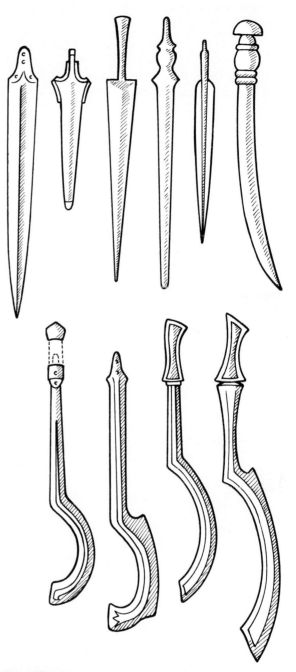

HAND WEAPONS
The Khopesh, or sickle-sword (bottom row), was used more in the manner of an axe than a true sword. As metallurgy improved, it was replaced by a range of iron hand weapons derived from the basic dagger shape (top row).

SPEARMAN
Spearmen (right) formed the backbone of most tribal military forces. Their equipment was very cheap and, more importantly to a nomadic people, easy to make.

ARCHER
Archers (left) were most commonly recruited from those who hunted with bows. The bow used by most tribal peoples was not very powerful, requiring the archer get quite close to the target before shooting. He might have to resort to his sword or dagger if his enemies closed in quickly.

Javelins, bows and slings were common missile weapons. All had applications to hunting, so the people of small villages and tribal groups were likely to include at least some individuals who were skilled with these weapons.

The javelin lacked range but could inflict a lethal wound. Its main drawback was its relative bulk. A man could carry at most two or three javelins and would have to drop or stick some of them in the ground while he ran up to make a throw. The result was a slow rate of fire coupled with rapid exhaustion of ammunition stocks. Nevertheless, javelinmen were common and could be effective on the battlefield.

In terms of lethality, there was not much to choose between the bow and the sling, although the mode of employment was quite different. A sling was much easier to carry as it could be coiled up and any suitably sized stone would do as ammunition.

A sling took skill to use effectively but many people learned to use one to protect their herds from predators. The flat trajectory of the sling stone meant that only direct fire was possible; it was not possible for warriors to shoot over their spear-armed companions, nor to shoot in volleys. However, these tactics were not available to tribal warriors, being more the province of trained professionals.

The bows used in war by tribal cultures were essentially hunting implements turned against human targets. Range and power were not great, though a killing or disabling wound was entirely possible. An archer could carry his bow and a reasonable number of arrows with relative ease, giving him a sustained firepower advantage over a javelinman.

Although body armour was not common, many warriors protected themselves with a shield. Designs varied, with rectangular, oval and round shields of various sizes all being common. A shield offered good protection against both projectiles and hand weapons and could be used offensively to push aside an enemy's weapon or to slam into him and drive him back.

Tactics and Techniques

The style of combat of these tribal warriors was highly individual. Archers, javelinmen and slingers would pick a target and attack him as an individual marksman rather than part of a disciplined volley-firing machine. Similarly, warriors engaged in what was effectively a large number of single combats. Individuals might help one another out or take advantage of a distracted foe, but where there were no complex manoeuvres nor unit tactics.

Although the manner in which war was made by tribal peoples was fairly primitive and lacked sophistication, the goals of a war were not very different to those of a more organized state. War-fighting was not a matter of inflicting a defeat on an enemy for the sake of it; there had to be a useful strategic outcome for the conflict to be worth fighting. In the case where a tribe's lands were invaded, then driving out the interlopers was the obvious goal. If they were sufficiently heavily defeated, the invaders could be driven from the tribe's lands and might decide that future raids or invasions would be better aimed at a weaker target.

If war was taken into the lands of a foe, the usual goal was to render the enemy incapable or unwilling to renew the conflict. The practice of 'laying waste' was not merely spite. By destroying the enemy's food supplies and burning his villages, the tribe weakened its enemies. An enemy recovering from a devastating invasion was unlikely to be a threat, and one whose lands had been laid waste before might be too afraid of the consequences to begin a new conflict.

Some tribes fought wars of conquest, taking the lands of their enemies for their own. Others did not, sometimes for religious reasons. However, plunder was a common denominator in almost all conflicts. Livestock, treasure and sometimes people could be captured to enrich the tribe. However, while cities tended to provide a suitable amount of plunder, the villages of a rival tribe were unlikely to yield much more than an assortment of livestock and a few slaves.

Thus, tribes went to war when they were threatened, when religious differences caused a conflict, or when there seemed to be a good chance to profit from it. The clashes that occurred were normally a chaotic meeting of lightly-armed warriors that were usually not strategically decisive but allowed towns and cities to be plundered and lands to be laid waste.

SLINGER
Within a tribe, many men owned a sling for self-defence or hunting. Slings were an effective alternative to bows, and were just as lethal in the hands of a skilled user. Their chief disadvantage was an inability to shoot over obstructions or friendly troops.

Waters of Merom (c.1400 BC)

The Hebrews were in many ways typical of the tribal peoples of the Middle East. For many years they wandered around the region, eventually heading northwards into Canaan (modern Palestine) where they came into conflict with the people they found there.

Canaan was nominally an Egyptian possession, but Egyptian control was very loose at the time that the Hebrews arrived. The Hittite empire to the north and the Mitanni kingdom to the northeast were also influential in the region, which was the cause

of much conflict. Canaan itself was home to a number of different peoples whose technological development lagged somewhat behind those dwelling in less troubled regions.

Canaan was a land of tribes and small city-states, presenting the Hebrews with an opportunity to conquer a region for themselves and make a home.

The Hebrews had not had an opportunity to settle and manufacture arms and equipment for their warriors, and so were lightly equipped. However, they had been in conflict for much of their wanderings as various peoples tried to drive the interlopers from their ancestral lands. As a result, the Hebrew warriors were experienced and toughened by their long trek. They also had religious conviction on their side.

Religion was a motivating factor in this conflict even without the Hebrews' belief that that Canaan was to be their Heaven-promised home. The Hebrews worshipped Yaweh, whilst the Canaanites

WATERS OF MEROM 1400BC

The Hebrew victory at the Waters of Merom was achieved by a combination of reckless aggression and confusion among the enemy. Faced with a Canaanite alliance, the Hebrews attacked before the Canaanites had organized themselves. Some Canaanite contingents fled without being engaged.

revered several gods including Ba'al. A collision of beliefs was inevitable and in societies where religion and politics were inextricably linked, war was all but inevitable.

Although relatively few in number, the experienced Hebrew warriors were able to defeat several city-states as they moved northwards. As was common at the time, the Hebrews laid waste to the lands of some of their foes, and put populations to the sword when the need was perceived. The result was that some cities surrendered without a fight or allied with the Hebrews. Others declared themselves neutral in the conflicts that unfolded. Some, however, formed hurried alliances and marched against the Hebrew tribes, beginning a new cycle of conflict, conquest and laying-waste.

An alliance against the Hebrews formed in northern Canaan, drawing in not only local cities and tribes but also contingents from the Hittite kingdom to the north. Although not unified in any real sense, the force fielded by the alliance did possess a significant advantage in that they could field chariots.

The Hebrews had no chariots, but they had managed to loot some military equipment from their defeated foes. Thus many of the Hebrew warriors were armed equivalently to their opponents. More importantly, the Hebrews were confident in their abilities. Even outnumbered and facing an army equipped with chariots, they decided to attack the enemy as they camped in the valley of the Waters of Merom.

The Canaanite host had no clear command structure and was composed of contingents from various states, leading to a certain amount of disorganization as the army prepared itself for battle. This provided the Hebrews with a perfect opportunity to attack.

Advancing rapidly, the Hebrews staked everything on a single blow, charging the disordered Canaanites. The Hebrews' leader, Joshua, engaged the King of the powerful city-state of Hazor in single

▶ It was common to execute the kings and leaders of defeated enemies as a warning to others and to prevent them rallying support. The Hebrews were no more brutal nor especially merciful than any other tribe of the times.

combat and killed him. The actions of leaders were of considerable importance in this kind of warfare, and the Canaanites were disheartened by this setback as well as by the ferocity of the Hebrews' assault.

The Canaanite army broke and ran, with the Hebrews in pursuit. As always in ancient warfare, casualties were much higher after one side broke than during the battle itself, and the Hebrews were particularly vigorous in their pursuit. The city of Hazor was razed and its population put to the sword as a warning to others who might be considering war against the Hebrews. Other cities in the alliance were also taken and the populations massacred, though the Hebrews chose to take these cities for their own rather than to burn them.

Victory over the northern alliance left the Hebrews in control of much of Canaan. Their dominance was completed by a campaign against those cities that would not ally with them. However, although they had gained several cities, the emergence of a centralized kingdom was many years in the future. The Hebrews remained very much a tribal people without much central organization, and continued to make war in the manner of a tribal people.

THE ASSYRIAN EMPIRE

Located on the upper reaches of the River Tigris, the region commonly known as Assyria was home to several city-states and small kingdoms, of which Ashur was the most important. From around 2000 BC, Ashur became the dominant power in the area, beginning what is known as the Old Assyrian Period (2000–1500 BC).

The city-state of Ashur's prominence was founded upon trade, and its political system reflected this. Power was concentrated in a small number of rich and highly influential individuals known as elders, with an hereditary ruler who executed the decisions of the elders. An additional office was held by an individual selected by lot each year, who dealt with economic matters. Ashur maintained trade relations with cities in Mesopotamia and Anatolia, gradually becoming a

◀ The characteristic conical helmet was often constructed from iron inlaid with bronze, or entirely from bronze. The shape of the helmet helped deflect a blow and also made the wearer look taller and thus more intimidating.

major power in the region. The city survived conquest by Amorite tribes but was later defeated by Babylon to become a vassal state.

When Babylon fell under Kassite rule, Ashur became a Hurrian possession. The destruction of the Mitanni kingdom in around 1300 BC enabled Ashur to regain its independence, beginning what is known as the Middle Assyrian Period (c.1300–911 BC). Military campaigns, mainly conducted against the Hittites, expanded Assyria's territory and prestige.

▲ **Assyrian archers. Each was protected by a shield-bearer, such as the man seen on the far left. His shield curves at the top to protect against plunging arrows.**

With the Hittite threat rapidly diminishing due to the collapse of their empire, Assyria engaged in a contest with Babylon for domination of the regions settled by the Amorite invaders. During this period, Tiglath-Pileser I came to the Assyrian throne.

Tiglath-Pileser is generally considered to be the founder of the Assyrian empire. His campaigns took him to the shores of the Mediterranean and he claimed to have reached the Black Sea. Conflict with Babylon in this period was frequent; after inflicting two defeats

on Babylon, Tiglath-Pileser claimed for himself the archaic title of King of Sumer and Akkad, claiming sovereignty over the whole region.

Assyria implemented a system of compulsory military service for all male citizens, and used an efficient bureaucratic system to control its territories.

However, competition with Babylon continued and Assyria's fortunes waned somewhat for a time.

The Neo-Assyrian period is considered to have begun in 911 BC, when Adad-niari took the throne. Under his leadership, Assyria began to expand once

▼ **King Sennacherib of Assyria is depicted during the siege of Lacshish in 701 BC. A strong bureaucratic apparatus governed the empire while the king was on campaign, but important matters had to be brought before the throne, wherever it was located.**

more. By 670–620 BC, Assyria controlled the whole of Mesopotamia.

Upon the ascension to the Assyrian throne of Tiglath-Pileser III, in 745 BC, the Assyrian Empire was reorganized. Power was centralized in each province, with a regional bureaucracy overseeing all matters. Each province owed tribute and obedience to the central authority represented by the king.

An Assyrian army marched into Egypt in 674 BC, taking Memphis and driving as far south as Thebes, but

within a decade the Assyrians had been pushed back out of Egypt, and a long war with the Elamites drained the resources of the empire.

The end of the Neo-Assyrian empire came relatively swiftly. Weakened by external conflict and civil war, under attack by the Scythians, Medes and Egyptians, and with a resurgent Babylon seeking independence, the Neo-Assyrian empire collapsed. The capital, which had been moved to Nineveh, fell in 612 BC.

The last emperor of Assyria, Ashur-Uballit-II, was crowned at Harran and held out for three years (612–609 BC) against the Medes and the Babylonians. The fall of Harran in 609 BC marked the end of the Assyrian empire and the beginning of a new period of Babylonian prominence.

Equipment and Organization

The Assyrians were the first power to make large-scale use of iron in war. This was an enormous advantage over their rivals; Assyrian weapons took a better edge and kept it longer. They were also lighter and more durable than their bronze counterparts. One of the key

ASSYRIAN GUARDSMAN
Although equipped with much the same weaponry as the militia – a spear and shield – the professional soldiers of the standing army were far more effective. In addition to their experience and training they benefited from the protection of body armour, a helmet and a stout pair of boots.

ASSYRIAN MILITIA
The Assyrian army was composed of a professional core plus extra forces raised as needed. For local defence, a militia was maintained by each city. Local governors were responsible for providing troops to the king's army.

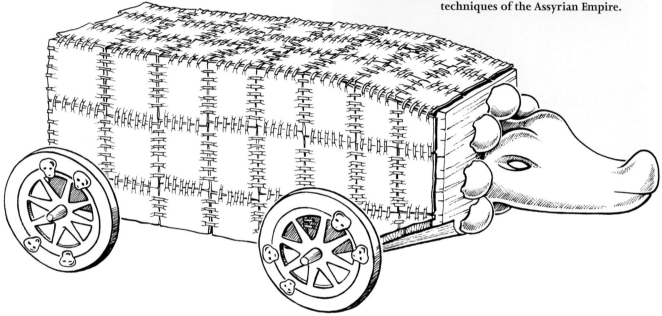

ASSYRIAN BATTERING RAM
The first 'rams' were relatively flimsy affairs designed to chip or scrape away parts of a mud-brick wall. Once stone fortifications became common, rams developed into heavy weapons designed to push stones out of a wall by the impact of the heavy head. Few fortresses could resist the well practised siege techniques of the Assyrian Empire.

advantages enjoyed by the Assyrian army was the use of military boots. Rather than sandals, which offered no protection to the foot, Assyrian soldiers wore a knee-high boot with hobnails in the sole. Boots supported the soldier's ankles in rough terrain and protected his feet from hazards on the ground as well as being stepped on in a fight or when manoeuvring in close order. Boots also provided a measure of protection to the lower legs. The use of boots allowed Assyrian troops be remain mobile and avoid casualties due to foot injuries even in very rugged terrain and bad weather.

Assyrian armour and protective equipment was also better than that of their enemies. Lamellar armour, formed of strips of iron, was highly effective but was only used by élite troops. However, even the rank and file benefited from better protection than their contemporaries elsewhere.

Logistical Superiority

Iron-tipped rams were also used against enemy fortifications. Initially these were not the weighty devices used to smash through walls as deployed by later militaries, but instead more like a spear whose point could chip away fragments of the wall surface. Such a weapon would be of little use against stone walls, but mud brick could be successfully attacked this way. An iron tip was of course far more effective than a softer bronze one. Later, as ever more solid fortifications became the norm, the Assyrians responded with heavy rams of a sort more familiar to later generations.

Engineering prowess was also beneficial when not engaged in siege warfare. The Assyrians became adept at crossing watercourses by using what was effectively a pontoon bridge, or by creating buoyancy aids from air-filled skin bags.

However, it was not simply technological superiority that made the Assyrian army the dominant force of its time. The army was well trained and backed up by an extensive logistical support system that ensured that sufficient supplies of arms and equipment, food and clothing were available for a field army at the beginning of a campaign.

The Assyrians were the first to make use of camels for logistical movements, and also established a system of mounted messengers, with changes of mount available at posts along the roads. This allowed orders and news to be rapidly passed to and from the capital, reducing response times to a revolt, crisis or invasion.

Reforms

Up until the reign of Tiglath-Pileser III, the Assyrian military model was fairly typical for the region, consisting of a small standing force of professionals, supported by additional troops raised at need. The main drawback of such a system was the limited training that could be provided to most of the force, especially if the troops had to return home to harvest their crops at the end of the campaign season.

Tiglath-Pileser III reformed the Assyrian army into an entirely professional force, which included large numbers of foreign troops. Some were provided as part of a tribute or the duties owed by a vassal state, but many were professional soldiers recruited from Mesopotamia, Asia and even Greece. The foreign contingents were mainly found in the infantry, where they were integrated with native Assyrians.

CAMPAIGNS IN PALESTINE AND SYRIA 734–732 BC

Tiglath-Pileser III was forced to put down a series of revolts from 734–732BC in Palestine and Syria. Such was the reputation of the Assyrian army that the rebels did not assemble a combined field army but instead took refuge in their fortresses, forcing the Assyrians to subdue them one by one.

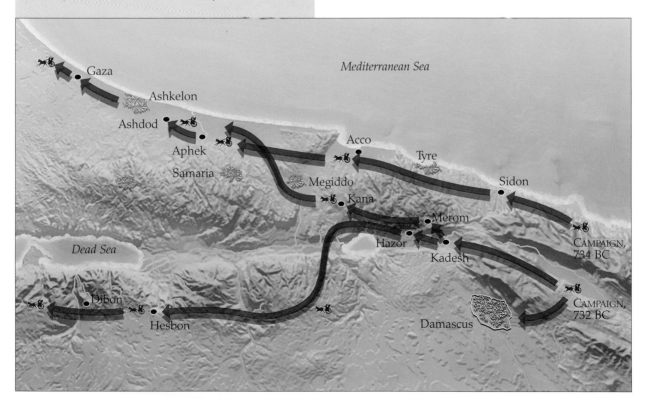

The majority of Assyrian infantry were spearmen who fought in close order, with body armour and helmets. They were supported by archers whose bows were of a superior design to those of most of their enemies. This, coupled with the use of iron for arrowheads, gave them an advantage in both range and striking power.

The mobile elements of the army were mainly chariot-based. The Assyrian chariot was a light design with a crew of two. Later, the chariot force was augmented by small numbers of horsemen. The latter tended to be drawn from the nobility and were highly efficient but not numerous.

The chariot force was used primarily to effect a breakthrough of the enemy line, which could then be exploited by infantry. The chariot assault was supported by archery, creating a combined-arms force that proved all but invincible.

Another Assyrian innovation was the combination of slingers and archers. Slingstones travel in a fairly flat arc, requiring that an enemy soldier hold his shield in front of him to protect himself. Archers shooting high in the air could then drop their arrows onto the unprotected enemy. The opposite also applied – shields held overhead to ward off falling arrows could not stop the direct fire of slingers.

ASSYRIAN CHARIOT
In addition to their battlefield function, chariots were used as mobile command posts and as transport for important officials. The chariot was as much a status symbol as it was a fighting platform. The Assyrian design was highly refined, with the axle in the optimum rear position.

ASSYRIAN ARCHERS
The main weapon of the Assyrian army was the bow, which was of a composite construction and thus more powerful than the weapons in use elsewhere. The bow also had a recurve shape, with the stave curving away from the user. This stored more energy for a given length of stave, giving the Assyrian bow advantages in terms of both range and power.

One result of the Assyrian dominance of the battlefield was that many enemies simply refused to fight in the open field, instead taking refuse in their walled cities. Extensive fortifications were not uncommon at the time, and required specialist techniques to breach them.

The Assyrian army deployed a range of siege weaponry including wheeled towers, battering rams and mobile shields to protect archers. The army was also extensively trained for siege warfare. Infantry, who had little to do until the wall was breached and an assault made ready, held shields to protect archers or those working at engineering tasks such as the construction of ramps to allow the rams and towers to reach the walls.

Psychological warfare was also used at the tactical and strategic levels. Massacres and the wholesale deportation of populations were used to encourage cities to surrender rather than resist. The Assyrians used their legend of invincibility to ensure that those they made war upon were halfway to defeat before any actual fighting took place. Many opponents simply refused to come out and fight, huddling in their fortifications while the Assyrians made preparations for a siege. Such passivity virtually ensured defeat.

One key to the success of the Neo-Assyrian empire was the gearing of the whole state towards warfare. Regional governors had a responsibility to provide a set level of logistical support to an army gathering for a campaign, and failure to deliver was considered an act of rebellion

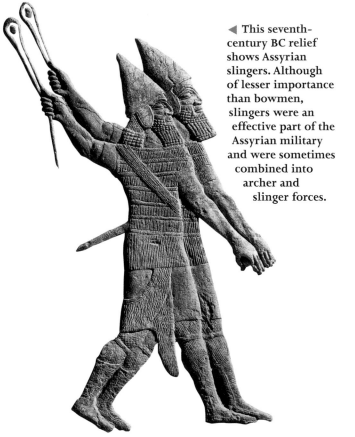

◄ This seventh-century BC relief shows Assyrian slingers. Although of lesser importance than bowmen, slingers were an effective part of the Assyrian military and were sometimes combined into archer and slinger forces.

that had dire consequences. The economy benefited from tribute and plunder gained in war, and this was ploughed back into supporting a well trained professional army.

THE CHALDEANS AND THE NEO-BABYLONIAN EMPIRE

After four centuries of Kassite rule, Babylon enjoyed a brief resurgence under a new dynasty. Nebuchadnezzar (1126–1104 BC) led a successful campaign against Elam which restored much of Babylon's lost prestige as well as more physical treasures. These included a holy statue of the god Marduk taken by the Elamites some years previously.

However, the resurgence came at a bad time. Records from this period are few, in contrast to more prosperous times from which written records are relatively common. A period sometimes referred to as a 'Dark Age' descended over much of Mesopotamia, characterized by a decline in the cities and the break-up of states. During this time the Chaldeans arrived in the region. The Chaldeans were absorbed by the Babylonians, as their previous conquerors had been, and Babylon began to regain its old power.

BABYLONIAN CHARIOT, SEVENTH CENTURY BC
This Babylonian chariot indicates the lack of efficiency inherent in chariot forces. Four horses and four men – a driver, a shield-bearer, a spearman and an archer – are required to deliver the same fighting power as two men each mounted on a single horse. In addition, the chariot itself was expensive to build and maintain.

Although dominated by Assyria, Babylon enjoyed considerable prestige as a holy place and one of the most important cities of the Assyrian empire. Aware of its importance, Babylon was always a difficult vassal, and rebelled on many occasions. Sometimes concessions and what amounted to bribery sufficed to bring Babylon back under Assyrian control; at other times the armies of Assyria were turned against the city.

In 626 BC, Babylon rebelled once again, but this time the Assyrian empire was in a state of upheaval and could not react effectively. The death of the Assyrian king Ashurbanipal resulted in a power struggle which, combined with external conflicts, weakened the Assyrian empire to the point where Babylon was able to establish independence under Nabopolassar, a nobleman of Chaldean descent.

In alliance with the Medes, Babylonian forces gradually defeated the Assyrians, taking the capital at Nineveh in 612 BC. The final defeat of Assyria came three years later, freeing Babylon to re-emerge as a regional power. At its height, the Neo-Babylonian empire stretched in a crescent from the Red Sea shores as far north as Syria and southeastwards into Judah and Arabia.

The Neo-Babylonian period was relatively short. From 549 BC, a new empire began emerging in Persia, founded by Cyrus the Great. By 539 BC, Cyrus' army was pushing into Babylonia. Defeated at Opis, Babylon's forces surrendered. The city became a province of the Persian Empire. Such was the significance of Babylon that Cyrus adopted the title of King of Babylon to assist in legitimizing his rule over the region.

True to form, Babylon revolted several times against Persian rule and was damaged by the resulting war. The city finally faded into insignificance as the tradition of

NEO-ASSYRIAN HORSE ARCHER
Horse archers combined mobility and firepower, enabling the warrior to strike the enemy and then make off rapidly to avoid retaliation. Cavalry were simply more cost-efficient than chariots, and supplanted them once horses capable of bearing a ride in combat became readily available.

consecrating Persian rulers in its temple was abandoned and the new regional capital was established at Seleucia.

THE MEDES AND THE PERSIAN EMPIRE

The region known to the Ancient Greeks as Medea lay to the east of Mesopotamia. Relatively little is known about the Medes for much of their history. The earliest definite reference dates from 836 BC, during which time the region was ruled by a succession of Elamite dynasties. The western lands of the Medes were conquered by the Assyrians but remained rebellious.

It is likely that up until the end of the Assyrian empire, the Medes were not a unified people. Many tribes, towns and regions seem to have existed. Herodotus suggests that the Medes became a single kingdom around 715 BC, though modern scholars consider 625 BC to be a more likely date.

The Medes began to move westwards as Assyrian power declined. They overran Mannae, a state allied with Assyria, in 616 BC and made an alliance with Babylon to destroy the Assyrian empire. This war of conquest gave the Medes domination of over most of northern Mesopotamia, and for a time Babylon and Medes co-existed with only minor conflict.

Cyrus the Great, King of Persia, rebelled against the Medes in 553 BC and captured their king, Astyages. Although now part of the Persian empire, the Medes

FALL OF JUDAH 588–586 BC

The Jewish kingdom of Judah rebelled against Babylon in 597 BC and again in 591 BC, forming an alliance with Egypt. The Jews took refuge in their fortresses, hoping for Egyptian assistance, but the relief army was defeated and forced to turn back. After reducing several cities, the Babylonian army besieged Jerusalem for 18 months before capturing it, ending Judah as an independent state.

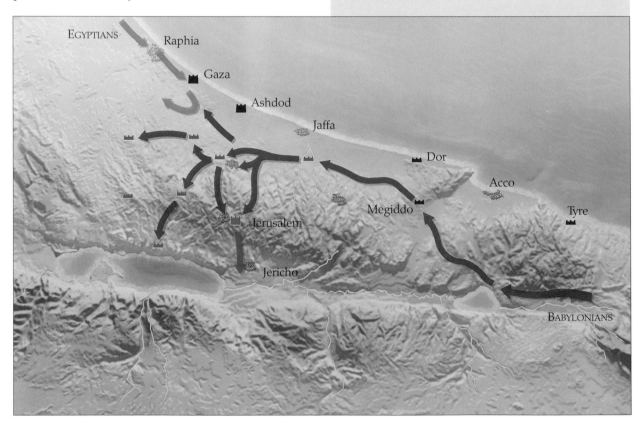

remained important. Many of their customs were adopted by the new Persian empire, and a significant proportion of the officials of the Persian empire were Medean nobles.

The Persian empire of Cyrus the Great and his successors is known to modern scholars as the Achaemenid Persian empire. It continued to grow under the rule of Cyrus' successors. Campaigns were mounted into Lydia, Thrace and Egypt, and even as far east as the Indus valley. An invasion of Greece was attempted in 490 BC but was defeated on the coast at Marathon. Later attempts to invade Greece resulted in the clashes at Thermopylae and Salamis in 480 BC.

The Persian empire was highly tolerant of cultural groups within its dominions, and allowed conquered people to retain their traditional way of life. This reduced the internal tensions within the empire, resulting in less rebellions than other empires had to deal with. Trade and communications between the regions of the empire were facilitated by a programme of road improvements. However, the empire was less unified than it might have been, and this could prove a disadvantage in war.

Conflict with Alexander the Great's Macedonian empire demonstrated the weaknesses of the Persian system. Although large, the Persian army suffered from command and control issues and never managed to bring its full strength to bear. The empire was rapidly overrun and became a Macedonian possession in 330 BC, re-emerging a few years later as one of the Successor States ruled by Alexander's generals.

Organization and Equipment
The Achaemenid Persian empire initially used Persian and Medean troops, which were augmented by mercenaries and units recruited in or supplied by conquered areas. These additional forces varied considerably in terms of equipment. Most fought in their traditional style and were armed and equipped with fairly basic weapons. The most common of these troops were javelinmen and archers who carried very little additional equipment. They generally fought as skirmishers.

PERSIAN IMMORTAL
The Immortals were given many privileges, such as being permitted to bring their wives on campaign, in order to ensure that there was no shortage of recruits to fill the ranks. As with other elite forces throughout history, the Immortals enjoyed high morale and were a formidable fighting force.

◀ This Persian dagger is a decorative item made from gold, based on a standard fighting weapon. Construction is very simple, with a broad blade and no hand protection. Daggers were carried mainly as tools and eating utensils, though they could serve as weapons for lack of anything better.

◀ The conical Persian helmet provided good protection against a downward blow, deflecting it outwards away from the head. However, it was of limited use against a horizontal thrust or slash aimed at the head or neck.

Many of the mercenaries in Persian service were Greek hoplites, equipped with a long spear and shield as well as body armour and a helmet. The hoplites fought as close-order infantry and were not, as a rule, unwilling to fight their countrymen. Other mercenaries came from Scythia, which produced well-respected bowmen. Some of the latter were hired as archery instructors to the Persian army.

The professional troops of the empire were uniformly equipped. The infantry fought with spears and shields and were armoured with quilted armour or scale mail attached to a quilted jerkin.

Professional archers were also included in the army, though they were not equipped with body armour.

Units were organized according to a decimal system, with units of 10, 100, 1000 and 10,000 men commanded by successively higher officers. Promotion to these ranks could be on the basis of merit or courage in battle, though the highest rank a commoner could hope to achieve was commander of 1000. Higher ranks were reserved for the nobility.

Within the army, regiments such as the Immortals were a prestige posting. The name 'Immortals' refers not to the longevity of the personnel in the unit – casualties in battle tended to be high – but to the fact that the regiment was kept up to strength by transfers from other units. The Immortals were paid regularly and given other privileges, such as being allowed to bring their wives and concubines on campaign with them, ensuring that service in the regiment was eagerly sought after.

▲ **The scythed chariot was intended to break up enemy formations with a combination of its mass and blades attached to the wheels. It was not widely used, though the Persian army valued it.**

The Persian army did not make much use of chariots, other than as a sort of mobile command post for senior officers. The exception to this was the scythed chariot, which was deployed as a weapon in its own right rather than a platform for soldiers to fight from. The driver stood in a wooden frame somewhat like a pulpit and guided the chariot. Blades on the wheels and under the frame made this a fearsome-looking weapon, although its effectiveness is open to question as the Persians made very limited use of it.

The Achaemenid Persians also made use of a battlefield version of the siege tower. Essentially a wheeled cart drawn by oxen, these could be used to transport and deploy siege engines but could also be used as high points to station archers behind the main fighting line.

SIEGE WARFARE

Any structure can function as a makeshift fortress. Walls built to keep out animals and the elements present an obstacle to an attacker. Thus as soon as humans learned to build shelters for themselves, they were on the road to the construction of fortifications.

The simplest defences could be constructed by using thorny bushes, either cut and dragged to make a barricade, or planted and allowed to grow into an obstacle. A fence, little more robust than one used to contain livestock, could be used to protect a settlement. Defences of this sort were easy to construct but also not very difficult to overcome. For a small village, little more might be possible as time spent building defences that might or might not be needed was time away from the more urgent work of tending herds and fields. However, well-organized towns and cities were able to construct more robust defences by making good use of division of labour.

Well-planned defences made use of natural features such as ravines, watercourses and hills. Height was important as it not only made the task of the attacker more difficult but also allowed the defender to strike downwards. Thus the siting of a fortified settlement was important as good natural features would not only strengthen defences but involved less building work.

▼ **This relief depicts fortifications defended by Assyrian soldiers. Height was a very significant advantage in combat, placing defenders out of the reach of hand weapons and giving their bows added range.**

A ditch, dug in front of the walls or other defences, fulfilled several useful functions. If it was close to the walls, it added to their effective height. Even if it were not, it imposed delay on the attackers as they scrambled down into the ditch and up the other side. Water or other obstacles in the ditch further added to the problems of the attacker. A ditch also made it difficult for an attacker to move siege weapons close to the walls, preventing a breach. A ditch could simply be an artificial ravine, or could be constructed with a more specific purpose in mind.

Some ditches were steeper on one side than the other, depending on their purpose. An 'offensive' ditch was built so as to be relatively easy for the attackers to pass if they were moving towards the city's walls, but if they wanted to fall back or retire to collect more arrows, siege ladders and so forth they would be confronted with a steep slope, making it difficult to get out of the ditch and away from the walls. The shallower slope towards the defenders gave them a clearer field of fire and allowed them to kill more of the enemy with arrows and javelins.

Conversely, a 'defensive' ditch had the steep side facing an attacker trying to reach the walls, making it as difficult as possible for him to approach and make an assault. Some fortification builders dug concentric ditches, one of each kind, to maximize the advantages of the defenders.

The earth from a ditch could be used to create a mound or rampart. This could be topped with a simple fence or palisade, increasing its effective height. However, such an obstacle was relatively easy to hack through with an axe and could be burned away. A solid wall was preferable.

Walls were initially built of mud bricks, which were easy to manufacture but relatively brittle. Stone walls eventually became prevalent, though these required more cost and effort to manufacture than those built of brick.

Of course, fortifications were merely an obstacle if they were not defended, so walls had to incorporate

▲ Assyrian troops attacking a fortress while a siege engine advances up a ramp to attack the walls. Another key weapon in the Assyrians' arsenal, terror, is indicated by the impaled enemies in the background.

MESOPOTAMIAN BATTERING RAM
This Mesopotamian ram is designed to attack mud-brick walls or to chip away at a joint in the construction of stouter walls. It is protected by thick timbers covered with hides, which can be wetted to prevent the enemy setting the engine on fire. Despite its wheels, the ram needs a smooth surface to run over, necessitating the construction of a siege ramp.

places for soldiers to stand and fight from, ideally while enjoying a measure of protection – easily visible troops would make tempting targets. Missile troops, notably archers, were the mainstay of fortification defence as they could strike the enemy at a distance. A position atop a wall or tower gave the archer an advantage in terms of range over those firing back at him, and he would usually be at least partially protected from return fire.

SIEGE OF JERUSALEM 1000 BC

Lacking a siege train, the Hebrew tribal warriors had only one chance to breach the fortifications of Jerusalem – raw aggression. Covered by archers and slingers, the Hebrew warriors rushed at the defences and managed to gain a foothold on the walls. Despite a counterattack they gradually expanded their lodgement, driving the defenders from the walls and gaining entry to the city.

Most fortifications were built with missile troops in mind. Towers that projected outwards from the walls allowed archers to shoot at enemy troops trying to sap the foundations or operate a siege engine as well as those involved in an assault.

If a breach was made in the walls, or if the enemy launched an assault, then troops armed for hand-to-hand fighting were necessary to repel the attack, at which point a breach could be barricaded. However, if things had reached the point where troops were fighting for the wall with hand weapons, then the situation was dire indeed.

Attacking Fixed Defences

Facing defences of this sort, the attacker had a daunting task ahead. Even a successful assault would be very costly, so the ideal way to deal with a fortified city was to obtain its surrender without a fight. The primary weapons in an attacker's arsenal were diplomacy, treachery, guile and starvation.

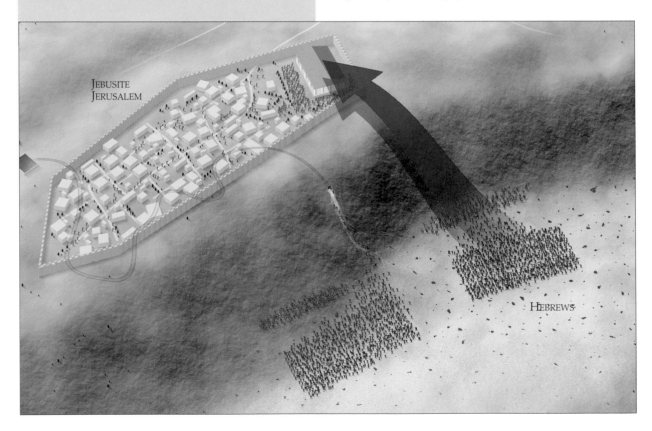

JEBUSITE
JERUSALEM

HEBREWS

One way to gain access to a city was to convince the defenders that it was in their best interests to allow this. Positive inducements might include outright bribery or the offer of preferential trade, territorial gain or other opportunities gained from throwing in their lot with the potential attackers.

The alternative was to inspire such fear that the defenders might prefer to open their gates rather than fight. For this reason many states made a practice of committing atrocities against those who defied them. Putting the whole population of a city to the sword or blinding everyone was not merely pointless viciousness; it was a means of obtaining the cooperation of others in the future. Faced with a choice between lenient treatment if they surrendered or a terrible fate after a failed resistance, many cities decided not to risk it.

Whether inducements, fear, or both were in use, the attacker needed to convince the defenders that their defence would be likely to fail. For this reason, shows of force were not uncommon. An army might parade its banners before the target city, demonstrating its vast numbers, or make a token attack before asking for surrender. Some states were so powerful that their name alone was a guarantee that sufficient force could and would be brought to bear.

If diplomacy was unsuccessful, the attacker might be able to nullify the defences by a ruse. A party of seemingly innocent merchants or farmers might be sent to infiltrate the city and open a gate during the night, or to capture one and keep it open while a fast advance force rushed up to take control of it.

The Biblical assault on Jericho may have been such a ruse. The Jewish army marched around the city each day, as if making a religious procession. No doubt this activity attracted attention and caused alarm the first few times, but eventually it was accepted as not posing any real threat to the defenders. Once complacency had set in, the Jewish host was able to use the procession to mobilize and get fairly close to the walls without the defenders responding. A rapid assault, signalled by the blowing of trumpets, carried the walls of Jericho before the defenders were able to make an effective response.

Treachery, Starvation and Disease

Treachery could also give the attackers a way into the city. Disaffected or frightened elements among the population might decide or be induced to open a gate or bring word of an unguarded entrance. This may have been a factor in the Hebrews' success against the cities of Canaan. A significant number of Hebrews lived in these cities at the time when their kin were wandering into Canaan, and may have decided to throw in their lot with the newcomers. This would help explain how an ill-armed tribal people were able to overrun well-fortified cities in rapid succession without a siege train.

> "BECAUSE HEZEKIAH, KING OF JUDAH, WOULD NOT SUBMIT TO MY YOKE, I CAME UP AGAINST HIM, AND BY FORCE OF ARMS AND BY THE MIGHT OF MY POWER I TOOK 46 OF HIS STRONG FENCED CITIES."
>
> SENNACHARIB OF ASSYRIA

If these measures failed, it was still possible to starve the defenders into submission. By surrounding the city and cutting off food supplies – sometimes water too, if the city had no supply within its walls – it was possible to induce the defenders to surrender. However, this could take a very long time as many cities were provisioned for several seasons. An army tied down in siege lines was not only unavailable for other operations and wearing out its boots and other gear, but was also prone to disease.

Disease was a serious threat to any army, especially one involved in a siege. The target city was under a similar threat, but where the attackers had the choice of accepting the risk, the defenders did not.

Thus the siege commander had to weigh up the alternatives. If other means had not worked, and if it was not desirable to spend months in a siege, then the only remaining option was to gain entry by force. Some civilizations became very skilled at siege operations. Among them were the Assyrians, who were

▲ Fortifications, such as the walls of Nineveh shown here, could not prevent a determined attacker from gaining entry, but acted as a 'force-multiplier' for the defenders. The inevitability of heavy casualties might be enough to deter the attacker from making an assault.

forced to undertake many sieges because most of their foes knew that to come out and fight in the field was certain to lead to defeat. The Assyrians were thus forced by their own reputation on the battlefield to also become masters of siege warfare.

Assaulting Gates and Walls

The weak point of any city's defences was the gates. By virtue of the fact that a gate was designed to open, no gate could be as strong as a wall of bricks or stones, so they had to be defended as well as possible. Fortified gatehouses and towers from which archers could shoot at enemies attacking the gate were necessary to secure the weak point.

Even if the gate were taken, it could be held by infantry or barricaded from within. Often a system of inner and outer gates was used, or additional fortifications jutting out from the walls to protect the gates themselves. These measures created a killing ground where the defenders could exact as high a toll as possible on the attackers. Nevertheless, the gates of a city were a prime target for any attacker. Once a gate was taken, access was relatively easy and the city was almost certainly doomed.

It was of course not practical for an attacker to concentrate entirely on the gates of a city. Indeed, in many cases the gate defences were sufficiently effective as to make an assault suicidal. Thus the gates were only one target.

ASSYRIAN SIEGE TOWER
Siege towers varied in size and construction. Most had more than one floor and mounted a range of artillery weapons as well as rams. The height of the tower negated some of the advantages gained by the defenders' position atop the wall, and allowed a bridge to be dropped onto the wall top. Troops could then ascend ladders within the protection of the tower before crossing to the wall top with relative ease.

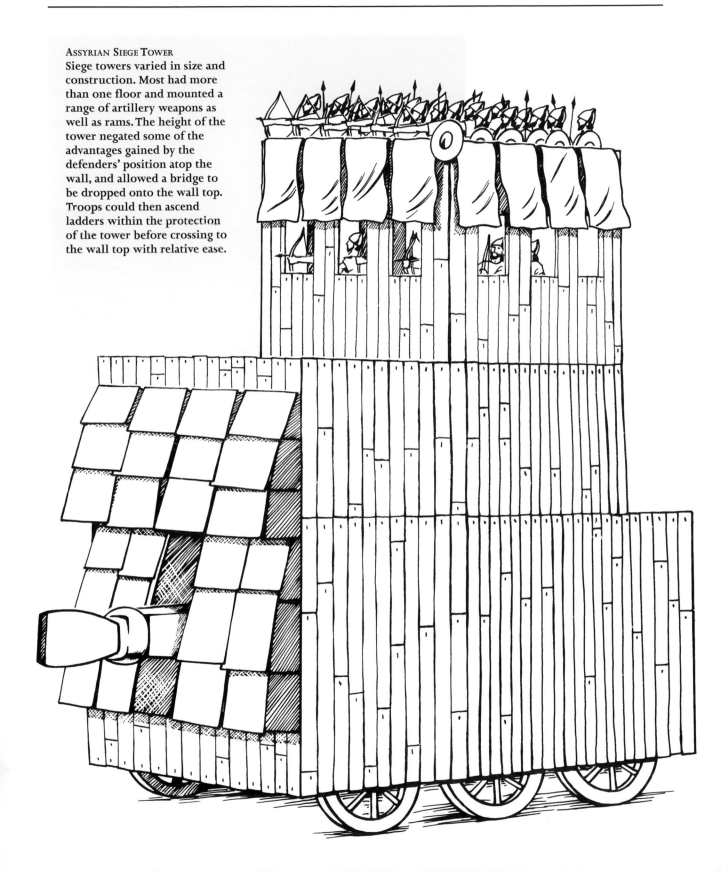

The walls presented a significant obstacle, which could be overcome in one of two ways. Either the attackers had to find a way to climb to the top of the wall, or they had to remove the obstacle by causing a section of wall to collapse.

Siege Weapons

The simplest, and most hazardous, method of ascending a wall was to use ladders. Men climbing a ladder were extremely vulnerable to attacks from above, and specialist tools were sometimes employed to deal with ladders.

Simply pushing a ladder away from the wall so that it fell outwards might cause consternation for those climbing it, but the ladder could be retrieved and re-used. It was more effective to pull the ladder into the fortress and thus deny it to the enemy. In a region with relatively little wood, finding materials to make replacement ladders was a significant problem. A ladder could be simply seized and pulled up the wall, but the weight of even a single man climbing or holding the ladder made this impractical. Hooked poles were sometimes used to snare ladders from the side and either pull them over sideways or lift them up into the city.

Using a siege tower was less hazardous than using ladders. Essentially a series of wooden boxes on a wheeled cart, with a ladder running up the inside, a tower was pushed against the walls. Archers or light siege engines on the top provided covering fire as the assault force rushed onto the wall top.

Getting a siege tower to the walls was a problem in most cases. If the wall was situated behind a ditch or on a slope, or simply with rough ground around it, then the tower could not approach. The answer was to create a 'ramp' or 'dam' by smoothing out the ground or creating a smooth slope up to the wall. This also allowed the tower to be matched to the height of the wall.

> "THE BLACK-HEADED PEOPLES I RULED, I GOVERNED; MIGHTY MOUNTAINS WITH AXES OF BRONZE I DESTROYED. I ASCENDED THE UPPER MOUNTAINS; I BURST THROUGH THE LOWER MOUNTAINS. THE COUNTRY OF THE SEA I BESIEGED THREE TIMES."
>
> SARGON OF AKKAD

Of course, creating an assault ramp was a significant undertaking, and one that had to be carried out under fire from the defenders. A similar and equally dangerous task was attempting to bring down a section of wall by digging away the foundations. In later periods this became known as 'sapping' a wall. The troops engaged in ramp construction or sapping work were exposed to missile fire from above and also objects dropped from the walls. Hot water or heated sand could be poured over the attackers from above. Boiling oil and lead were rarely, if ever, used due to cost and limited availability.

In order to protect the workers, and also to wear down the numbers of defenders, the attackers used archery and siege engines that threw javelins or clusters of small rocks. Workers, archers and engines of destruction were protected, where possible, by earthworks or large shields manhandled into position to give them cover from enemy fire.

Battering Rams

The walls could also be brought down by engines such as battering rams. In their original form these were more like a pick or spear on a frame that could be used to chip and dig at the surface of a mud-brick wall. Digging through a wall like this was a slow process, and once stone walls became prevalent it was impractical. Rams thus became heavier, delivering a powerful impact rather than scraping away the surface of the wall.

A heavy ram could push stones out of a wall, or batter through a gate. In its simplest form, a solid wooden beam, with a metal cap over the impact surface, could be driven forward by several men. However, it was much more useful to suspend the ram in a frame, with a roof overhead to protect the crew. The ram could then be pulled back and then released to swing forward under the influence of gravity.

▲ **This Neo-Assyrian relief depicts a ram in action against the defences of Lachish in 701 BC. The basic tools of siege warfare – mining, rams and towers – were developed early in history and did not change greatly until the invention of cannon.**

In some cultures, a convention developed that it was not merely acceptable but expected for the defenders to surrender when the first ram touched the wall. A force that held out up to this point had behaved honourably and put up a decent fight, but not forced the attackers to suffer the torment of taking part in an assault. They could expect to be treated leniently, and often were.

However, if the defenders decided that they could win, or that they had nothing to lose, they might refuse to surrender. The attackers would then be forced to make wall assault, or drive a breach through the walls and storm it; usually at terrible cost. The defenders could expect little mercy in this case. This convention was not universal, nor was it always respected. Many garrisons surrendered honourably and were massacred anyway.

The defenders had relatively few options when dealing with siege engines and work parties. They could try to kill enemy workers with archery, hurl missiles down onto the siege engines as they approached the walls, sally out in sudden attacks to harry the work parties and engine crews, or try the wholesale destruction of the siege engines themselves. The usual method in this case was to shoot flaming arrows at the engines in the hope that they would catch fire. This was not all that likely at the best of times. An engine that was constructed of stout timbers was fairly fire resistant to start with, and the attackers would usually protect the timbers with hides or cloth soaked in water. Any fire that did break out was usually extinguished fairly easily by an alert crew.

Mining

The attackers had one additional means of entry to a city. They could dig a tunnel under the walls. This practice has conventionally become known as mining. It was not usually practical to dig an entry tunnel and send troops into the city that way. Instead the attackers would tunnel until they were under the walls then enlarge their tunnel into a small cavern. This would be supported by flammable timbers. When all was ready, the supports would be fired and the attackers would retreat down their tunnel. Ideally, the cavern would then collapse, causing a section of wall to fall down. Once the wall was breached, a conventional assault could be made.

If the defenders detected mining operations, they could take countermeasures. The key was early detection of a mine. Bowls of water placed on the ground near the walls would display ripples caused by the vibrations of digging operations, allowing the defenders to determine the approximate location of the mine. Countermining operations allowed the defenders to intercept an enemy mine and collapse the tunnel before it reached the walls. If the enemy tunnel was occupied at the time, a desperate close-quarters fight was the inevitable outcome.

Thus a siege was more than a matter of encircling a city and waiting for the defenders to starve. Even if a relief army did not come to the rescue, the defenders might launch a breakout attempt. Smaller forces might sally out to attack the siege engines or destroy supplies. Meanwhile the attackers gradually encroached on the walls, filling in ditches and gradually moving their engines closer to the walls.

Archery and siege engines would impose a constant stream of casualties as the attackers worked to breach a wall or gate. Sapping and mining parties would attempt to bring down a section while other workers prepared ramps for the rams and towers.

Final Assault

Finally, an assault would be made. It was not uncommon to attack at several points, using ladder escalades against unbreached sections of wall while the main assault force stormed the breaches. Multiple assaults split the

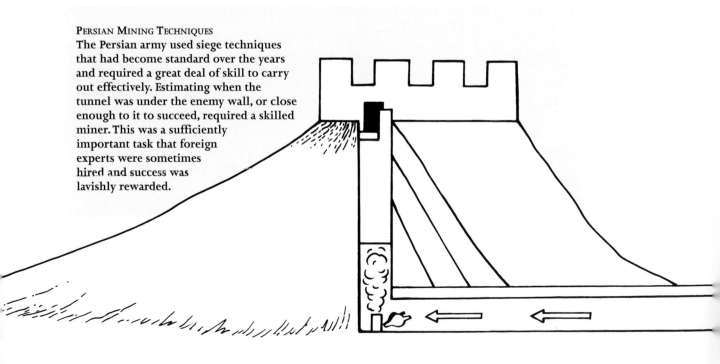

PERSIAN MINING TECHNIQUES
The Persian army used siege techniques that had become standard over the years and required a great deal of skill to carry out effectively. Estimating when the tunnel was under the enemy wall, or close enough to it to succeed, required a skilled miner. This was a sufficiently important task that foreign experts were sometimes hired and success was lavishly rewarded.

defenders' force and weakened the response to the main thrust, though sometimes a diversionary assault succeeded instead of the main attack.

In any case, if the attackers gained a section of wall, the defenders had to make an immediate counter-attack to drive them out, or the whole wall would be lost. If this happened, the attackers would quickly gain relatively free access to the city and the defenders would be doomed, though they might hold out in a citadel or other strongpoints for a time.

Cities that resisted to the last were usually sacked and the population subjected to atrocities. Even if the attacking commanders wanted to be lenient, troops that had just emerged from the stress of a breach assault tended to run wild. This was one reason for the garrison to surrender once the walls were under attack by engines – an enemy that had got that far was likely to take the city, so the decision to fight on was a fateful one. A successful defence might turn the campaign or become the stuff of legend, but failure had terrible and bloody consequences.

▼ **This depiction of the Siege of Lachish is more reminiscent of a European castle assault than an ancient siege, suggesting that the painter was more familiar with medieval siege warfare than ancient conflicts.**

Siege of Lachish (701 BC)

The Assyrian empire was massively successful on the battlefield. This was due to many factors including the use of iron for arms and armour, good training and organization, and the creation of a professional army that could retain experience gained in one campaign rather than losing it as men went home to tend to their farms and workshops.

The ability of the Assyrian army to drive any foe from the battlefield led to a necessity to develop good siege tactics, as many foes took refuge in their fortresses as soon as the Assyrians approached. Military colleges within the empire taught siege engineering skills and the tactics of capturing a city.

The kingdom of Judah remained precariously independent of Assyria by paying tribute and trying to keep a low profile, but it was obvious that at some point the Assyrians were going to annex Judah. In order to forestall this, Judah joined an alliance composed of Egyptians, Philistines and Phoenicians.

The Assyrians quickly defeated Egypt, the major partner in the alliance, and Judah sued for peace. Unusually, this was granted. However, the King of Judah tried to take advantage of political turmoil in Assyria and joined another alliance, which was also defeated by the Assyrians.

Again Judah escaped retribution, but only briefly. The new King of Assyria, Sennacherib, soon decided to punish Judah for its actions and launched an invasion. Some 46 fortresses were taken by the Assyrians. They did not manage to capture Jerusalem, whose fortifications had been improved, but Lachish was taken.

> "THEN THE ASSYRIAN KING'S PERSONAL REPRESENTATIVE SENT THIS MESSAGE TO KING HEZEKIAH: "THIS IS WHAT THE GREAT KING OF ASSYRIA SAYS: WHAT ARE YOU TRUSTING IN THAT MAKES YOU SO CONFIDENT?"
>
> **THE BIBLE, 2 KINGS 18:19**

The siege of Lachish began in the usual manner. The Assyrian army paraded in a display of strength before the city, and a request to surrender was sent to the defenders. This outlined their slim chances of victory and the terrible consequences of defeat, and contained a promise of leniency if the city surrendered without a fight.

Lachish did not surrender, forcing the Assyrians to begin siege operations. The first task was to surround the city and cut it off from outside assistance. Once this was done, it was necessary to decide how best to proceed with the attack. An assault on the gates was impractical; they were very heavily fortified. So it was decided to attack the walls.

The Assyrians began construction of a ramp up to the walls, which would allow their rams and other siege engines access. The defenders did their best to interfere with the construction of the ramp, shooting arrows and hurling objects from the walls. However, the workers were protected by heavily armoured archers who shot at anyone exposing himself on the walls.

The workers themselves were largely captives taken in previous assaults, and were considered expendable by the Assyrians. As the earthen ramp took shape it was surfaced with slabs of stone to allow siege engines easier access, and once the ramp was complete, rams were brought up to begin smashing the wall.

As the rams worked on the wall, the defenders did all they could to prevent a breach. They built a ramp of their own to shore up the wall, but to no avail. The wall was breached and assault

LACHISH 701 BC

The siege of Lachish demonstrated several ancient siege techniques: isolating the city, construction of a ramp, use of rams and the harsh treatment of the defenders to deter others from defying Assyrian rule. There was nothing unusual about any of this; Lachish is of note primarily because good records remain rather than for any remarkable aspects of the siege.

preparations began. As the main breach was stormed, other sections of wall were attacked using ladders, diluting the defenders' response. Covered by the fire of archers, Assyrian infantry stormed onto the walls and through the breach. The defenders fought as best they could, but they were overrun and the assault troops ran wild through the city, putting the populace to the sword. The city's leaders were impaled upon stakes as a warning to others who might defy the might of Assyria.

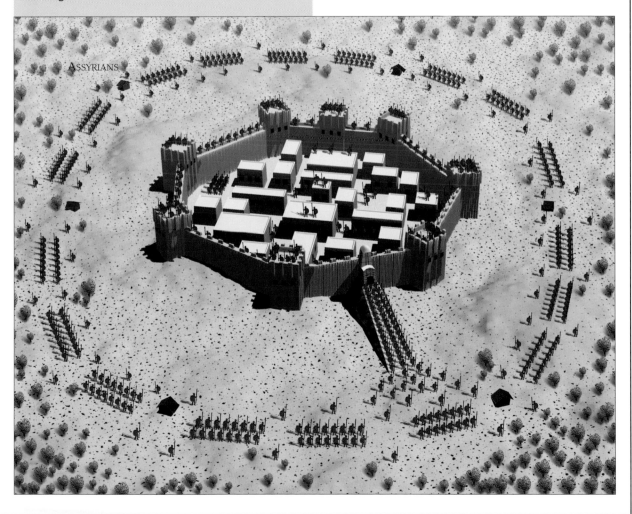

ASSYRIANS

CHAPTER 2

Warriors of Ancient Egypt and Palestine

From unsophisticated beginnings, Ancient Egypt developed an advanced military system with trained officers and a highly effective logistics corps. New challenges forced the Egyptians to learn to fight from chariots and even at sea.

L ike most ancient civilizations, that of Ancient Egypt arose along the course of a great river. The River Nile rises as two separate rivers, the Blue Nile and the White Nile, which come together in modern Sudan before flowing northwards to the Mediterranean Sea.

THE RISE OF CIVILIZATION ALONG THE NILE

The Nile watered what would otherwise be barren desert, and while its periodic floods made life difficult for local farmers, they also made agriculture much more productive than would otherwise be the case. Sediment deposited by the flooding Nile made the local soil extremely fertile. This promoted the early

◀ The Pharoahs of Egypt recorded their deeds in stone as a form of propaganda as well as historical record. These figures are servants carrying supplies, from a temple commissioned by Ramses III.

settlement of the region, as bands of hunter-gatherers abandoned their nomadic lifestyle in favour of a settled existence.

The productivity of the Nile region permitted a rapid expansion in population and also facilitated the rise of an organized society. The ability of agricultural workers to produce a surplus freed a segment of the population to undertake more specialist tasks such as construction, industry and trade. In turn, this economic activity created a need for metal and stone which had to be mined, shaped and transported to wherever it was needed.

The communities and trade routes needed protection of course, leading to the creation of a warrior class capable of waging organized warfare as well as defending their own holdings. It was this warrior class that led the conquests of nearby towns and cities, gradually creating a centralized kingdom. The prosperity of this kingdom is evident to this day in its great pyramids and temples.

The manpower and resources required to undertake such projects, even building at a modest rate over a long period, was prodigious. In order to be able to take the people involved away from agricultural and industrial activities, an effective system of transportation and bureaucracy had to be in place to ensure that there was no shortfall, and that the workers' needs were met.

▼ A society that could direct manpower in the construction of great works such as the Pyramids and the Sphinx had little difficulty funding, raising and supplying an army.

This in turn required a strong central government capable of creating stability, if not peace. The existence of an effective warrior class, dedicated to dealing with internal and external threats, was essential if the building work – and indeed, the day-to-day running of society – were not to be disrupted by banditry or invasion.

Thus the existence of an organized military force was vital not only to the security of the kingdom but also to its prosperity. Great works such as the Pyramids were to a large extent made possible by the soldiers of Egypt and the commanders who led them.

The history of Egypt is a long one, broken into a series of fairly distinct periods. These are based on the ruling dynasties of the time, which were not always native to Egypt itself. Foreign invaders, upstart local leaders and disaffected members of the ruling class all made their challenges for the rulership of Egypt, and some succeeded.

From the first beginnings of the kingdom around 3150 BC onwards, the warriors of Egypt developed new techniques and learned from their foes, for example by adopting the chariot from the Canaanites. The Egyptian military system was also influenced by a succession of invaders and conquerors.

However, despite the occasional change of dynasty, Egypt endured as a recognizable political entity for many centuries, until the armies of Rome ended the reign of the Ptolemies in 31 BC and Egypt became a province of the Roman Empire.

THE FIRST DYNASTIES

The climate change we talk about today is nothing new. Northern Africa around the Nile Valley had been drying out for millennia when the first of the great

▲ Egypt recruited foreign troops wherever possible to back up its own armies. This mural from Thebes depicts a band of Nubian mercenaries in Egyptian service.

Egyptian dynasties arose. What had once been grassland gradually became desert, forcing humans inward towards the fertile and well-watered region along the Nile.

The Nile Valley became home to various tribes, of which the Naqada became prominent. Originating in the southern reaches of the Nile Valley, the Naqada gradually expanded along the river, beginning around 4000 BC. This expansion was not without conflict, and other tribes were conquered or displaced as the numbers and territory of the Naqada increased. The expansion was very gradual, with several centuries elapsing between the initial expansion and the rise of a unified civilization.

By around 3150 BC, lower Egypt was unified under a dynasty considered to be the first Pharaohs, who made Memphis their capital. These Pharaohs, of what is known to historians as the Early Dynastic Period, were extremely wealthy. Their riches came from the industry of their own people and from trade

▲ **Overseas trade was important to Egyptian prosperity. This relief from around 2494–2345 BC depicts a trade boat entering port with goods and passengers aboard.**

with outsiders. The latter included the peoples of the eastern end of the Mediterranean as well as those dwelling in the nearby desert.

The early dynasties adopted the written language of the Naqada, which gradually developed into the classical hieroglyphs used for centuries thereafter. They also introduced the concept that a dead Pharaoh became a god. This was a useful tool in legitimizing a dynasty as it meant that the current ruler was descended from gods and presumably could call on their favour or even assistance.

During this period of Egyptian history, known as the Old Kingdom, a middle class of literate individuals arose to fill the need for scribes, bureaucrats and government officials. Central authority was only possible over a fairly limited area, so regional governors were appointed and gradually increased in power. By the end of the Old Kingdom period, a significant fraction of the economic powerbase rested not with the Pharaoh but with the governors and literate classes.

This gradual shift in the balance of power permitted the regional governors to challenge the authority of the Pharaoh. Around 2200–2150 BC, a period of drought severely disrupted the Nile Valley's agricultural base, and conflict over food sources began to break down the traditional system. Central authority collapsed and the newly independent provinces fought one another as well as the Pharaoh's forces.

As conditions improved, the independent former provinces began competing for control of a larger area. Eventually Lower Egypt became unified under their own dynasty while another ruled Upper Egypt from Thebes.

This situation persisted for a century or so, before the two kingdoms clashed. The forces of Thebes were

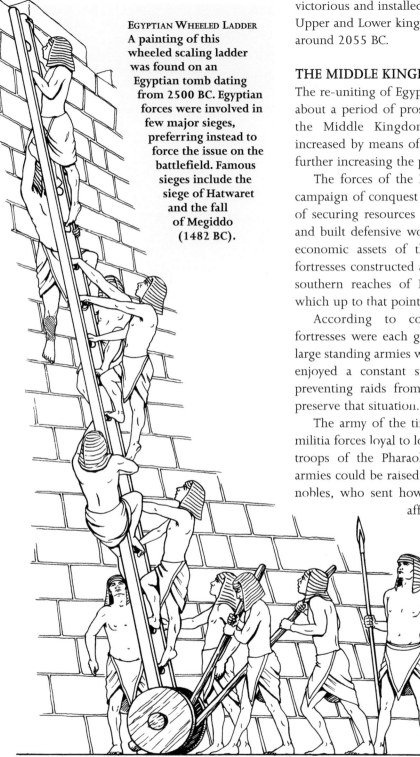

EGYPTIAN WHEELED LADDER
A painting of this wheeled scaling ladder was found on an Egyptian tomb dating from 2500 BC. Egyptian forces were involved in few major sieges, preferring instead to force the issue on the battlefield. Famous sieges include the siege of Hatwaret and the fall of Megiddo (1482 BC).

victorious and installed their own ruler over both the Upper and Lower kingdoms of Egypt. This took place around 2055 BC.

THE MIDDLE KINGDOM AND THE HYKSOS

The re-uniting of Egypt under a single ruler brought about a period of prosperity known to historians as the Middle Kingdom. Agricultural output was increased by means of large-scale irrigation projects, further increasing the power of the kingdom.

The forces of the Middle Kingdom undertook a campaign of conquest into Nubia with the intention of securing resources of stone and precious metals, and built defensive works to secure the borders and economic assets of the kingdom. A chain of 20 fortresses constructed around 2200 BC protected the southern reaches of Egypt from Nubian invasion, which up to that point had been a significant threat.

According to contemporary sources, these fortresses were each garrisoned by 3000 men. Such large standing armies were only possible in a state that enjoyed a constant state of prosperity – and by preventing raids from the south, they also helped preserve that situation.

The army of the time was primarily made up of militia forces loyal to local nobles, plus the household troops of the Pharaoh and the great lords. Large armies could be raised by requesting troops from the nobles, who sent however many militia they could afford – at least in theory. In practice, the militia system depended greatly upon internal politics and the state of relations between the Pharaoh and his nobles.

This system worked well enough for the defence of local areas or a small kingdom, but Egypt was too large for the system to work efficiently against a large-scale threat.

◀ **This carving on a ceremonial footstool celebrates victory over Syrians, Libyans, Nubians and Sudanese by depicting them prone, indicating that they have been defeated by the footstool's owner.**

A gradual evolution therefore took place in the period 2000–1700 BC. Professional generals and officers were appointed to deal with logistical matters and threats not requiring the personal attention of the Pharaoh.

The Middle Kingdom began to seriously decline economically as a result of drought from about 1650 BC. As the power of the Pharaoh faded, foreign workers living in the Nile Delta rose up and overthrew the rule of the Pharaoh, gaining control of northern Egypt. These foreigners became known as the Hyksos, meaning 'chiefdom of a foreign hill country'.

The Hyksos were a tribal people, probably originating in the lands to the north and east of Egypt. They were relatively few in number and could not field the large armies of the Egyptians, but they had significant advantages in combat.

The Hyksos had access to advanced military technology originating in Canaan and Mesopotamia. This included the socket axe, which was much more effective than the blade axe of the Egyptian forces. The Hyksos wore body armour and helmets,

rendering the Egyptians' maces and weak bows ineffective. They themselves also used more powerful bows, enabling them to strike at greater distance with improved lethality.

In addition to these advantages, the Hyksos used chariots, which the Egyptians had up to then not encountered. Outranged by enemy firepower, their weapons unable to penetrate Hyksos body armour and frightened by the mass of wheeling, speeding chariots the Egyptian army could not stand up to the Hyksos.

The Hyksos thus gained control of northern Egypt. Knowing little of the governance of a large state, they wisely adopted the practices and institutions left over from the rule of the Pharaohs, essentially overlaying their own authority on a barely altered system. The Pharaohs were not entirely defeated, however. Retaining some territory around Thebes, they survived the next century or so by paying tribute to the Hyksos, until finally they were able to expand once more.

Beginning in 1555 BC, the Pharaohs waged war against the Nubians to their south, finally breaking their power. This freed the forces of Thebes to march northwards against the Hyksos. A 30-year war ensued, in which the Pharaohs were eventually victorious.

THE NEW KINGDOM AND THE DECLINE OF EGYPT

Having regained control of Egypt, the Pharaohs set about enlarging their territories. This required a major change in the Egyptian military system. Adopting some concepts from the Hyksos, the Egyptians also created a military class in society. These families received land grants on the condition that they provided candidates for the army's officer class.

Troops were raised by conscription, using a system whereby one man in ten (rather than the more common one in 100) was eligible for service. Organizational and political reforms were also undertaken. The regional militia forces were incorporated into a system of military districts, making it much easier for the Pharaoh to raise local forces. No longer could a regional noble withhold militia troops, which not coincidentally reduced the ability of nobles to revolt effectively.

With a newly re-equipped and reorganized army, Pharaohs Tuthmosis I and Tuthmosis III campaigned northwards into Syria and Canaan, and south into Nubia. They established a series of buffer states to protect Egypt's borders and forced even powerful states such as Assyria, Babylon and the Hittite kingdom to pay tribute. Coupled with new trade links, the wealthy Pharaohs spent lavishly on temples and statues.

Ramses II, who became Pharoah at the age of 18 in around 1279 BC, was perhaps the most lavish of them all but was almost immediately confronted with a military challenge from the Hittites, whose power had begun to reach south through Canaan from their homelands in the north. Responding with impressive speed, the young Pharaoh mustered an army 20,000 strong and marched against the Hittites. The resulting battle, fought at

◀ **Pharoahs liked to portray themselves as warriors or conquerors. This relief from around 2050 BC depicts Mentuhotep smiting a Nubian foe with his mace.**

Kadesh, was inconclusive but demonstrated to both sides that they were up against a strong and determined foe. The result was the first peace treaty known to historians.

Although peace was made with the Hittites, Egypt came under attack from the Libyans to the east and the Sea Peoples, who raided along the Mediterranean coast. Egyptian control of Canaan and Syria was gradually weakened until the provinces were finally lost.

Meanwhile, the balance of power was shifting. The priestly caste were accumulating power and wealth at the expense of the Pharoah, and by 1078 BC the southern part of the kingdom was effectively ruled by the priests of Amon who had a capital at Thebes. The

northern realm was ruled from Tanis, but control of even that reduced area was slipping away.

By 945 BC, Libyan tribes who had been migrating into the Nile Delta region for many years had become the main power in the area, setting up a Libyan dynasty. Rather than challenge the priestly rulers of southern Egypt, the Libyan dynasty infiltrated them, gradually working trusted people into the priesthood until the south, too, was under the control of the Libyan dynasty.

However, by 727 BC, the Libyan dynasty had been seriously weakened by local conflicts. Kushite forces began pushing northwards up the Nile, conquering Egyptian territory all the way to the Mediterranean shore. Soon afterwards, the Assyrian empire began pushing into Egypt from the northeast.

The Assyrian invasion of Egypt did not last long. Beginning in the 670s, Assyrian forces marched down the Nile, conquering the cities they encountered.

▼ In this relief from around 1257 BC, Ramses II is depicted as not merely killing his enemies, but crushing them underfoot as they beg for mercy.

However, the Assyrians soon departed, leaving local governors in place. These governors were supposedly vassals of the Assyrian empire, but instead fought to remove Assyrian influence. By 653 BC they had succeeded, creating a new kingdom with its capital at Sais.

IRREGULARS, MILITIA AND CITIZEN-SOLDIERS

Most organized states maintained a body of trained professional troops, or at least a warrior caste whose duties included being prepared for war at all times. In some cases, these regular troops were all that was needed to win a battle or successfully prosecute a campaign. However, there was usually a need to put more troops into the field than could be maintained in the long term.

In a reasonably well organized society, it was not difficult to find enough manpower to create an army, but simply handing men a weapon does not make them soldiers in anything other than name. Various partial solutions to this problem were available.

One option was to give the new recruits at least a little training before they were sent out to fight. It was not possible to train a newly raised force to undertake complex manoeuvres or to fight in close order in a short time. An inadequately trained unit would simply break up in confusion under the stress of battle, and if its members were armed with weapons that were only effective in a massed formation, they would simply become targets for the enemy at this point.

Instead, men were issued weapons that were simple to use and, often, also cheap to manufacture. This was important when the state had to arm large numbers of troops in a short time. Thus, in Sumeria the professionals fought with long spears in a tight phalanx and were protected by expensive body armour while the supporting troops had no armour and were armed with the simple and easy to use – but far less effective – sickle-sword.

Recruitment, Training and Tactics

Various means were tried to ensure that the men liable to be called up for military service had at least some

CANAANITE IRREGULAR Many of the foes Egypt faced were tribal peoples who could not field organized forces. The typical opponent was therefore a tribesman armed with a spear and shield, who fought as an individual or part of a small warband.

experience or training. The commonest method was to maintain a militia. Whether men were offered inducements to join or were required to do so, a regional militia that trained at least occasionally both maintained some level of military skill and also provided a defensive force if the region were attacked.

Militias of this sort were no match for an army of professionals, of course, but they were roughly on a par with the irregular supporting troops of an invading army, and could offer useful support to the army's regular units.

Some states took the militia concept a stage further and implemented a system of citizen-soldiery, whereby every male citizen had a duty to report for training at intervals and to be ready to fight. In many ways this was an extension and a dilution of the idea of a warrior class; rather than a segment of society having a duty to prepare for war at all times, everyone was thus required.

The level of training that could be maintained by citizen-soldiers was necessarily lower than that of full-time professionals as the citizens still had to tend their fields or work at their trades. Taking men away from these activities for long periods of time to fight in a campaign was a serious drain on the economy in wartime, but this was offset in some states by a reduced need to pay for full-time professionals.

A form of martial training could be implemented by encouraging sports that were useful in war. Wrestling, javelin-throwing and so on had obvious military applications and kept the men fit and healthy as well as creating an aggressive, confident and competitive mindset.

The alternative was to recruit supporting forces from segments of society that would already have the requisite skills. Hunters would likely be skilled with bow, sling or javelin and would be able to provide their own weapon. Throughout history, tribal peoples and those who made their living from the hunt have provided sharpshooters, archers and skirmishers to the armies of their own or nearby states.

Even a state that could maintain a large number of trained regulars would usually augment this force with irregular troops. These were often used for supporting tasks such as guarding camps and supplies and for scouting. In battle, they usually fought as skirmishers, exchanging missile fire with their opposite numbers, or covered the flanks of better-equipped units.

A tribal force might be made up entirely of irregulars, in the form of tribesmen who came at the call of their leaders and fought as best they could. These individuals might be very experienced for all their lack of formal training, and under the right conditions irregulars could be more effective than a formed body of professionals. However, they were also more prone to flee when the situation turned against them, lacking the discipline and sense of unity engendered by long training.

Thus while the professional soldier was generally more effective on the battlefield, the irregular, equipped to a lower level and almost entirely untrained, was still a useful part of an army. Irregulars could and did defeat professionals upon occasion, but far more often the professional force, often with militia or irregular skirmishers in support, justified its upkeep by winning battles and preserving the security of the state.

CONQUEST AND DECLINE

Egypt enjoyed a brief period of renewed power and prestige after driving out the Assyrians, but the Achaemenid Persian empire was at that time the greatest state of the region. The Persians expanded into the Mediterranean and overland into Egypt.

The Persian conquest started in 525 BC. After defeating the Pharoah in battle, the Persian emperor took the title for himself. After this, Egypt was governed, along with Phoenicia and Cyprus, as a satrapy of the

◀ **Egyptian soldiers in training, as depicted on the temple of Ramses III at Medinet Habu. Formal training gave the Pharoahs' armies the edge over their tribal enemies.**

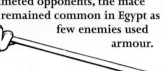

RAMESSIDE MARINE
The Egyptians used boats for logistics and learned to launch amphibious landings from them, requiring specially trained troops. This marine is armed with a mace to back up his spear. Ineffective against helmeted opponents, the mace remained common in Egypt as few enemies used armour.

ownership for Egypt; in 332 BC the province was ceded to Alexander's Macedonian empire. This move met with little opposition in Egypt itself.

After the death of Alexander, Egypt remained under Greek rule in the form of the Ptolemaic dynasty. The capital at Alexandria was not only a seat of government but also an economic and cultural centre. The famous lighthouse was built, at least in part, for the benefit of seagoing traders. The Ptolemies also invested heavily in the economy, increasing the prosperity of their dominion.

The Ptolemaic dynasty, much like the Persians, did not greatly interfere with local religion and practices. Some cultural mingling was of course inevitable, but the intent was to avoid offending local sensibilities in the hope of reducing tensions. The Ptolemies were only partially successful in this endeavour, and were forced to deal with a number of revolts as well as rather vigorous internal politics among the ruling class.

The increasingly unstable situation in Egypt worried the rulers of Rome, which obtained large quantities of grain from Egypt. The involvement of Queen Cleopatra of Egypt in Roman politics, arising from an affair with Mark Antony, resulted in Egypt being occupied as a province of the Roman Empire in 31 BC.

Although many local customs were retained, Egypt ceased to be a power in its own right and became a part of the huge Roman Empire. The Roman military system replaced one that had evolved over the

empire. Persian control over Egypt was much more complete than Assyrian, but for almost four decades (380–343 BC), a native Egyptian noble house held the throne.

Persian rule was restored in 343 BC, marking the end of rule by native Egyptians. The conquest of Persia by Alexander the Great resulted in a change of

Battle of Meggido (1457 BC)

Upon the death of Pharaoh Tuthmosis II, his young son Tuthmosis was sidelined by his aunt Hatshepsut. Officially Hatshepsut co-ruled Egypt with Tuthmosis, but in practice she wielded power and he was kept occupied elsewhere.

One of the tasks to which Tuthmosis III was put was as general to the Egyptian army, in which capacity he conducted successful campaigns and gained considerable experience as a commander. He would need it when he became Pharaoh in his own right.

Shortly after the death of Hatshepsut, revolt broke out in Canaan. Many of the city-states there were vassals of Egypt, and some of them felt that they could use the disruption caused by the death of Egypt's ruler to quietly assert their independence. However, Tuthmosis had been Pharaoh, in name at least, for the past 22 years and was well positioned to take up the reins of power with no period of disruption.

Using his military experience, Tuthmosis set about preparing an expedition to Canaan. Scouts marked a route, with particular reference to water sources, and provisions were prepared. In a remarkably short time, an army of 20,000 men was assembled and set out.

The élite striking arm of Tuthmosis' army was his chariot force. The chariot was a relatively new weapon and experimentation was still underway into the best designs and tactics, but what Tuthmosis did know was that his chariots needed good maintenance in the field, so a chariot workshop accompanied the army.

Tuthmosis' army advanced rapidly into Canaan and swung north towards the city of Megiddo. Here, the rebels were assembling their army. It was led by the King of Kadesh and was composed of contingents from many cities and tribes.

The Rebel Army

The rebel army was large but it was not unified. Its command structure was virtually non-existent, with each contingent answering to its own prince or tribal leader, who argued with his peers over who had precedence and therefore the right to give orders to the others. Thus important matters were sometimes overlooked in the general disorganization of the army.

The rebel army contained a sizeable proportion of professional troops, mainly among the household of the princes that had come to fight, but the force had been hastily raised and included large numbers of militia, irregulars and barely trained soldiers. Coupled with a weak command structure this made the Canaanite army very vulnerable to setbacks and unexpected circumstances, to which it would be unable to react quickly or effectively.

Had it been possible to draw up the host facing the enemy and fight it out in a simple, linear battle, things might have gone differently. However, Tuthmosis had no intention of meeting his enemies in a simple set-piece battle when he could gain an advantage by doing the unexpected.

Lying directly across the Egyptian line of march was the formidable obstacle posed by Carmel ridge. There were three possible routes through the ridge. The northern and southern passes offered relatively easy transit and were wide enough that the army could not be easily ambushed. The central pass, on the other hand, was so narrow that a small force could easily bottle up the Pharaoh's army. Nevertheless, Tuthmosis took the audacious decision to advance through the central pass, which offered the fastest route.

Despite misgivings on the part of his subordinates, Tuthmosis' plan worked perfectly. The Canaanites were watching the northern and southern passes, which were the logical approach routes, but had disregarded the central one. Whether this was due to disorganization or because the Canaanite commanders thought that no commander would be so reckless as to push his army though what could easily become a death-trap, the pass was unguarded and not even watched.

As a result, Tuthmosis' army debouched onto the plains in an unexpected position, and earlier than expected. They reached the plains after nightfall, and rested through the night as the Canaanites attempted to redeploy to meet the unexpected threat. At daybreak the Egyptians were drawn up in good order on high ground, and the Canaanites were still milling around in confusion.

Egyptian Attack

The Egyptian attack opened with a chariot charge. As the Egyptian chariots raced along their unsteady front, shooting at will into the confused mass of troops, the Canaanites became increasingly demoralized by the vigorous onslaught. No coherent response emerged, and as casualties mounted elements of the Canaanite army were unable to stand the pressure. Groups began to melt away, and soon a general rout began.

The Canaanite army dissolved and was vigorously pursued by Egyptian chariots and infantry. Some of the Canaanite force was able to enter Megiddo and shelter inside its walls, while the rest was scattered. For the next seven months Tuthmosis left Megiddo under observation as he mopped up pockets of resistance elsewhere, before returning to take the city's surrender.

Egyptian authority was firmly stamped on the region and governors were installed to ensure that the revolt was not repeated. Although this process took some months, the revolt was really ended at the moment when the Egyptians appeared out of the wrong pass and threw the Canaanites' preparations into chaos. Their forces were simply too disorganized to cope with a rapidly changing situation and were doomed to defeat from that moment onwards.

MEGIDDO 1457 BC

By taking an unexpected route to the battlefield the Egyptians altered the tactical situation from what the Canaanites were expecting. The well drilled Egyptians were able to form up efficiently and strike as their disorganized opponents struggled to make ready for battle.

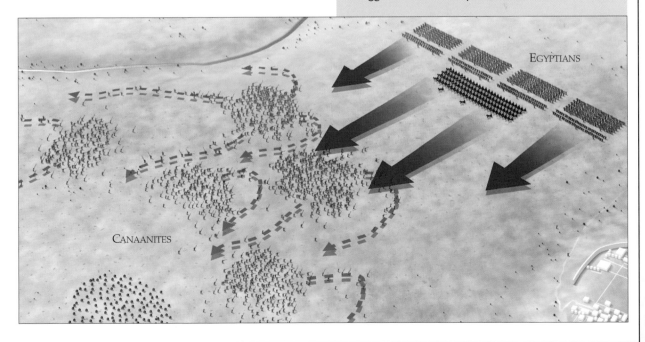

EGYPTIANS

CANAANITES

centuries from traditional Egyptian warfare, modified by Persian and then Greek rulership.

Egypt remained a province of one empire or another until the modern era. Fittingly, modern interest in the activities and culture of Ancient Egypt owes much to a great warrior, for it was Napoleon Bonaparte who took with him scientists as well as soldiers on his expedition to Egypt. These men uncovered many of the mysteries of Ancient Egypt and founded modern Egyptology.

Equipment and Organization

The Egyptians had a highly organized culture and were well practised at undertaking great construction projects. These required that thousands of workers be recruited, housed and fed. They also had to be directed according to a central plan, in order to avoid setbacks, bottlenecks and inefficiency in the work of construction. The same principles applied to the raising, equipping and organizing of a military force.

The Egyptians faced mainly tribal enemies in their early history. Unlike the soldiers of Sumeria, who had to deal with armoured opponents, the armies of early Egypt faced unarmoured men. Thus there was no impetus to construct armour-piercing weapons such as the socket axe.

The primary infantry weapon was the spear. Cheap to manufacture and needing little metal, spears were highly effective, especially against unarmoured opponents. Early Egyptian infantry fought in fairly close order compared to groups of tribal warriors, but they did not use a tight phalanx of the sort employed by the Sumerians and, later, the Greeks. The infantry of early periods did not receive armour, relying on shields instead. When the Egyptian army was reformed under Tuthmosis III, armour began to be issued along with more potent weapons, such as socket axes.

In addition to his spear, an infantryman might be issued a basic sidearm. This could be a dagger or a mace, or a weapon referred to as a sword but which was somewhat different from the modern design. The sword of an Egyptian soldier was very simple, consisting of a handgrip and a blade, with no hand protection nor any form of crosspiece.

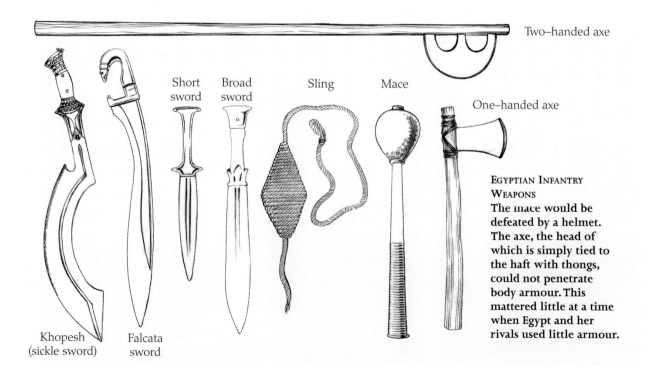

Short sword

Broad sword

Sling

Mace

Two-handed axe

One-handed axe

Khopesh (sickle sword)

Falcata sword

EGYPTIAN INFANTRY WEAPONS
The mace would be defeated by a helmet. The axe, the head of which is simply tied to the haft with thongs, could not penetrate body armour. This mattered little at a time when Egypt and her rivals used little armour.

The mace was a popular hand weapon. Consisting of little more than a spherical cast copper or bronze head and a handgrip, a mace was ideal for smashing the skulls and bones of unarmoured enemy soldiers. This weapon became obsolete in Sumeria, where helmets and armour were in use, but in Egypt, where this was not the case, the mace persisted as a standard sidearm until war with the Hyksos demonstrated that it was no longer useful.

If a sidearm was not issued, most soldiers had a knife that could be used at need. This was primarily a tool which could be pressed into service as a weapon if nothing better was to hand.

The spearmen were generally formed into lines, which were supported by archers. The bows of Egypt were relatively weak. Until the invention of the composite bow by the Assyrians, archers lacked the ability to shoot over great distances or penetrate armour. However, the latter was not necessary against most of the opponents an Egyptian army might face, so the lack was not keenly felt.

The archers were unprotected, relying on the support of spearmen and their own mobility to keep them out of the reach of infantry armed with hand weapons. Their task was to move close to the enemy and shoot down as many men as possible whilst avoiding any attempt to attack them with hand weapons. Once the enemy line was weakened, the spearmen could charge home decisively and defeat the enemy.

The flanks of the army were held by lightly equipped troops. These might be native Egyptians conscripted from the lower echelons of society or troops recruited from allied tribes. Slingers and javelinmen were common. Their main function was to prevent the main force from being flanked and to counter the effectiveness of their opposite numbers in an enemy force.

The light troops and some of the infantry and archers came from the lower classes. A form of conscription was used to raise the required numbers. However, many of the archers and spearmen came from a warrior class which held a higher place in society, and some were drawn from the personal households of important nobles.

The war chariot was invented in Canaan, and imported to Egypt by the Hyksos. Having been rather graphically shown the potential of this weapon, the Egyptian army adopted it with enthusiasm. The chariot corps was the élite of the army, in much the same way as heavy cavalry were the élite of many later forces.

EGYPTIAN ARCHER
The bow used by Egyptian archers was a fairly weak weapon with a short range. Archers had to be constantly ready for a quick retreat in the face of an enemy determined to close to spear-throwing range.

The Egyptian chariot was fairly light, drawn at considerable speed by a pair of horses. Although less stable and durable than those in use by the Hittites and other foreign powers, the Egyptian chariot was fast and manoeuvrable. This permitted a line of chariots to break through the enemy line, then wheel and return the way they had come without collisions or becoming disordered.

The Egyptian chariot was primarily a missile platform, so its speed was useful in avoiding contact with more heavily equipped troops. This included the heavier and slower chariots of enemies such as the Hittites. In theory the Egyptian chariot force could harass the enemy, wearing him down to eventual defeat, without ever being brought to close action.

Organization, Command and Control

The Egyptians understood the value of command and control, having gained experience in large-scale construction projects. Their army was subdivided into units under commanders who had a vested interest in success. In addition to the obvious consequences of defeat, commanders who were related to the Pharaoh stood to lose status if his army were defeated, while those with large holdings were inclined to fight hard to protect them.

The importance of unit identity was well understood. At the battle of Kadesh, Ramses II assigned each of his four 5000-man divisions the name of a patron god. In addition to suggesting divine assistance, the creation of unit identity helped improve morale by giving the men a sense of belonging.

It is unclear exactly when the use of 5000-man divisions became standard, but by 1300 BC the system was well established. Within each division, troops were further subdivided into regiments of 200 men, which themselves were formed of 50-man units. The training level of a regiment was noted in its title, with regiments being rated as formed of recruits, trained men or élite shock troops.

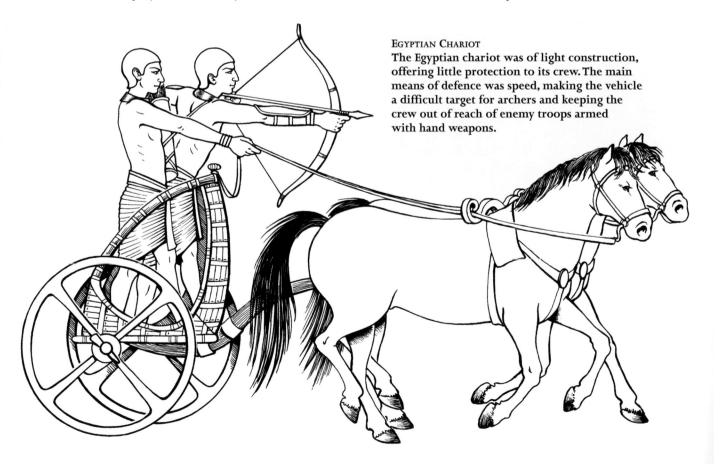

EGYPTIAN CHARIOT
The Egyptian chariot was of light construction, offering little protection to its crew. The main means of defence was speed, making the vehicle a difficult target for archers and keeping the crew out of reach of enemy troops armed with hand weapons.

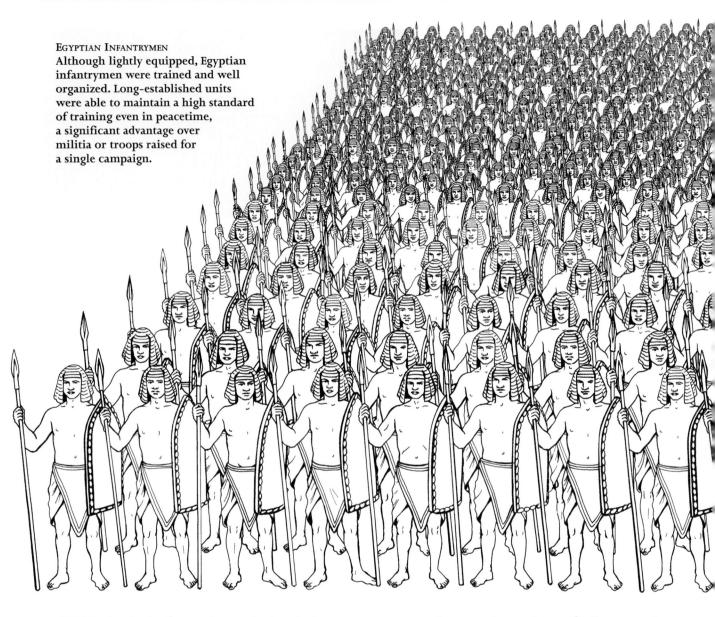

EGYPTIAN INFANTRYMEN
Although lightly equipped, Egyptian infantrymen were trained and well organized. Long-established units were able to maintain a high standard of training even in peacetime, a significant advantage over militia or troops raised for a single campaign.

Within the chariot forces, the standard tactical unit was a squadron of 25 chariots, which were then grouped into units of 50–150 as necessary. The army also included a logistics corps which used ox-carts and, where feasible, water transport to maintain an effective supply chain. Officers were professionally trained at military schools where logistics were emphasized alongside tactics and strategy.

The Egyptian officer corps was also adept at using intelligence. Doctrines were in place for using

scouts as well as routine and specifically targeted reconnaissance patrols. Agents and spies were maintained and their information formed an integral part of military planning. Officers were even trained to use deception techniques to confuse the enemy and deny him information.

The main assets of the Egyptian army were organization and numbers. It was relatively easy to gather a huge number of warriors together, but a different matter entirely to maintain a large force in the field or to make effective use of numerical superiority. Egyptian organizational techniques permitted troops to be efficiently raised, supplied and deployed for a lengthy period.

Thus although the Egyptians fielded forces that were lightly equipped, they were effective in the field and could cover long distances rapidly due to good logistics. Although perhaps not so potent man for man as the armoured phalanxes of Sumeria, as a whole the Egyptian army was a powerful fighting force.

CHARIOT WARFARE

The first chariots probably originated in Canaan, though there is evidence of a chariot-like vehicle among the steppe peoples of Asia. Whatever their point of origin, chariots were sufficiently useful that they were adopted by most states that found themselves likely to fight in suitable terrain.

Two broad types of chariot developed. Heavy chariots, often drawn by up to four animals, were relatively slow but could crash through an enemy line using their mass or act as a mobile rampart from which the crew would fight with bows, javelins or spears. Heavy chariots commonly had a crew of two or three personnel. Usually this was a driver, an archer and either a shield-bearer or an additional archer.

The crew were also equipped with hand weapons in case close combat occurred, but other than spears, hand weapons were not very effective in this role. In any case, if the crew were fighting with axes and swords then something had gone badly wrong.

Ancient AFVs

The heavy chariots of some states resembled four-wheeled wooden trucks and were not capable of great speed. Some states actually did field

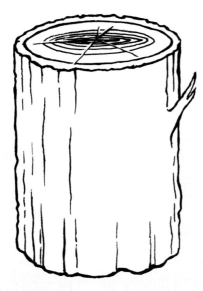
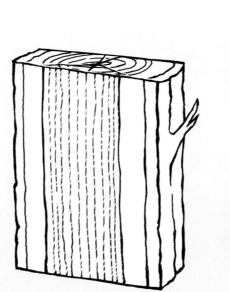
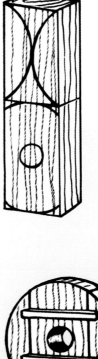

MAKING A WHEEL
Before the invention of spoked wheels, chariot wheels were formed from a section through a suitably large log. The resulting wheels were strong but very heavy. This was acceptable for a cart or heavy chariot pulled by four animals, but for a fast missile platform a lighter alternative had to be developed.

CANAANITE CHARIOT

The Canaanites are sometimes credited with the invention of the chariot. Their vehicles were fast and light, serving as mobile missile platforms for the most part. Encounters with the Canaanites probably influenced Egyptian chariot development.

NEO-JUDEAN CHARIOT

The Hebrews had no chariots upon their arrival in Canaan, and resisted the temptation to introduce them for many years. Indeed, Hebrew leaders at times issued explicit instructions to burn captured chariots rather than press them into service. However, as the Hebrews settled into domination of the region they began to use chariots from the Canaanite model.

SEA PEOPLES' CHARIOT

Many incursions of the Sea Peoples took the form of a tribal migration, with families following the warriors in the hope of finding a good place to settle. The Sea Peoples used slow, heavy chariots that served as mobile forts and were also used to transport supplies and dependants.

ox-drawn war wagons crewed by archers or spearmen, though these were uncommon. Asses were sometimes used to pull heavier chariots, rather than horses. Although slower, asses had greater endurance when hauling a large, heavy vehicle about the battlefield.

Lighter chariots were fielded by many states, sometimes alongside the heavy units and sometimes as the entire chariot force. A light chariot crew consisted of a driver and an archer, who also had a spear for close combat or in case his arrows ran out. The usual mode of combat for chariots was as mobile archery platforms, employing tactics that would be familiar to the horse archers of later years. Chariots could approach the enemy force at speed, wheel parallel to the front line and race along it delivering a hail of arrows before swerving away to reload, rest the horses or escape from a counter-attack.

The light structure of the chariot offered little protection from enemy arrows and javelins, though it might serve to confuse the enemy's aim a little as there would be tendency to aim at the chariot as a unit rather than either of the crew members. Far more important was the speed of the chariot, which made it a hard target for all its size. The dust thrown up by the massed charge of a chariot force also confused the enemy and could conceal the number of chariots in use.

Chariot Tactics

The adoption of the chariot granted its users a new set of capabilities in war. Rapid mobility on the battlefield allowed firepower to be brought to bear at a crucial spot and enemy weaknesses to be exploited.

◀ **This stele from the eighth century BC depicts an Assyrian two-man chariot. The chariot is of the classic form, with a rear-mounted axle and six-spoked wheels.**

> "I WAS BEFORE THEM LIKE SETH IN HIS MONUMENT. I FOUND THE MASS OF CHARIOTS IN WHOSE MIDST I WAS, SCATTERING THEM BEFORE MY HORSES."
>
> **RAMSES II ON THE BATTLE OF KADESH**

Chariot forces could also act as mobile reserves if things were going badly. Chariots were sometimes deployed as a screen for the infantry, but rather than protecting the main striking arm, the chariots were the main force. The infantry was there to exploit opportunities made by the chariots as they disrupted the enemy line and to provide cover if the battle went badly.

Strategically, chariots could move no faster than the rest of the army unless they left behind their supporting infantry, but a chariot force could be quickly detached for reconnaissance or to make a surprise flanking attack. Similarly, the speed of the chariot force allowed it to disengage from a disaster, permitting the nobles and their households to retire behind the protection of the infantry – or abandon it completely and flee.

As well as this, chariot forces could pursue a beaten enemy much faster than infantrymen could run. The heaviest casualties on the enemy's side were always taken after an army broke rather than during the battle itself, so with a swarm of chariots in pursuit, their crews shooting and spearing at will, a fleeing army was sure to suffer terribly.

Napoleon Bonaparte observed about his own horsemen than 'without cavalry, battles are without result', but he could equally have been speaking of chariots – a vigorous pursuit would turn a marginal victory into a strategic success.

The chariot was eventually eclipsed by cavalry, though the two existed side by side for a time. However, once horses large and strong enough to bear soldiers and their equipment in combat were available, the chariot disappeared from the battlefield fairly quickly, although it remained a symbol of power and prestige for a long time; Roman generals used chariots for ceremonial processions and chariot races remained a popular form of entertainment well into the later years of the Roman Empire.

Battle of Kadesh (1285 BC)

Both Egypt and the Hittite empire had an interest in Palestine and Canaan, and both were powerful states in 1285 BC. In Egypt, Ramses II sought to make his reign at least as glorious as those of his predecessors. The Hittites, however, were intent on expansion and were not afraid of conflict with Egypt.

Deciding to remove the Hittite presence from what he considered to be his territory, Ramses gathered an army of about 20,000 men, divided into four 5000-man divisions each named after Egyptian deities. These were each self-contained, allowing them to march dispersed and concentrate to fight, a principle that would still be in use thousands of years later.

The Egyptians were able to advance rapidly thanks to their good logistics system, reducing the time available to the Hittites for preparation. They also hired as many mercenaries as possible which not only swelled their own ranks but deprived the Hittites of this ready supply of trained fighting men.

Nevertheless, the hurried preparations of the Hittite king, Muwatallis, enabled him to assemble a force of comparable size to meet the Egyptian advance. Muwatallis deployed his army in front of the walled city of Kadesh and awaited the Egyptian approach. However, he was not inactive during this period. Instead he took advantage of the Egyptians' habit of obtaining all possible information to carry out a deliberate deception operation.

Muwatallis placed two spies where they would be captured by the advancing Egyptians' patrols. When questioned, the spies told their captors that the Hittite army was still far off, leading Ramses to believe that he had time to make a rush to Kadesh and capture it before any real opposition arrived. Ramses and his bodyguard force duly hurried to Kadesh. The remainder of the army was still on the march, leaving the Pharaoh and his small force dangerously exposed.

Surprise Attack

The Hittite army was hidden from Ramses' view by the city itself, and was able to strike by surprise as the division of Ra, the first to arrive, approached the city. The Egyptians were struck in the flank by a superior force and put to flight.

The remnants of the division of Ra sought safety with the division of Amon, which probably saved them from a murderous pursuit, but their sudden arrival also caused severe disruption in the division of Amon. The Hittites, meanwhile, positioned themselves to the south of the division of Amon, cutting it off from the rest of the army. Ramses, to the north, was unable to command his army, though his own élite bodyguard force was with him and under his personal control.

The Hittites had problems of their own, however. Their forces had become disordered

◄ **Although the battle of Kadesh was essentially a draw, Ramses ordered carvings depicting it as a victory in which his enemies begged for mercy.**

in the fight with the division of Ra, and their lead elements had become involved in an engagement with Ramses' bodyguard in the vicinity of the Pharaoh's camp. Worse, Muwatallis had crucially failed to realize that he only faced part of the Egyptian army.

The line of retreat for the division of Amon, which Muwatallis had cut, was also the line of advance for the rest of the Egyptian army. The divisions of Ptah and Sutekh were marching straight into his rear, and a force of mercenaries hired by

KADESH 1285 BC

The Egyptians were skilled at using reconnaissance and intelligence, but fell for a deception at Kadesh. As a result the Egyptian army was badly compromised. Disaster was averted when a similar reconnaissance failure caused the Hittites to be attacked in the rear by the rest of the Egyptian army.

Ramses was also approaching from the coast. Despite this, Ramses was in desperate trouble, and resolved to fight his way out of it. Leading his bodyguard in a charge, Ramses showed by heroic example what he wanted his forces to do, and they responded. In a somewhat disorganized manner, the Egyptians counter-attacked, enabling the southern divisions to attack Muwatallis' rear.

The Hittite army rapidly collapsed under this unexpected assault, though much of it was able to take shelter inside the walls of Kadesh. There was thus no devastating pursuit, and the strategic situation remained unchanged.

Both Ramses and Muwatallis knew that they faced a potent foe, and decided that a negotiated settlement was in their best interests. Thus came about the first peace treaty known to history, creating a lasting peace between Egypt and the Hittite empire, while both commanders returned home and proclaimed a great victory.

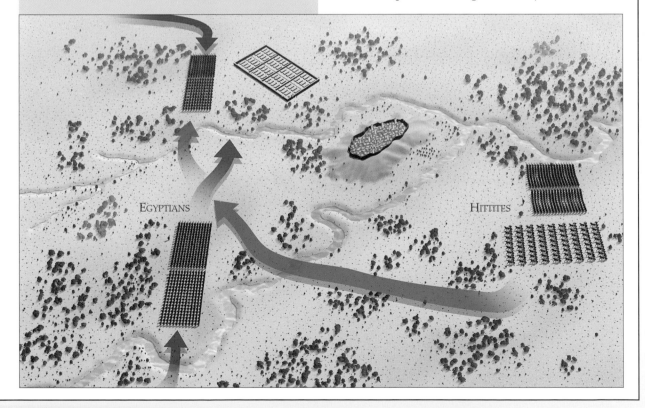

▲The identity of the Sea Peoples remains unclear, but their attacks and the Egyptians' development of sea warfare tactics are recorded in the temple of Ramses III.

THE SEA PEOPLES

The group known to historians as the 'Sea Peoples' raided the coasts of the Eastern Mediterranean, sometimes moving far inland and bringing settlers to take over conquered lands. They are thought to have raided Cyprus and Greece, Anatolia, Syria and Mesopotamia, as well as Egypt.

Raiding by the Sea Peoples has been suggested as the cause of the Bronze Age Collapse, an event which occurred around 1200 to 1150 BC. Large numbers of cities were sacked, and in many cases abandoned afterwards, around this time. Literacy and trade also dropped off rapidly, along with centralized economies in several areas.

All this suggests massive upheaval of a sort that could be caused by large-scale raiding over the whole area. If travel became dangerous and central authority was unable to deal with the problem, trade and communications would suffer. This could spell doom for a centralized empire or kingdom. It is known that raids by the Sea Peoples contributed to the collapse of the Hittite empire, and may have also hastened the downfall of other kingdoms at around the same time, such as the Mitanni.

Egyptian sources refer to the Sea Peoples as a confederation of tribes including the Peleset, Tjecker, Shekelesh, Denyen and Weshesh. However, the origins of the Sea Peoples are debated by historians. It may be that the label was applied to several groups undertaking similar activities in the same region, all with different origins.

It has been hypothesized that the Sea Peoples may have originated in Crete or the islands of Greece, spreading out to conquer new lands. Other historians believe that the Sea Peoples were remnants of Greek or Minoan city-states, displaced by warfare or the destruction of their homes, or Anatolians who had sought new homes due to overpopulation or famine. If any of these theories are correct, the confederation of tribes referred to by Egyptian sources may represent contingents from colonies or conquered lands in different areas, united by a common cultural identity.

There are references to raids against Egypt by the Sea Peoples during the reign of Ramses II, which began in 1279 BC, but the attacks may have started earlier. The Sea Peoples themselves left no records. Or perhaps, nothing that has been definitely

INVASION OF THE SEA PEOPLES 1190 BC

After sacking Troy, the Sea Peoples migrated overland and by sea along the coast, including Hittite territories, destroying and looting cities as they went. Their rampage was halted at the Nile delta by an Egyptian fleet while their land force was overrun in the Sinai desert.

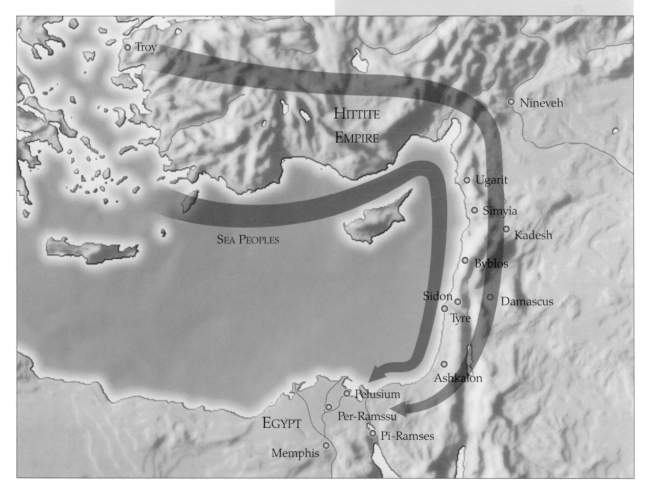

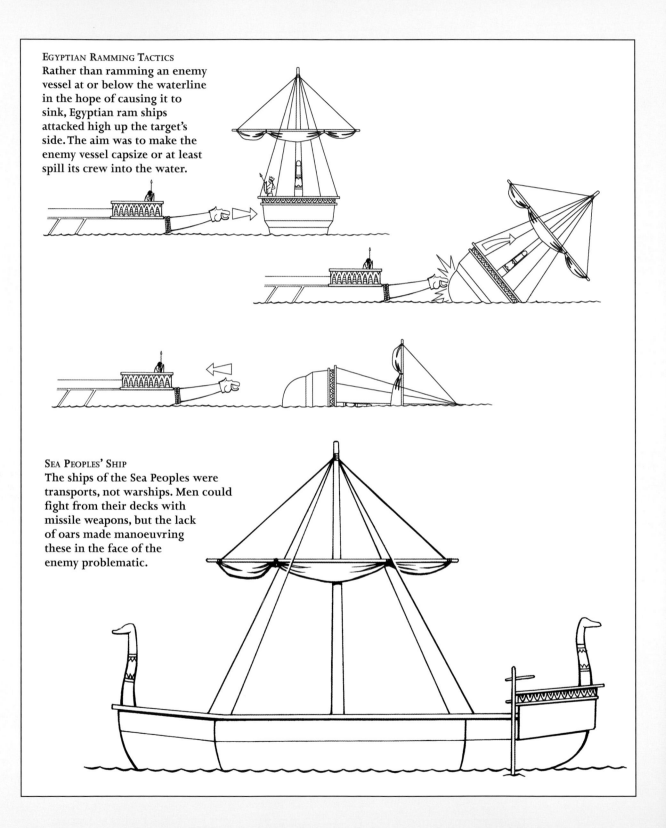

EGYPTIAN RAMMING TACTICS
Rather than ramming an enemy vessel at or below the waterline in the hope of causing it to sink, Egyptian ram ships attacked high up the target's side. The aim was to make the enemy vessel capsize or at least spill its crew into the water.

SEA PEOPLES' SHIP
The ships of the Sea Peoples were transports, not warships. Men could fight from their decks with missile weapons, but the lack of oars made manoeuvring these in the face of the enemy problematic.

▲ **The success of a commander could be measured by the numbers of captives taken and kept or sold as slaves. This depiction of Ramses III leading prisoners thus shows him to be a great war leader.**

recognized as a record of their activities. It may be that the raiders were a faction offshoot of a known civilization. If so they are unlikely to have referred to themselves by the same name that their victims used.

Egypt was a prime target for the Sea Peoples due to its prosperity. Not only were raids into rich lands more lucrative, but the Sea Peoples were also interested in conquering areas to settle. Once an area had been softened up by a period of raiding, it was relatively easy for the Sea Peoples to take a region for their own and fend off any attempts to dislodge them.

Attacks on Egypt

Of all the kingdoms raided by the Sea Peoples, Egypt was the only one to have much success against them. This was for precisely the same reasons that it was such a good target; the wealth of Egypt allowed a strong military force to be maintained and a well organized response made to any incursion.

In 1178 or 1175 BC, the Sea Peoples sacked the Hittite vassal state of Amurru and began moving towards Egyptian territory nearby. Pharoah Ramses III

marched his army to meet them as they approached the Egyptian border. The two armies clashed at Djahy.

Perhaps the Sea Peoples were used to enemies that were half-beaten by their reputation for invincibility, or perhaps they were caught by surprise by the aggressive Egyptian attack. Whichever was the case, Ramses III launched his chariots at the forces of the Sea Peoples and inflicted a serious defeat which was followed up by a vigorous pursuit.

Ramses III did not want to merely defeat the force that was marching against him; he wanted to send a message to the invaders that to attack Egypt was a losing proposition. However, the Sea Peoples remained undaunted. Defeated on land, they launched a naval assault on the Nile delta.

Ramses III had prepared for this possibility, and had ordered the construction of a fleet. His ships were probably very primitive, but so were those of his enemies, being intended as transport to a land objective rather than naval combat assets. There are no recorded instances of naval combat before this event, which became known as the battle of the Delta, so warship technology would be in its infancy if it existed at all.

The Egyptians wisely did not risk action in the open sea against an enemy that would certainly handle their ships better. Instead, the Egyptian fleet was hidden in the delta and attacked from ambush as the Sea Peoples attempted to land. The Egyptians used their ships as floating archery platforms, and it is likely that the Sea Peoples did likewise.

The Egyptian force was supported by additional archers on the shore, who shot at any ship that came close enough and moved to counter any attempted landing. Any of the Sea Peoples' warriors who made it to shore were rounded up and executed.

Further invasions of Egypt were attempted but met with the same effective resistance. A second expedition into the Nile was dealt with in much the same way as the first, while land forces were defeated at the border. There are also indications that Ramses III used his fleet to launch expeditions against the holdings of the Sea Peoples.

The cost of repelling the incursions of the Sea Peoples all but bankrupted Egypt, and greatly reduced its power. One result was that the Egyptians were unable to prevent the Sea Peoples settling in Palestine and Canaan.

The Sea Peoples gradually faded from the scene. They may have settled and stopped raiding, or run out of targets to pillage. In either case, they ceased to be a major factor in the history of the Eastern Mediterranean. However, their influence was felt for centuries. Not only did their war with Egypt weaken the Pharaohs to the point that they never regained their power, but the destruction wrought by the Sea Peoples eventually created the conditions necessary for new empires such as those of the Neo-Assyrians and the Neo-Hittites.

Equipment and Organization

There is relatively little information on the Sea Peoples and their military system. It is known for certain that they were very effective in combat; city-states and even empires fell before them and writings from the period lament the destruction wrought by the raiders.

The Sea Peoples used ships for mobility, but probably had no organized naval warfare capability. Their targets lay on land and had to be attacked there. Thus it is likely that the Sea Peoples would simply land their forces on the coast near the objective, using their beached ships as a supply depot.

When fighting on land, the Sea Peoples used fairly conventional forces for the most part. Their infantry was primarily composed of spearmen and unarmoured warriors armed with bows and javelins. Some men fought with sword and shield, though armour was uncommon.

The Sea Peoples were warriors rather than soldiers, and tended to fight as groups of individuals rather than in close-ordered formations. Command and control was also rather loose, with leadership exercised by example and battlefield manoeuvres limited to responding to the immediate situation rather than following a complex plan.

Chariots and Ox-carts

The Sea Peoples also used chariots, which were similar to the Egyptian design. Light, fast and manoeuvrable, they were used as missile platforms and crewed by an archer and a driver. The chariot forces were well suited to a rapid advance, inflicting fear on their opponents with the noise and dust of their approach, then delivering a hail of arrows before withdrawing.

> "THE UNRULY SHERDEN WHOM NO ONE HAD EVER KNOWN HOW TO COMBAT, THEY CAME BOLDLY SAILING IN THEIR WARSHIPS FROM THE MIDST OF THE SEA, NONE BEING ABLE TO WITHSTAND THEM."
>
> **RAMSES II ON THE SEA PEOPLES**

The Sea Peoples also deployed four-wheeled ox-carts. These are depicted as carrying women and children behind the army in some inscriptions, but were also used as slow-moving mobile forts from which archers could shoot in safety.

The presence of their families was an added incentive to win for the Sea Peoples. Defeat could mean a massacre, whilst victory might result in prime land to be settled. This was an important facet of the Sea Peoples' mode of warfare; they were not merely plundering the riches of the lands they attacked but were seeking places to settle and make a home.

THE HEBREWS

According to the Bible, the Hebrews had first been enslaved in Egypt and then had wandered for 40 years before arriving in Canaan, which they viewed as their promised land. Decades of wandering about in a harsh wilderness had toughened the Hebrews but nomadic life was not conducive to creating an effective technological base.

Thus the early Hebrews were ill-equipped when they first reached Canaan some time in the 13th century BC. Their war gear was basic, consisting mainly of spears and shields in addition to the tools of the hunt, such as javelins and bows. The most prevalent missile weapon among the Hebrews, however, was the sling. They certainly had no chariots or anything that could be considered a siege train.

What advanced equipment the Hebrews had available had been captured from the enemies they encountered in the course of their long wanderings. Some tribes and states had attacked the Hebrews, hoping to drive them away. This was a matter of self-preservation, as no state could afford to have a large, land-hungry horde setting up camp and consuming local resources. In other areas, disputes arose between the Hebrews and the local tribes, often over religious differences. The outcome was the same in each case; conflict began and the Hebrews were forced to move on.

The region into which the Hebrews wandered had always been a turbulent and troubled one, lying as it did on the land bridge between Africa, Asia and Europe. Canaan and Palestine

SHERDEN WARRIOR
The warriors of the Sea Peoples were well equipped, with long swords and leather shields reinforced with metal. Protection was afforded by leather or metal body armour and a helmet.

had seen many armies march through on their way to wars elsewhere, and had been fought over as frequently.

Egypt had been the main power in the region until recently, having annexed Palestine as a buffer zone against the Hittites and other powers to the north and east. However, Egyptian power was weakening as a result of conflict with the Sea Peoples and their hold on Palestine could be considered shaky at best.

The Sea Peoples had also broken the Hittite empire, which might otherwise have taken over control of the region, and had destroyed many of the cities of Canaan. They had settled along the coastal plains of Palestine, becoming known as Philistines. In time they would become enemies and

rivals of the Hebrews, but at the time of the Hebrews' arrival the Sea Peoples' colonies were confined mainly to the coastal strip and were bypassed.

Whether or not it was promised to them by divine authority, the Hebrews found Canaan in a state of chaos and ripe for the taking. They also discovered fellow Hebrews already living there. Some of these local relatives assisted the Hebrews or came to join them, swelling their numbers in a short time.

Hebrew Incursions

As had happened elsewhere, conflict broke out between the new arrivals and the native residents. This was partly a matter of dislodging the interlopers and partly a religious matter. The Hebrews were monotheists with rather strict moralistic practices, while the Canaanites were fond of religious orgies and worshipped multiple gods of whom the Hebrews did not approve.

Inevitably, the first cities encountered by the Hebrews sent armies out to fight them directly. Convinced that the land was theirs, and desperate to find a place to settle, the Hebrews fought hard and refused to be driven off, eventually gaining control of a small area.

MICHMASH 1040 BC

The Philistines were thrown into disorder by the panic of an outpost garrison, who were attacked from an unexpected direction by a tiny force. This created an opportunity for a frontal attack by the main Hebrew force. Local villagers then fell on the fleeing Philistines, killing many.

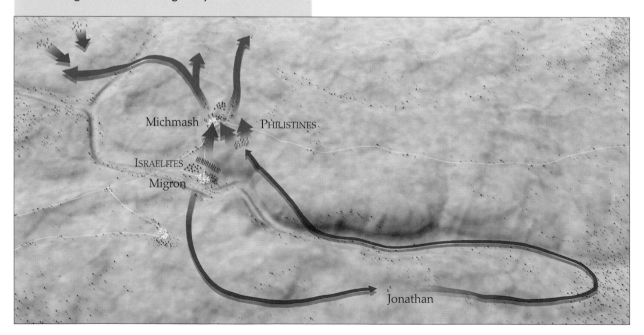

At that time it was not uncommon to massacre the population of a defeated city, though this was not always done. However, the religious dimension to the conflict made the fighting even more savage. This helped perpetuate the conflict as nearby city-states became convinced that they were next on the Hebrews' list of targets.

Word spread that the Hebrews intended to force their religious beliefs on the cities of the region, overrunning and massacring any city that would not join them. This worked in favour of the Hebrews at times, as some cities made alliances with them in the hope of avoiding total destruction, but more cities formed their own alliances and sent their armies against the invaders.

The Hebrews were thus forced to fight their way northward through Canaan, as each alliance they broke spawned another one. Although the time was right for conquest, the Hebrews had a hard task ahead of them as the towns and cities of Canaan were fortified with good walls and defended by forces better equipped than the tribal host. Nevertheless, they were able to overrun all of Canaan and take it for their own.

The Hebrews were ill-equipped but they were tough and desperate, and they had the advantage of belief on their side. They had been told by their Prophets that they would defeat their enemies and take the land for their own, and it seemed to be happening. Each success strengthened their self-belief. Meanwhile their enemies began to see the Hebrews as an invincible force. Many sought alliances while others took the field half-defeated by their enemies' reputation.

The Hebrews also benefited from local sympathizers and their own cunning. Having few material advantages they became adept at using terrain to their advantage, and at scouting for an enemy weakness that could be exploited. Aggression and confidence helped make up for a lack of advanced weapons.

As the Hebrews won battles they gained more advanced military equipment, until they were able to equip themselves in the same manner as their enemies. At first the Hebrews disdained the use of chariots. Indeed, after capturing a great many in battle at the Waters of Merom (c. 1400 BC), the Hebrews destroyed them. Later, the Hebrews did make use of chariots as other Canaanite peoples had done.

WARS WITH THE PHILISTINES

After overrunning Canaan, the Hebrews remained a loose tribal confederation rather than an organized state. Although they now dwelt in cities the Hebrews retained many aspects of their former tribal existence until forced to change by external pressures. This pressure came from the Philistines, who now expanded out from their coastal holdings and began to conquer Hebrew cities, forcing many to pay tribute or live under harsh restrictions.

The Philistines were far more organized than the Hebrews, with central authority resting with a king. A formal and well-equipped army opposed the ad hoc contingents sent by the Hebrew tribes to assist their neighbours.

To counter this threat, the Hebrews appointed Saul as their war leader in c. 1040 BC. Saul set about creating an organized military force but was eventually defeated. The Hebrews had always been suspicious of the idea of having a king,

CAMEL RIDER
Camels were used as beasts of burden or archery platforms by some armies. Their long endurance and ability to operate in difficult terrain made them useful, but they were surly and difficult to control at the best of times.

PHILISTINE SPEARMEN

In common with most other ancient societies, the Philistines relied on spearmen as the backbone of their forces. Philistine infantry were organized and trained, and thus more than a match for Hebrew tribesmen under most conditions.

PHILISTINE ARCHER

Philistine archers fought as skirmishers and supported the spear-armed infantry. They used relatively weak bows which were primarily useful against opponents who had little or no armour.

PHILISTINE CHARIOT

The Philistines occupied the coastal plains, where chariots were highly effective. Philistine chariots may have been derived from Hittite designs, and used iron for some fittings, which made them more durable than earlier Bronze Age chariots.

but Saul's example paved the way for a new order, and his successor, King David, undertook some major military reforms.

Israel and Judah

Under King David, the Hebrews became much more organized and fielded troops equipped with armour and swords as well as archers armed with the new composite bow. The Philistines had been using armour of bronze strips and the world's first true slashing sword for some time, which had given them a significant advantage. The Hebrews could now meet them on equal terms.

The Hebrews also began using chariots, and made war to enlarge their kingdom. Their conquests were, however, short-lived. After the death of David's successor, Solomon, in 931 BC, the Kingdom of Israel, as it was now known, broke into two. Judah, in the south, was small and relatively weak. Israel, to the north, was larger and more populous.

Israel and Judah fought one another as well as outsiders. Judah built fortifications to keep the Egyptians at bay while Israel was a major player in the politics of the region and became the main force in a coalition against the increasing power of the Neo-Assyrian empire.

Israel succeeded in remaining outside the Assyrian empire for many years by a combination of diplomacy and military strength. Fortifications were built and improved, moving from mud-brick construction to solid stone for walls. Allies as far afield as Phoenicia added to the strength of the kingdom and helped deter Assyrian aggression. However, eventually Assyria moved against Israel and overran its cities. This was no minor undertaking – the siege of Samaria lasted three years – but eventually the kingdom was conquered in 721 BC. The Assyrian practice of deporting rebellious populations ensured that the Hebrews of Israel were scattered and their kingdom ceased to exist.

Judah still remained independent for a time, but in 701 BC the Assyrians invaded. They reduced the fortresses of Judah one by one, including the city of Lachish which guarded the approaches to Jerusalem.

SIEGE OF SAMARIA 890 BC

Attacking as the Syrian leaders were drunk or asleep, an elite group of Hebrews caused disorder in the Syrian army. The main force then made an assault, routing the Syrians and pursuing them from the field.

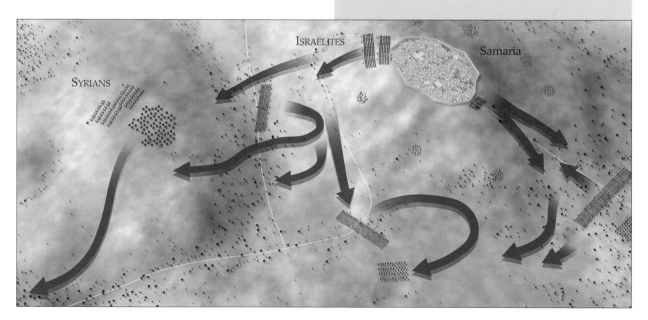

Jerusalem itself was not taken, permitting the Hebrew kingdom to continue in a greatly diminished form. It was not until 586 BC that the city was taken by forces from Babylon. Deportations were again undertaken, effectively ending the Hebrews' kingdom.

The region became a possession of the Persian empire when it conquered Babylon and took its holdings, including Palestine. The tolerant Persians allowed many of the displaced Hebrews to return home, though the region remained a province of the empire. Alexander's conquest of the Persian empire changed little for the Hebrews, though their homeland became a battleground where Alexander's successors in Persia and Egypt fought for supremacy.

A revolt against Seleucid Persian rule in 167 BC led to a period of guerrilla warfare between the rebel Hebrews and the formidable Persian army, which could field elephants as well as Greek-style hoplite phalanxes. The Hebrews eventually won independence and remained a minor but free state until the Roman intervention which began in 63 BC.

The Romans intervened in a political dispute between Hebrew princes to help ensure that their favoured candidate would win. This helped make sure that Judea would remain friendly towards Rome. Not many years later, in 37 BC, the Judean kings were finally deposed and a puppet answering to a Roman governor was installed.

A series of uprisings failed to dislodge the Romans despite great heroism such as the defence of Jerusalem and the fortress of Masada (AD 66–74), and by AD 135 the Hebrew people, also known as Jews or Israelites, were dispersed yet again. They would not have a state of their own again for nearly 2000 years.

Equipment and Organization

The early Hebrew armies were simply large groups of tribal warriors with no armour and only basic equipment. Spears were the main infantry weapon. These were fairly short, as they were intended for use in a fluid melée rather than a close-order formation.

HEBREW INFANTRY, 167 BC
The early Hebrew forces were composed of tribesmen armed with whatever they had managed to make or capture from previous battlefields. Most men had nothing more than a spear or sling to fight with.

For most of the time, spearmen fought as individuals, though the Hebrews' experience in many conflicts instilled a level of discipline and co-operation that substituted for training to some extent. Most men carried only a knife as a secondary weapon, and this was a tool more than a weapon.

Bows and javelins were in use, but the commonest missile weapon was the sling. The sling had the advantages of being very easy to carry and that its ammunition was readily available, but there was no time to look around for suitable stones in the middle of a battle, so men carried a pouch that could be filled on the march. Cast lead shot was also used in some cases. In addition to requiring more skill than a bow to shoot accurately with, a sling was restricted to a more or less horizontal trajectory. However, many Hebrews had used the sling since boyhood and were extremely skilled, and it was as lethal as a bow if it scored a direct hit.

The early Hebrew army was well suited to guerrilla warfare in hills and rough terrain. When drawn out into open battle against a more formally trained and better-equipped army such as that of the Philistines or Phoenicians, the tribal force of the Hebrews was likely to be defeated.

The essentially light-infantry nature of the Hebrew army made it very mobile, allowing surprise attacks and ambushes to be made on an enemy who thought the Hebrews were miles away. The Hebrew style of combat was also reasonably well suited to storming cities, where a close-quarters scramble tended to ensue once the attackers got inside the fortifications. However, getting onto or past the walls was a serious problem for the Hebrews, who resorted to all manner of stratagems and ruses to get inside, or were sometimes assisted by their kin dwelling in the city.

Leadership tended to be loose and of an heroic nature. A tribal leader was expected to lead by example, fighting among his (or her) troops against the enemy's leader or champion. No tribal leader could command other tribes to send men to his assistance, but a request for aid usually resulted in at least a small contingent from each tribe, and more from those that were friendliest to the requesting tribe or felt that it was in their interests to respond.

The greatest leaders – Prophets and the semi-religious, semi-political leaders known as Judges – could raise a massive host from the tribes, but it was not possible to maintain a large force in the field for long as the Hebrews lacked a sophisticated logistics system. Men started drifting home almost as soon as they had arrived, so even the largest army would quickly evaporate unless a very charismatic leader kept it together, or a truly desperate situation existed.

Later Hebrew armies were much better equipped, with armour and weapons taken or copied from their enemies. Once the tribes were reorganized into a kingdom, a formal army could be fielded, with contingents of trained and well-equipped infantry backing up a chariot force.

However, the Hebrews involved in the revolts of their later history would be unlikely to be able to field well-equipped forces with a large chariot arm. They would have to rely on captured weapons and the same sort of irregular, guerrilla warfare that their ancestors had used to defeat the cities of Canaan.

Although the Hebrews' military system changed over time, the main feature of the way they made war remained unchanged. They were extremely good guerrilla fighters who made excellent use of terrain and circumstances. Their main assets were not so much technical or organizational as personal; the Hebrews were resourceful and determined to make the best of what little they had to work with.

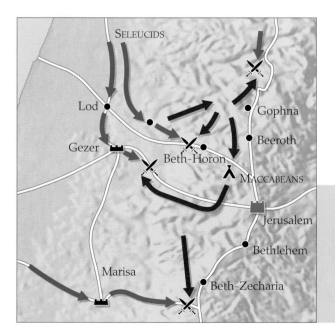

CAMPAIGN OF JUDAH MACCABEE 167–164 BC

Advancing into Judea from the north, Babylonian forces captured several cities before embarking on an 18-month siege of Jerusalem. A relief army marching up from Egypt was defeated and driven off, leaving the kingdom of the Jews to its fate.

CHAPTER 3

Warriors of Ancient Greece

Greece and the surrounding lands and islands were inhabited by Stone Age hunter-gatherers for centuries before the beginnings of civilization. Around 2900 BC, the Bronze Age began in Greece, with the use of metal weapons and tools gradually becoming more prevalent.

The first known Greek civilization was that of the Minoans. It centred on Crete and spread to the surrounding islands. The Minoans probably arrived on Crete from the lands of Asia Minor to the east, around 3000 BC. Over the next ten centuries they learned to use metal and build cities.

The written language of the Minoans was a form of hieroglyphics, possibly derived from contact with the Egyptians. It has, however, defied interpretation. As a result historians know relatively little about the Minoans and their culture, other than from the structures they built.

The Minoans built palaces that seem to have been the centres for government. It is thought that their government

◄ **Greek warriors training with spear and shield, protected by helmets and greaves. This depiction is from a vase dated around the fifth century BC, from the period of the Peloponnesian War (431–404 BC).**

▲ A late Minoan sword, dating from 1500–1450 BC. The design is simple, with no hand protection. The blade is made of bronze, with a gold handle.

was a monarchy backed up by a strong bureaucratic apparatus. The main function of this government was to facilitate and regulate trade.

MINOANS AND MYCENEANS

The Minoans built a large fleet. Their vessels were not warships, though they had some combat capability to defend themselves against pirate attacks, but merchant ships. In these vessels, the Minoans traded along the coasts of the eastern Mediterranean. Their goods have been found by archaeologists in Egypt and throughout Asia Minor. Large-scale maritime trade made the Minoans very wealthy. Their surviving structures suggest that standards of living were high even for the mass of the population. The Minoans even invented plumbing, an innovation that was lost for centuries when their civilization collapsed.

Perhaps due to the location of their homelands, on islands that could not be easily reached by enemies, the Minoans do not seem to have been greatly concerned with military matters. They presumably had some kind of military system, since their cities were protected by defensive works. However, these were much less formidable than those of the mainland civilizations. The smaller towns and the palaces of the ruling class do not seem to have been fortified at all.

The Minoans seem to have managed well enough without a powerful military for centuries, but eventually they met with disaster. It is thought that several of their palaces and major cities were destroyed by earthquakes around 1500 BC, and that a massive volcanic eruption caused tsunamis that devastated coastal areas and destroyed much of the Minoan trading fleet.

The Minoans, weakened by these disasters, were overrun by the Myceneans, a civilization that had arisen in coastal Greece. The Mycenean civilization was named by archaeologists after the site at Mycenae, where a palace and city were excavated.

The Myceneans built several cities, including Athens and Thebes, and were a much more warlike people than the Minoans. Authority was centralized in a king, who exercised power through a bureaucratic system. The Myceneans fortified their palaces and cities, and maintained military forces for conquest as well as defence.

The Myceneans were adept traders, who brought home wealth from far afield. This was less than equally spread throughout society, however; the upper echelons were very rich whilst there was a large poor class. Nonetheless, society as a whole was affluent compared to many contemporary civilizations. This enabled great works and large structures to be built.

Although more is known about the Myceneans than the Minoans, there are still a great many gaps in the data available to archaeologists. Even the later Greeks knew of the Myceneans mainly through legends. The most famous of these is that of the Trojan War. Homer's epic poems depict the legends as they were known centuries later, but it is likely that his writings were based on tales handed down since the Mycenean age.

Legends of the Mycenean age depict warriors wearing armour of bronze and armed with spears, javelins and swords. Chariots and warships are also mentioned. It is not possible to be certain whether or not this is due to later Greeks superimposing their contemporary images of warfare on legendary events, but the Myceneans probably did possess the technology to manufacture military equipment of this sort, and if so they would certainly have made use of it. Archaeological finds corroborate the writings of

CORINTHIAN ARMOUR
The best-equipped Greek warriors enjoyed the protection of a helmet and body armour formed of two halves. These were joined by leather straps locked in place by a bronze pin.

EARLY GREEK WEAPONS
The primary weapon of the Greek warrior was a spear, which might have a variety of heads. Longer swords such as that shown were popular until around 1300 BC, when they were replaced by the shorter design.

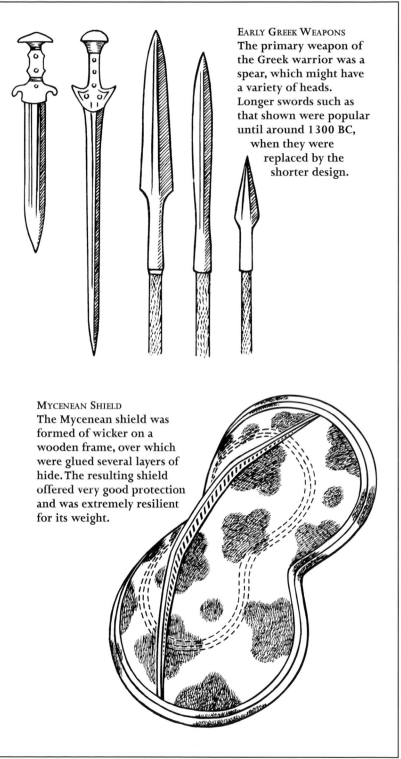

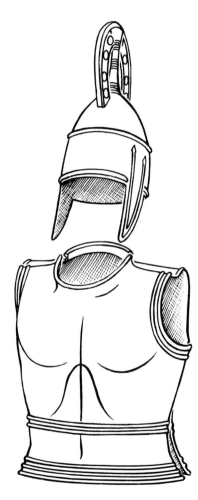

MYCENEAN SHIELD
The Mycenean shield was formed of wicker on a wooden frame, over which were glued several layers of hide. The resulting shield offered very good protection and was extremely resilient for its weight.

Homer to a great extent; Mycenean weapons and armour have been found which match the claims of the *Iliad* and the *Odyssey*.

THE GREEK 'DARK AGE'

The Mycenean age came to a rather abrupt end, ushering in a period known as the Greek 'Dark Age'. During this time the cities were abandoned and people went back to a small-village or even nomadic existence. There is of course little in the way of written record from this period.

The 'Dark Age' began around 1100 BC. There are various theories about its cause. The Sea Peoples are often blamed, as they were very active around this time and are thought to have destroyed many cities and even civilizations elsewhere in the eastern Mediterranean. A similar theory suggests that the Dorians, a warlike people from the north, may have raided the Myceneans' cities to the point where their civilization simply broke down.

Other causes are postulated, including an internal revolt or civil war. Whatever the reason, Mycenae and Tirynth were completely destroyed and the rest of the Mycenean civilization rapidly disintegrated. A massive drop in population then occurred. This may have been due to plague but the collapse of civilization could simply have resulted in starvation, as food grown in one area could no longer be transported to where it was needed.

Whatever the cause, the result was a period in which literacy was virtually non-existent. Thus not only is little known of the 'Dark Age' itself, but much

▼ **Although more warlike than the Minoans, the Myceneans were great traders. Their ships brought home wealth from the ports of the eastern Mediterranean, but were not capable of open-sea navigation.**

of what went before is now lost to history other than as folk tales and legends.

THE ERA OF THE CITY-STATES

While some of the tribes of the Greek 'Dark Age' wandered around the countryside following their herds or hunting for game, others settled in small villages that gradually grew into towns and then cities. From about 750 BC onwards, a return to urban living began. New cities were founded and older ones reoccupied as the population grew.

These small independent cities, or *polis*, gradually grew in power. Trade links and alliances were formed, and conflicts broke out between the city-states. Internal conflict was also not uncommon. Initially, the usual form of government was a monarchy but many of the new city-states deposed their kings and set up their own form of government. This ranged from an oligarchy composed of the few most powerful individuals in the city to a democracy, albeit one in which only free men could vote.

Tyranny, the rule of one man alone, was also a common form of government. Tyrants seized power through a variety of means. Sometimes they were appointed by the general population to deal with a crisis, and then clung to power. Others took advantage of an unstable situation to manoeuvre and connive their way into power. Some tyrants managed to legitimize themselves and to make their position hereditary, essentially becoming kings. Others were quickly replaced by other ambitious tyrants or eventually deposed by a disaffected population.

Thus the politics, internal and external, of the city-states tended to be rather vigorous at times. An effective military force was essential to maintain order and deter enemies – or

defeat them if war proved unavoidable. However, the small city-states could not maintain the same sort of large army that a unified civilization could support. Thus a rather different system evolved.

One way to offset weakness is to use force-multipliers, i.e. factors that make a military force more effective. Defensively, the most obvious means was fortification. Even a small or ill-trained force could hold a set of good walls against a much more numerous foe, especially if the enemy lacked siege equipment to breach the defences. However, no *polis* could afford to be besieged for any length of time. A mobile military force was necessary to break a siege or prevent it being imposed. The alternative was to starve within the walls while the fields lay untended outside, beyond the besieging army.

Military Systems

In order to raise the necessary numbers of troops, a system of militia or citizen-soldiery was implemented, with men being required to make themselves available to fight at need. It was the duty of each free man to provide himself with weapons and a shield – and armour, if he could afford it.

The majority of troops fielded by the city-states were hoplites, named for their large round shield called a *hoplon*. They fought in close order with a long spear, forming a deep formation known as a phalanx. The phalanx was supported by lighter troops which protected its flanks.

Clashes between the phalanx of one *polis* and another tended to be swift and decisive, with one side broken and

◀ **Symbolic objects, known as votives, were often used as religious offerings. This eighth century BC votive shield is decorated with a centaur and hunters.**

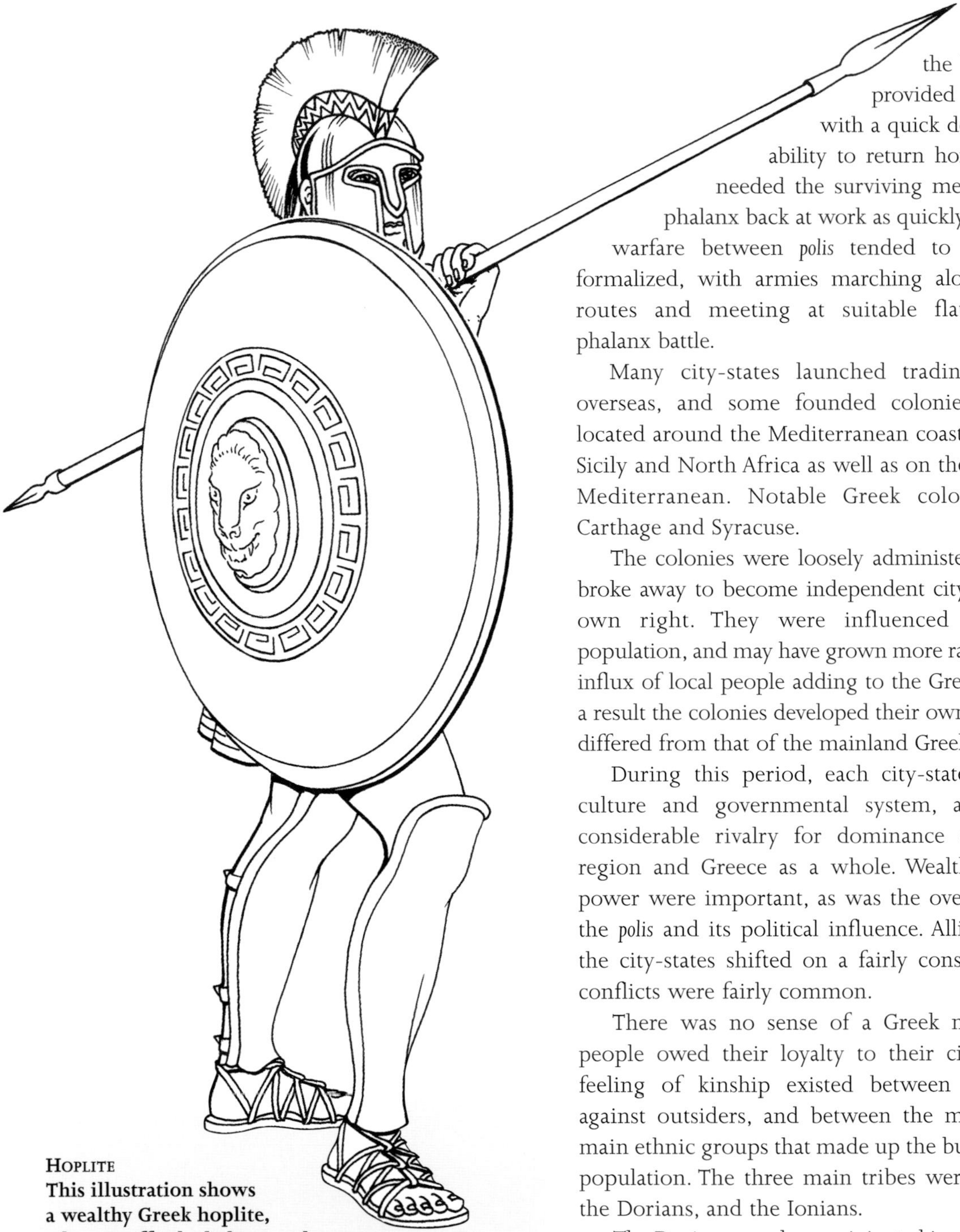

pursued from the battlefield. This provided the city-states with a quick decision and the ability to return home. Both sides needed the surviving members of their phalanx back at work as quickly as possible, so warfare between *polis* tended to be somewhat formalized, with armies marching along predictable routes and meeting at suitable flat areas for a phalanx battle.

Many city-states launched trading expeditions overseas, and some founded colonies. These were located around the Mediterranean coast in Ionia, Italy, Sicily and North Africa as well as on the islands of the Mediterranean. Notable Greek colonies included Carthage and Syracuse.

The colonies were loosely administered, and many broke away to become independent city-states in their own right. They were influenced by the local population, and may have grown more rapidly due to an influx of local people adding to the Greek colonists. As a result the colonies developed their own culture which differed from that of the mainland Greek city-states.

During this period, each city-state had its own culture and governmental system, and there was considerable rivalry for dominance over the local region and Greece as a whole. Wealth and military power were important, as was the overall prestige of the *polis* and its political influence. Alliances between the city-states shifted on a fairly constant basis, and conflicts were fairly common.

There was no sense of a Greek nation as such; people owed their loyalty to their city. However, a feeling of kinship existed between fellow Greeks against outsiders, and between the members of the main ethnic groups that made up the bulk of the Greek population. The three main tribes were the Aeolians, the Dorians, and the Ionians.

The Dorians may have originated in northern Greece and Macedonia, or perhaps in Asia Minor. They migrated southwards, displacing other Greek tribes and establishing themselves in the Greek heartlands. Raids or migrations by the Dorians have been postulated as a

HOPLITE
This illustration shows a wealthy Greek hoplite, who can afford a helmet and greaves as well as a cuirass to protect his body. Possession of good armour earned a man the honour of fighting in the front ranks where the danger was greatest.

possible cause of the Greek 'Dark Age'. The Dorians founded or conquered many of the major city-states of Greece, including Sparta, Corinth and Argos.

The Ionians were displaced from their original homelands by the Dorian migrations, settling in Ionia and Anatolia. The Aeolians originated in Thessaly and were also displaced by the Dorians, eventually settling in uninhabited regions or areas abandoned by other peoples, including islands off the coast of Asia Minor. These two groups are sometimes collectively referred to as Achaeans, though other peoples were also included in the group given that name.

Ethnic and cultural links did influence the politics of the city-states to some extent. For example, a Dorian city that found itself at war could generally expect assistance from other Dorians. This did not prevent conflict within the ethnic group itself, nor were alliances between Achaean and Dorian cities unknown.

Overall, cultural and ethnic links were little more than an influencing factor in the politics of the Greek city-states. Self-interest and local politics were far more important in determining which cities would assist their neighbours and which would exploit the situation, even when Greece was threatened with foreign invasion.

WAR WITH PERSIA

In 539 BC, the Persian empire was expanding and sought to conquer the Greek colonies in Ionia. Having overrun Lydia, Persian forces moved against the Ionian Greeks and quickly captured their cities along with some of the Greek islands.

In 521 BC Darius became King of Persia, and began seeking to expand his domain. Scythia was invaded in 513 BC, and Thrace in 511 BC. The disunited Greek city-states seemed like a good prospect for conquest, but Darius ceased his expansion for a time, leaving a governor in charge of his conquests.

Peace between Persia and the Greek city-states lasted for over a decade, but in 499 BC revolt broke out among the conquered Greek colonies of Ionia. The exact reasons for the revolt are lost to history, though some sources suggest that Persian rule was fairly oppressive. It is also possible that the Ionian cities were encouraged to revolt by their kin in Greece itself.

SCYTHIAN ARCHER
Scythians were hired as mercenaries by various Greek city states and the Persian Empire. They were renowned as archers; so much so that Scythian instructors were appointed to train the archers of the Persian army.

Certainly, other Greek cities sent assistance, even though the colonies had long ago become independent of mainland Greece.

The Ionian revolt went on until the rebels were decisively defeated at the battle of Lade in 494 BC. Within a year, Persian rule had been firmly restored in Ionia and Darius began looking towards mainland Greece as an avenue for expansion. It is highly likely that Darius also wanted to pay the Greeks back for interfering in the Ionian revolt.

An invasion of Greece from Persian territories in Asia Minor was no minor undertaking. It was theoretically possible to march north, cross the Hellespont and come around via Macedon, but this would mean a long campaign just to secure a route. A direct approach across the Aegean sea was much more practical, especially since Persia already possessed a large fleet that was ideal for the job.

Persian emissaries toured the city-states of Greece, demanding submission to Persia. This was usually on generous terms, being mostly an agreement to pay lip-service to the Persian empire and remain neutral in any conflict between Persia and those who would not submit. Many Greek states agreed to Darius' terms, including the strategically important island of Aegina. This worried Athens, whose trade was threatened by Persian control of Aegina. Athens and Sparta demanded that Aegina withdraw from its agreement with Persia, creating a diplomatic incident. This may have been what Darius wanted as a pretext for war.

Marathon

Darius opened his campaign in 490 BC by crossing the Aegean to land at Eretria, which surrendered to his army. The city was destroyed and the population enslaved, after which the Persian army re-embarked for the short crossing to the Greek mainland.

The Persian army landed at Marathon, and a Greek army marched to meet them. This force came almost entirely from Athens, as the Spartans were unwilling to go to war until they had finished their religious

MARATHON 490 BC

Not waiting for their allies to come up in support, the primarily Athenian force advanced rapidly and crushed the Persian wings before falling on the enemy centre. The Persian force was driven back to its ships, where a desperate stand allowed an equally hurried re-embarkation.

ATHENIANS

PERSIANS

celebrations. As a result, about 10,000 Greeks arrived as around twice that number of Persians were still on shore.

Despite misgivings about the numbers facing them, the Greeks chose to fight and advanced aggressively. Historical sources claim that the Greek hoplites charged at a run for a whole mile (1.6km) to strike the Persian army, but this seems unlikely given the heavy arms and equipment they used. However, it is reasonable to assume that the Greeks advanced rapidly and charged home with great ferocity. Their force was almost entirely of heavy infantry, with no cavalry or missile troops in support, so a head-on attack with levelled spears was the only real option.

The Greeks had thinned their line to match the length of that of the Persians, resulting in a dangerously weak centre. There, the Persian heavy infantry recovered from the shock of impact and began to push the Greeks back. However, the Greek hoplites on the flanks drove off their lighter-armed opponents and closed in on the Persian centre like a giant pincer. The Persian army was broken and pursued to its ships, where a desperate rearguard action permitted many of the Persians to board their ships and escape.

Defeat of the Persians

For ten years there was no further attempt by the Persians to invade Greece, but Darius' successor, Xerxes I, made a renewed attempt at conquest in 480 BC. An alliance of Greek city-states, including Athens, Corinth and Sparta, formed to resist the invasion.

Sea power was vital to this undertaking as the Persian army had to be transported and supplied across the Aegean. The allied Greek fleet moved to prevent the Persians from passing the straits of Artemisium, though numbers were heavily in the Persians' favour.

▲ King Leonidas of Sparta bids farewell to his allies before the battle of Thermopylae. The greatly outnumbered Greeks were able to hold up the Persian invasion for a week.

This was evened up somewhat by storms, which cost the Persians several hundred ships wrecked or scattered, but even so the 271 Greek vessels were outnumbered nearly three to one.

After two days of skirmishing, a full-scale naval action was fought which ended in a tactical stalemate. Strategically, however, the Persians came off best as they could afford the casualties and the Greeks could not. The remnant of the Greek fleet withdrew to the island of Salamis where it was joined by reinforcements from other cities.

Meanwhile, the Persian army, possibly 300,000 strong, was met at the pass of Thermopylae by a force of about 7000 Greeks under Spartan leadership. This tiny force was able to delay the Persians for a week, much of which time was spent in a stand-off in the narrow pass.

After breaking through at Thermopylae and opening up the seaward supply route, the Persians advanced through Boeotia and captured Athens, though the city had been evacuated in anticipation of invasion and stood empty.

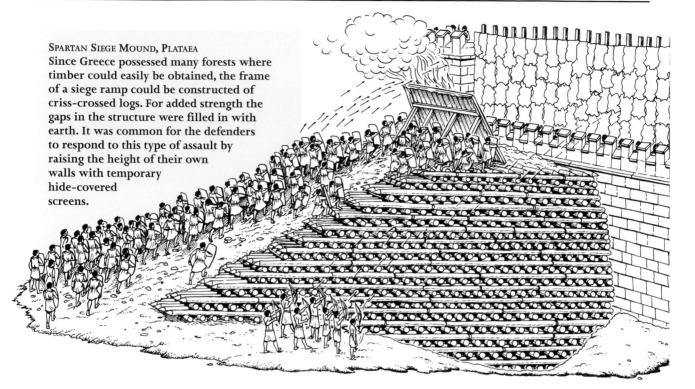

SPARTAN SIEGE MOUND, PLATAEA
Since Greece possessed many forests where timber could easily be obtained, the frame of a siege ramp could be constructed of criss-crossed logs. For added strength the gaps in the structure were filled in with earth. It was common for the defenders to respond to this type of assault by raising the height of their own walls with temporary hide-covered screens.

The fleets clashed again at Salamis, this time resulting in a Greek victory and serious losses for the Persians. Convinced that the naval campaign was lost, Xerxes withdrew his fleet. This in turn meant that the army could not be supplied or supported, so most of it was also withdrawn.

The remnant of the Persian army was defeated at Plataea in 479 BC, by a large army of Greek allies. After a long stand-off the Greeks began to withdraw to preserve their supply lines. This drew out the Persians into a pursuit. The Greeks turned and inflicted a sharp defeat, then overran the enemy camp and destroyed the Persian army.

Defeat at Plataea was accompanied by disaster at sea. A naval battle at Mycale shattered the Persian fleet. These two battles effectively ended the Persian threat to Greece, and allowed the Greeks to begin a campaign against Persia.

The Delian League

To this end, the Delian League was formed, so-called because its treasury and meeting-place were on the island state of Delos. Led by Athens, the League was an alliance dedicated to making war against Persia, though many members made financial contributions only. As the forces of the Delian League removed Persian garrisons from captured territories, the Ionian cities revolted again, this time successfully.

Egypt also revolted against Persian rule, and the League sent forces to assist the Egyptians. These were mostly captured after four years of war, when the revolt was finally put down in 456 BC. A naval campaign fought over control of Cyprus was more successful, and afterward the Graeco-Persian conflict wound down. It is not clear whether or not a formal treaty was ever signed, but there was no more war between Greece and Persia after 450 BC.

SEA WARFARE

The development of fighting ships was a continual process, with specialist warships emerging from merchant and fishing vessels. The earliest known designs date back to around 3000 BC. These were trading vessels that hugged the coast; open-sea navigation was not developed for many centuries. With

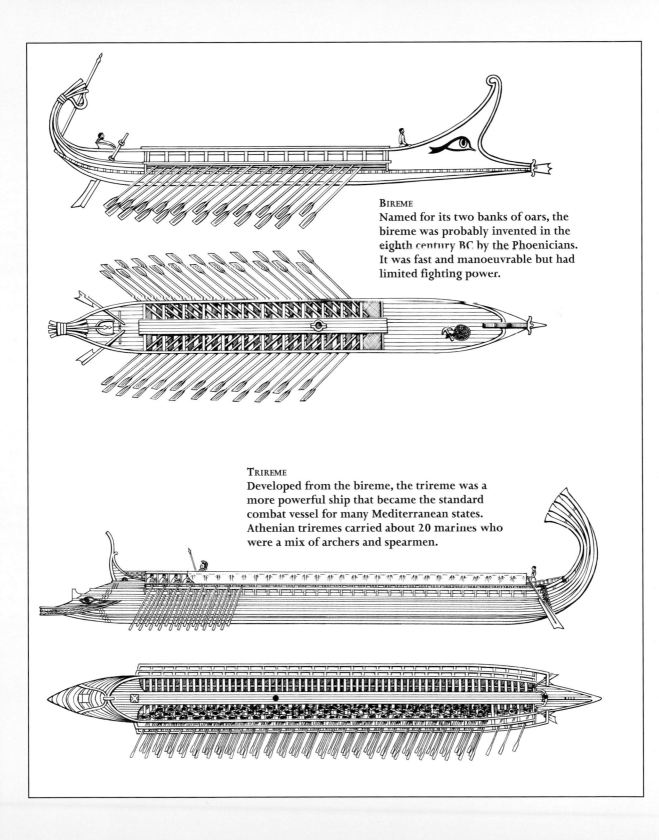

BIREME
Named for its two banks of oars, the bireme was probably invented in the eighth century BC by the Phoenicians. It was fast and manoeuvrable but had limited fighting power.

TRIREME
Developed from the bireme, the trireme was a more powerful ship that became the standard combat vessel for many Mediterranean states. Athenian triremes carried about 20 marines who were a mix of archers and spearmen.

their shallow draught they could enter almost any waters and navigate rivers as well as being dragged up on the shore at night.

The various designs of vessel in use in the Mediterranean are known as galleys. There were several broad types of galley and many individual designs. What they all had in common was the ability to be propelled by oars or sails.

Rigging was very simple and the sails were only useful in a favourable wind. Thus naval galleys used their sails for strategic movement where possible but relied on oar power much of the time. Sails were not deployed in combat. Where possible, they were left ashore before battle.

Early galleys with a single row of oars on each side were termed penteconters. These were gradually supplanted by more powerful ships with two banks of oars, referred to by modern historians as biremes. Triremes, with three banks of oars, appeared soon afterward.

> "SIRE, BE NOT GRIEVED NOR GREATLY DISTRESSED BECAUSE OF WHAT HAS BEFALLEN US. IT IS NOT ON THINGS OF WOOD THAT THE ISSUE HANGS FOR US, BUT ON MEN AND HORSES."
>
> PERSIAN GENERAL MARDONIUS AFTER DEFEAT AT SEA OFF SALAMIS

New Weapons and Tactics

The move towards more powerful ships was prompted largely by a change in weaponry and tactics. Up until 800 BC or so, there were only two modes of attack for a warship; missile fire and boarding. These remained viable options, but with the invention of the ram, a more decisive attack could be made.

A ram-equipped galley could ram an enemy vessel from the side, smashing in its timbers and sinking it, or could pass close alongside with its own oars shipped, snapping off the enemy vessel's oars and causing mayhem among the rowers as their oars flung them about. This manoeuvre required a highly skilled crew to avoid self-inflicting the same fate on its oarsmen or coasting to a stop halfway along the side of the enemy vessel.

Some rams were designed to break off in the target, allowing the ramming vessel to back oars and avoid becoming entangled with the target and its crew, who might resort to boarding in an effort to escape their crippled vessel. Other rams were more robust, allowing repeated ramming attacks. It was still possible to avoid entanglement by good shiphandling.

A ship with more oars could theoretically generate more power, enabling it to avoid ramming attacks and to get into position to make an attack of its own. However, much depended on the skill of the crew for this to happen. Slaves were not likely to possess the necessary skill and motivation, so free professional rowers were often used.

Experiments were made with quadriremes and quinqueremes in the hope of creating an even more powerful ship. It was impractical to build a vessel with four or five banks of oars, so additional oarsmen were added on the upper oars. Thus a quinquereme ('fiver') may have had a single man on the lowest oar in a set, and two men on each of the upper ones. The ship still had three banks of oars but these were more powerful than those of a trireme – at least in theory.

In practice, the large crews required to man these vessels produced diminishing returns, as did the huge vessels built by some of the successor states. Ptolemy IV of Egypt built a multi-hulled 'polyreme' with the equivalent of 40 rowers at each station. Whilst impressive, this was not a practical vessel of war.

The ships of the Greek, Macedonian and Persian fleets were more modest but highly effective triremes. The majority of the crew were oarsmen, with a contingent of marines aboard. The design of the ship depended on how important the marines were considered to be. Marines were trained to deliver missile fire and to take part in – or resist – boarding actions. Navies that preferred to fight in this way designed ships to make the best use of their marine contingent whilst other navies relied on the ram for their striking power.

Thus at the battle of Salamis the Persian ships, built for boarding actions, had high sides and prows, and carried 30 or so marines. The Greeks preferred to ram and sink their opponents rather than exchange arrows and javelins with the crew or to attempt boarding (although all options remained open to a captain who spotted an opportunity), and only carried eight or so marines and were built lower in the water.

Favoured tactics of the Greek galley forces included the *periplous*, essentially a flanking movement allowing a ramming attack from the side and the *diekplous*, which involved concentrating several ships at a single point in the enemy line, breaking through it and throwing the enemy force into confusion.

As a general rule, ramming tactics required a higher standard of shiphandling and skill among the rowers as they depended greatly upon the ability of a crew to accelerate at the right time then back oars and disengage. Those nations that lacked such skill tended to deploy bigger, heavier ships with greater troop numbers aboard in the hope of defeating their enemies with missiles or boarding.

Much also depended on local sea conditions. At Salamis, the heavy Persian ships were hampered by a heavy swell that made them hard to row. This affected the lighter Greek ships less severely. A knowledge of local conditions was every bit as vital to a galley force commander as the fighting ability of his crews.

Ultimately, although the Graeco-Persian wars were fought mostly on land, it was sea power that defeated the Persian invasion and allowed the Greeks to take the offensive. Sea power also enabled the Greek city-states to prosper through trade and establish colonies all around the eastern Mediterranean. The galley, as much as the hoplite, was the symbol of Greek power and prowess for several centuries.

ATHENIAN TRIREME
Three sets of rowers, one above the other, would have created a vessel that was top-heavy. Instead, the rowers' positions were inclined.

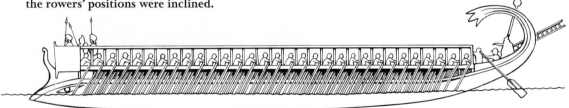

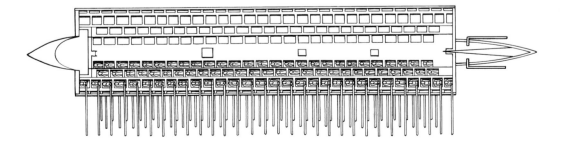

Battle of Salamis (480 BC)

Defeated at sea in the battle of Artemisium and on land at Thermopylae, the Greek city-states were in a dangerous position. Their fleet, built up to resist the Persian invasion, was heavily outnumbered and had taken refuge off the island of Salamis. Several city-states were considering withdrawing their vessels to protect their own interests. Meanwhile the Persian army was marching towards Athens.

Athenian statesmen argued that the Greeks needed to stand together and persuaded the other city-states to leave their contingents in place at Salamis. These vessels assisted in the evacuation of Athens, ferrying the population to the tenuous safety of the island.

Even though the Persian fleet had lost many ships in a series of devastating storms, and had been further reduced by the actions of Greek naval forces, it was still larger than the fleet of the city-states. However, the Persian invasion of Greece depended upon sea power to keep the army supplied, and the Greek fleet was still a serious threat to the Persians' supply line.

SALAMIS 480 BC

A combination of deception and excellent seamanship allowed the Greeks to defeat a greatly superior Persian force at Salamis. Drawing the Persians into narrow waters, the Greeks ambushed them in conditions that favoured the Greek ships over the more powerful but top-heavy and less manoeuvrable Persian vessels.

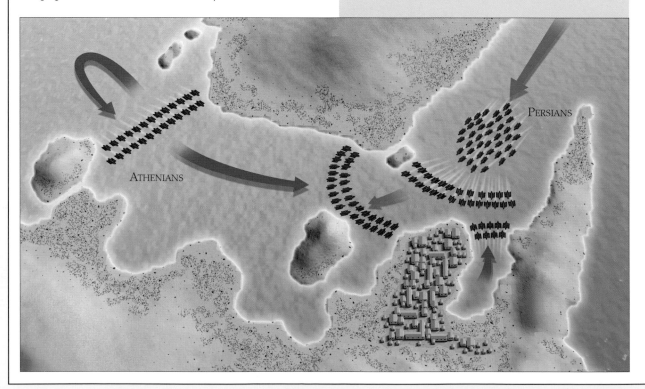

ATHENIANS

PERSIANS

The Persian fleet needed to eliminate the Greek naval capability, to make sure that the supply route to the army was not disrupted. With the whole Greek fleet bottled up in the straits off Salamis, there existed an opportunity to strike a knockout blow, removing the threat at a stroke rather than chasing down small numbers of ships or dealing with nuisance attacks for months or years to come.

Besides, revenge upon Athens was one of the goals of the invasion. Not only would destruction of the Greek fleet at Salamis eliminate the Athenian navy but it would give the Persians access to the island and the Athenians sheltering on the island.

Greek Weakness

The Greeks had managed to muster a very considerable force of ships, though many fled when the Persian fleet arrived, leaving about 310 to fight. At least 700 Persian ships were available to take part in the battle, and they were in better condition than their Greek counterparts, having been overhauled recently.

The Greek command structure was fragmented, with leaders from various city-states arguing over what was to be done and over matters of precedence. Thus it came as no surprise to the Persian commanders when the Athenian leader Themistocles sent a message offering to defect to their side.

Themistocles told the Persians that some of the Greek fleet planned to escape under cover of darkness, prompting them to deploy ships to pursue any that fled. The following morning a Corinthian squadron began retiring up the Salamis channel, and other Greek ships began to follow them.

The Persians had ships positioned to trap the escapees, and launched their main force into the channel to crush them between hammer and anvil. However, it became apparent that the flight was a ruse when the fleeing ships came about and formed into a battle line. Other Greek ships came out of a side channel where they had lain concealed and fell on the Persian flank. The Persian fleet had greater numbers, but this was not such an advantage in the confined waters as it would have been on the open sea, and their squadrons were disordered which prevented effective use of their strength. Although the Persian ships generally carried twice as many marines as their opponents, the Greeks had put every fighting man they had aboard their ships, gambling everything on victory at sea. Even the sea was against the Persians, whose top-heavy vessels were at a disadvantage in the morning swell.

The Greek ships attacked with ramming and missile fire, killing the Persian admiral and adding to the confusion among their enemies. With the fury of desperation the Greeks broke some of the Persian squadrons, opening gaps through which to fall upon others. Soon, the whole Persian fleet was in chaotic retreat, with the Greeks in pursuit.

The next morning, the Greeks began repairing their ships for a renewed clash, but the Persians were beaten. Their battleworthy vessels were now outnumbered by the Greeks and morale had been crushed by the sudden and shocking defeat.

The Persian fleet withdrew the following night, which also brought the land campaign to an end. Without a secure supply route across the sea, the army could not be maintained on Greek soil. Thus naval power secured victory on land and defeated the Persian invasion.

▲ **A modern painting of the battle of Salamis, showing a Greek vessel ramming a taller Persian ship. Sails were not normally carried in battle, ideally being left behind on shore.**

THE PELOPONNESIAN WAR

Over time, the Delian League became more or less an Athenian empire. Athens dictated policy to other members of the League and punished those who sought to secede. Contributions in the form of troops and ships were discontinued; members paid what was effectively tribute to Athens, which used a large portion of these funds for non-military purposes.

Disaffection grew, and in 465 BC Thassos not only left the League but aligned itself with Persia. Sparta, meanwhile, had dissociated itself from the League, becoming increasingly hostile towards Athens. In 457 BC the conflict became open, with a Spartan army marching against Athens. By 431 BC, the Delian League, dominated by Athens, and the Spartan-led Peloponnesian League were becoming increasingly hostile to one another. A supposedly 30-year treaty of peace collapsed and open warfare broke out.

The armies of the Peloponnesian War were more varied than those that had existed at the beginning of the Graeco-Persian war. Hoplites were still the core of the army, but they were now supported by contingents of lighter infantry and cavalry.

There was also a disparity between the forces involved in the war. Athens was primarily a naval power, whilst Sparta was the pre-eminent military

▼ **The Peloponnesian War (431–404 BC) was caused by tensions between Sparta and Athens. The conflict spread to every corner of the Greek world and resulted in an eventual Spartan victory.**

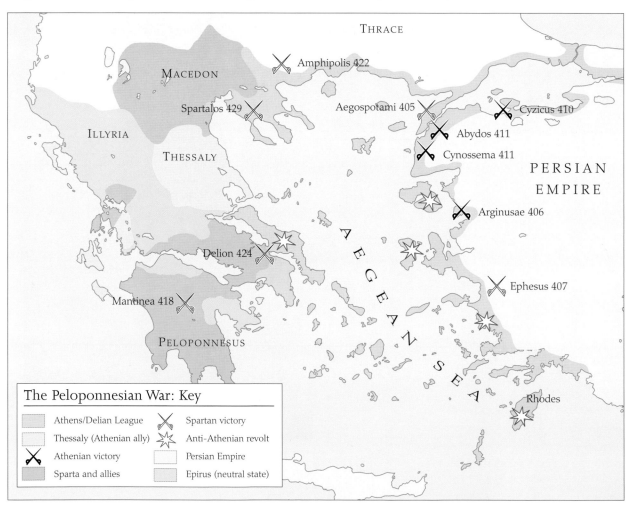

THRACE

MACEDON

✕ Amphipolis 422

Spartalos 429 ✕

Aegospotami 405 ✕

Cyzicus 410 ✕

ILLYRIA

✕ Abydos 411

THESSALY

✕ Cynossema 411

PERSIAN EMPIRE

✕ Arginusae 406

Delion 424 ✕

A E G E A N   S E A

✕ Ephesus 407

Mantinea 418 ✕

PELOPONNESUS

Rhodes

The Peloponnesian War: Key

▨ Athens/Delian League	✕ Spartan victory
▢ Thessaly (Athenian ally)	✸ Anti-Athenian revolt
✕ Athenian victory	▢ Persian Empire
▨ Sparta and allies	▨ Epirus (neutral state)

power on land. Both sides made use of their advantages as best they could, with the Athenians maintaining naval blockades while the Spartans and their allies sought a decisive result on land.

The Athenian strategy involved cutting off supplies to the Peloponnesian League, and capturing their overseas territories. The expedition to Syracuse in 415 BC was one such attempt, albeit an ill-advised one.

Syracuse (415–413 BC)

Seeking to increase its power by conquering the rich city of Syracuse, a Corinthian colony, the Athenians sent a fleet to Sicily carrying a small army. This was a considerable undertaking; an amphibious operation had never before been launched over such a great distance. The fleet made slow progress through coastal waters, beaching each night to rest ashore. Thus the Syracusans had time to prepare for the attack.

The operation went well at first. The Athenians allowed the Syracusans to march out to attack their camp, then boarded their ships and advanced rapidly up the coast, establishing themselves ashore in front of the city without much resistance while the Syracusan army could only trudge back homewards.

An attempt to dislodge the Athenians failed, but nothing could be achieved before winter set in. By the spring, the Syracusans had improved their fortifications. The Athenians were able to re-establish their positions after some fighting, and a period of fortification-building ensued as both sides tried to secure vital terrain. The outposts, forts and walls built by both sides became the focus of intense fighting, in which the Athenians were eventually victorious.

As the siege closed in on Syracuse, reinforcements arrived from Sparta and began attacking the Athenians while the Syracusans mounted frequent sallies from within their walls. These were largely unsuccessful but helped wear down the Athenians.

Spartan and Corinthian ships continued to arrive, to the point where a battle against the Athenian fleet offered a reasonable prospect of success, and additional Athenian forces were also sent to Sicily. Athenian support for their expedition was reduced due to a need to counter Spartan attacks on Greek mainland targets.

After more fighting, the Athenian fleet became bottled up in the harbour, while several of their fortifications were overrun. Athenian supply convoys were intercepted and gradually their army became besieged in its own siege works while their fleet was gradually whittled down by naval attacks.

SYRACUSE 415–413 BC

The Athenians attempted to cut off Syracuse with encircling walls, prompting the defenders to construct 'spoke' walls intersecting those of the attackers. Once their fleet became trapped in the harbour, the Athenians found themselves on the defensive. They were finally driven inland and forced to surrender.

SYRACUSAN FORCES

ATHENIANS

▲ **Cornered in the harbour at Syracuse, the Athenian fleet fell prey to repeated attacks which reduced its strength until a naval breakout became impossible.**

Despite the arrival of Athenian reinforcements and a vigorous assault on the city's defences, the Athenians were unable to regain the upper hand. With sickness in their camp, morale collapsing and the army short of supplies, the Athenians were attacked from land and sea until the only option left was a breakout.

A desperate attempt to break through the Syracusan fleet failed after intense fighting, forcing the Athenians to abandon any hope of escaping the island and returning home. Instead they began to retreat inland. As they did so, the Athenians were harassed by cavalry and light troops until they were finally cornered between forces blocking a pass and the pursuing army.

After a determined attempt to break through and escape, the Athenians tried to escape along the coast. Their rearguard was surrounded and compelled to surrender, and soon afterwards the main body, its will to fight completely gone, was brought to action. After what amounted to a massacre, the surviving Athenians surrendered.

Defeat at Syracuse not only dented Athenian prestige and morale; it more or less emptied the treasury and cost Athens large numbers of ships and men that could not be easily replaced. Attempts to do so caused resentment among allies who felt that they had already contributed quite enough to the war.

During the last years of the war, around 410–406 BC, the Spartans encouraged Athens' allies to revolt and gradually chipped away at her ability to make war by cutting off supplies of grain and silver. Bankrupt, Athens was forced to surrender and Sparta became the dominant power in Greece.

Sparta Ascendant

Sparta could not control all of Greece in the manner of a centralized empire, but it was possible for it to maintain a position of dominance by forbidding alliances that might allow other cities to challenge its military might. However, Sparta's position was not completely unassailable.

Only a year after surrendering, a greatly weakened Athens was nonetheless able to restore its own chosen form of government and dispose of the oligarchy that had been imposed by the victorious Spartans. This challenge to Spartan authority, which went unanswered, may have been a factor in the decision of Argos, Athens, Corinth and Thebes to form an alliance.

The result was what became known as the Corinthian War, which ran from 395 to 387 BC. At first Sparta was victorious; her hoplite phalanx was more than a match for those of the allies and inflicted the expected defeat. However, tactical innovations worked in favour of the allies. At the battle of Lechaeum in 391 BC, a force of lightly equipped peltasts defeated a Spartan hoplite force by using hit-and-run tactics.

The Corinthian War was a relatively low-intensity conflict after the first year. It

came to an end when the Persian empire, which had been supporting the allies, switched its allegiance to Sparta. A treaty was signed, which essentially restored the pre-war situation, although Athens made some gains.

Thebes gradually grew in power, until it began to be seen as a threat by Sparta. In 382 BC, Spartan forces occupied the citadel of Thebes in response to this threat, though by 378 BC the Spartan presence had been removed. This made war between the two cities more or less inevitable.

Theban forces captured former Spartan territory in Boeotia, prompting a demand from Sparta that she withdraw her forces. This was not done, so a Spartan army advanced on Thebes. This force was mainly composed of hoplites, with some cavalry and light troops in support. The Thebans had more light forces but less troops overall, and were forced to innovate in order to avoid defeat. At the battle of Leuctra in 371 BC, by refusing one flank and strengthening the other, the Theban army was able to defeat the supposedly invincible Spartan phalanx.

As a consequence of this victory, Theban forces were able to carry the war into Spartan territory, though this

▶ The hoplites' body armour, helmets and greaves are clearly evident in this carving. Hoplites enjoyed a status equivalent to that of heavy cavalry in some other armies and were given prominence in military art.

was a fairly low-key offensive with no decisive outcome. The war gradually wound down leaving both Thebes and Sparta as major players in Greek affairs, though Sparta never regained her former prestige and power.

Theban forces again defeated the Spartans at the battle of Mantinea in 362 BC. Both had many allies at this battle, which was the largest encounter between the armies of the Greek city-states. Thebes briefly displaced Sparta as the main power in Greece, but the conflict weakened the Greek city-states as a whole and created an opportunity for the forces of Macedon to launch a successful invasion.

HOPLITE WARFARE

The citizen-soldier system used by the Greek city-states allowed large numbers of troops to be raised quickly by a general muster, and at little cost to the government. However, it was not possible to deliver much training to a volunteer force of this nature, and the economic disruption of a long campaign would be disastrous. As a result, a quintessentially Greek form of warfare arose. This worked very well against others who also played by the same rules, and against any opponent foolish enough to try to tackle the phalanx head-on. Indeed, the only formation able to survive the onslaught of the phalanx was another phalanx of comparable size.

This form of warfare was eminently suitable for resolving disputes between city-states, who all adopted similar tactics to each other. When conflict arose with outsiders, however, or when a commander deviated from the conventional form of warfare, the weaknesses of the system were made apparent.

Service as a hoplite was a matter of social standing, and a man's conduct in battle had a major influence on his civilian life. Being part of a phalanx that was defeated was not too shameful, as more or less the entire male population of the city had shared in the defeat, but a hoplite who dropped his shield to flee was shamed in the eyes of his peers.

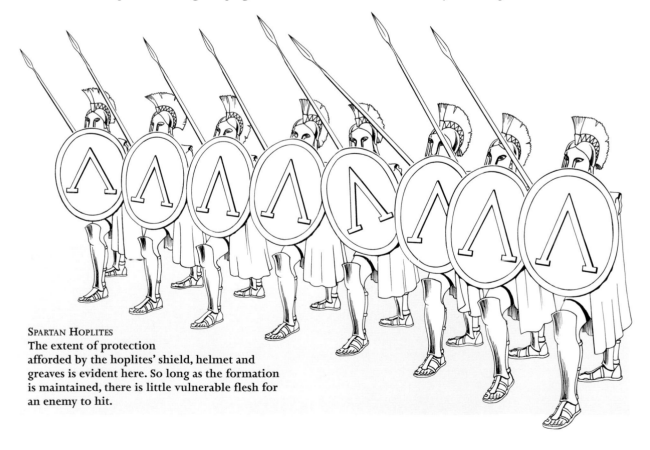

SPARTAN HOPLITES
The extent of protection afforded by the hoplites' shield, helmet and greaves is evident here. So long as the formation is maintained, there is little vulnerable flesh for an enemy to hit.

▶ The battle of Plataea was the final land action of the Persian invasion of Greece. Decisively beaten, the Persians were driven back into their camp and then massacred.

In addition to the spear and shield, which were necessary to stand in the phalanx and were symbols of manhood, additional military gear was important to those who cared about their social standing.

Possession of full armour granted the honour of standing in the front rank of the phalanx, with lesser-armoured

men behind and those who had no armour making up numbers at the back. Whilst there were social advantages to being seen in the front lines of the phalanx, this was something of a mixed blessing as those in the front ranks faced several spearpoints at the moment of contact and were liable to be speared or trampled underfoot in the ensuing clash.

The concept that the position of greatest risk carried with it social advantages was by no means unique to hoplite warfare; later in history, troops would eagerly volunteer for units engaged in high-risk operations or as members of 'forlorn hope' assault parties in the expectation of winning promotion or recognition for their bravery.

In the forces of the city-states, where the social order and military system were so intertwined, a man who did not perform to the expectations of his peers was effectively ruined when the campaign was

◀ This iron breastplate, dating from the fourth century BC, is decorated with symbols of King Philip II of Macedon. It may have been a ceremonial item or actually worn in war.

over, so there was a strong social incentive to seek a dangerous, exposed position to fight from.

Training and Tactics

Hoplite tactics were straightforward. Wars tended to be somewhat formalized, with an army marching along a predictable route so that its opponents could intercept it at a place suitable for a battle. After drawing up in battle order on fairly flat ground the two forces advanced towards one another with spears levelled.

Each hoplite was partially protected by his own shield and partly by the shield of the man on his right. This led to a tendency for a phalanx to angle to the right as it advanced, as each man tried to ensure he remained protected behind his neighbour's shield. If possible, a phalanx would attempt to overlap the enemy right, enabling its members to attack the enemy's shieldless side.

To counter the rightwards drift and the tendency to become disordered, a leader was posted at the front and rear of each file of hoplites, and the most experienced men were placed at the right of the line. This tradition of placing the best men and units on the right carried over into other forms of warfare, long after the phalanx had been abandoned.

One consequence of positioning the best men on the right was that, all else being equal, two phalanxes would tend to revolve around a central point as the strong right flank of each defeated the weaker left of the opposition.

The advance to contact was usually at a steady and deliberate walk, to maintain unit cohesion, though if the enemy looked weak or shaky then the hoplites might

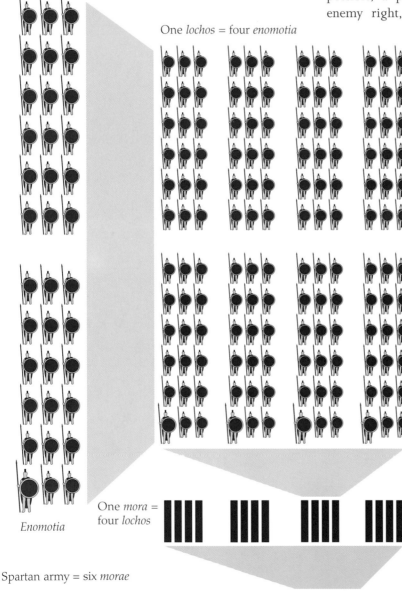

One *lochos* = four *enomotia*

Enomotia

One *mora* = four *lochos*

Spartan army = six *morae*

◀ **Spartan unit structure. The smallest unit was the *enomotia*, consisting of three files of 12 men. *Enomotia* were coupled to form *pentekostyes*, two of which made up the basic unit of the phalanx, a *lochos*. A *morae* consisted of four *lochos*.**

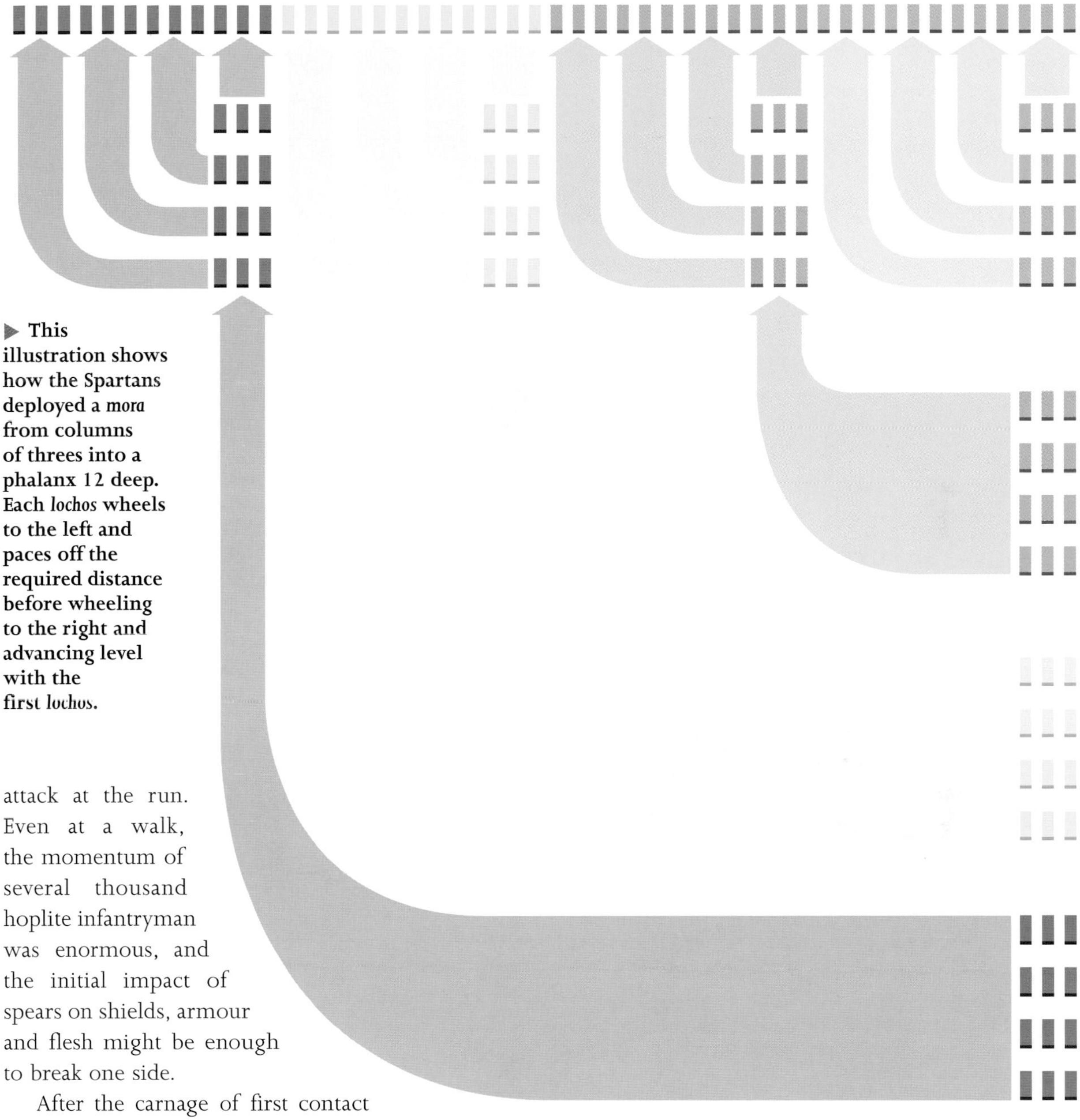

▶ **This illustration shows how the Spartans deployed a *mora* from columns of threes into a phalanx 12 deep. Each *lochos* wheels to the left and paces off the required distance before wheeling to the right and advancing level with the first *lochos*.**

attack at the run. Even at a walk, the momentum of several thousand hoplite infantryman was enormous, and the initial impact of spears on shields, armour and flesh might be enough to break one side.

After the carnage of first contact the forces might recoil apart and clash again, or else would become locked together in a giant pushing match. Long spears allowed several ranks of men to present their points to the enemy, but the depth of the formation was mainly important to allow the men in the rear to brace those in front of them and shove them forward.

Push and Shove

Success in a close-fought hoplite battle depended greatly on 'pushing power' provided by the strength of numbers, but this had to be delivered in a coherent way to avoid a phalanx simply collapsing under the stress of its own efforts. A considerable degree of trust between members of the phalanx was necessary, and the shared danger and exertion was a powerful factor in bonding members of a community after a battle.

Hoplites trained to carry out the *othismos*, a manoeuvre whereby every man in the phalanx took a number of deliberate steps forward. Keeping the unit organized and in formation whilst moving was essential, so this evolution was of extreme importance. There were few other battlefield manoeuvres, but the *othismos* could deliver victory if performed correctly, or doom the phalanx to defeat if it became disordered.

Forward movement was the heart and soul of hoplite warfare. A force that pushed its opponents back gradually gained the advantage. It was harder for a hoplite to keep his footing going backwards than forwards, so men would stumble and fall. Not only did this weaken the force as a whole, it was very likely to result in death or injury for the unfortunate hoplite.

A downed man also risked being trampled to death by his own side, and if the enemy advanced over him he would simply be finished off with the spiked butt of an enemy spear. The weight of a spear was such that if it were driven downwards with determination it would have no trouble punching through a thick bronze cuirass.

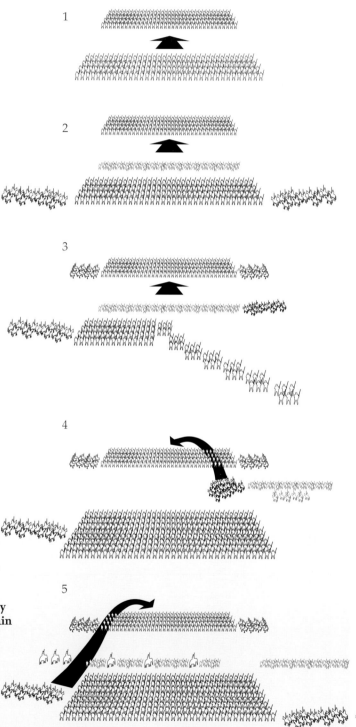

DEVELOPMENT OF GREEK BATTLE TACTICS
1. Phalanx as seen at Marathon, four ranks deep.
2. Phalanx with a peltast screen and cavalry to protect vulnerable flanks.
3. A Theban formation where peltasts and cavalry pin down the enemy's flanks while the the main phalanx advances in an oblique formation.
4. Macedonian phalanx – eight ranks deep, with heavy cavalry seeking a breakthrough.
5. Successor state formation – elephants and cavalry employed to gain a breakthrough and hit the enemy in the rear.

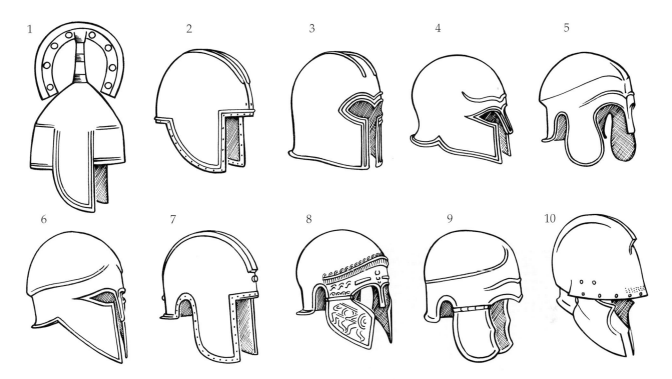

As men fell and the pushing power of the hoplite formation decreased, the enemy gained momentum until finally men began to break away from the back of the phalanx and flee. A collapse was certain at this point, and would be followed by a pursuit. Casualties were heaviest at first contact and after a force broke, with men speared as they ran or finished off on the ground as the enemy phalanx rolled over them.

The graphic collapse of a phalanx made it very clear who had won, and a peace treaty usually followed. Terms were rarely very onerous and dealt mainly with the resolution of disputes. If the terms were too high, the losing *polis* could simply close its gates and accept a siege, which would cost the attacker more than the outcome would be worth.

Thus, the clash of hoplite phalanxes was in many ways a bloody form of negotiation which strengthened the bargaining position of the winning side. The cycle of dispute, phalanx battle and treaty might be repeated year after year, sometimes between the same opponents. It was an essential part of the political system.

If light troops were present at all, they were normally used to harass the enemy phalanx or to fight

HOPLITE HELMETS
1. Cone-shaped helmet (Argos, 700 BC); 2. Illyrian-style helmet, made from two halves riveted together (Olympian, 650 BC); 3. Corinthian-style helmet, covering eyes and jawline (600 BC); 4. Corinthian-style helmet (550 BC); 5. Chalcidian helmet, allowing for better hearing (500 BC); 6. Corinthian-style helmet (500 BC); 7. Later Illyrian-style helmet (480 BC); 8 & 9. Chalcidian helmet with hinged cheek guards (450 BC); 10. Thracian (300 BC).

their own opposite numbers. They did, however, occasionally play a more important role in a battle. If lightly equipped psiloi could get in among the hoplites they could wreak havoc in the phalanx. A man concentrating on his role in the phalanx, wearing a helmet which restricted his vision and hearing, might not even be aware of the knife at his back until too late.

On other occasions, light troops were able to defeat hoplites by simply refusing to fight them on their own terms. Heavily equipped hoplites could not catch lighter troops who ran in to throw javelins and then retreated in the face of any counter-attack. This occurred very rarely in internal Greek conflicts during the city-states

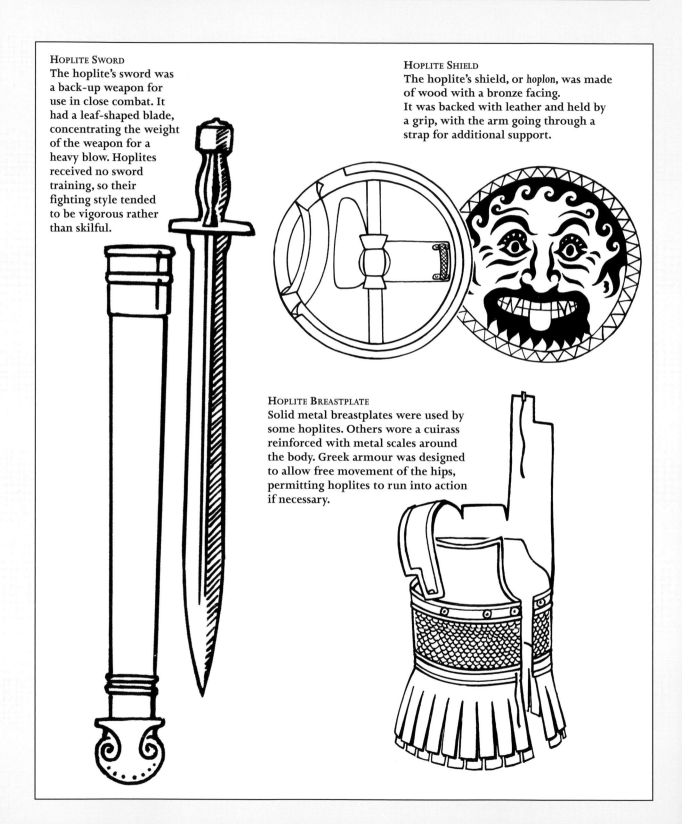

HOPLITE SWORD
The hoplite's sword was a back-up weapon for use in close combat. It had a leaf-shaped blade, concentrating the weight of the weapon for a heavy blow. Hoplites received no sword training, so their fighting style tended to be vigorous rather than skilful.

HOPLITE SHIELD
The hoplite's shield, or *hoplon*, was made of wood with a bronze facing.
It was backed with leather and held by a grip, with the arm going through a strap for additional support.

HOPLITE BREASTPLATE
Solid metal breastplates were used by some hoplites. Others wore a cuirass reinforced with metal scales around the body. Greek armour was designed to allow free movement of the hips, permitting hoplites to run into action if necessary.

period. However, when the Greeks fought enemies who did not subscribe to their system, the vulnerabilities of the hoplite phalanx were ruthlessly exploited.

Equipment and Organization

The principle weapon of the Greek citizen-soldier was a long spear known as a *doru*. He fought in close order with this weapon and a large round shield called a *hoplon*. Troops were therefore known as hoplites.

Hoplites fought in a close formation called a phalanx. Men who could afford additional protection in the form of greaves, cuirass (breastplate) and helmet fought in the front ranks, with less well protected individuals behind them.

The phalanx was not a manoeuvrable formation, but this was not really necessary in the stylized warfare of the city-states period. Phalanxes simply lined up by mutual agreement and charged into one another, reducing the outcome to a straight contest between the phalanxes of both sides.

Later in the period light troops became increasingly important, though they were always eclipsed by the hoplites. The best regarded of the lighter forces were peltasts, named for their lighter, crescent-shaped shield, the *pelta*. Peltast equipment was cheaper than that of the hoplites, so poorer members of society could serve in this role if they could not afford to join the phalanx.

Peltasts fought primarily with javelins, harassing the enemy phalanx and protecting the flanks of their own hoplites. Some peltasts were armed with swords for close combat; others carried a knife or dagger. However, their main role was as skirmishers; close combat was the preserve of the hoplite heavy infantry.

Peltasts were sometimes recruited as mercenaries from lands outside Greece, and at times mercenary peltast forces from Greece itself became available for hire. Mercenary peltasts were sufficiently common that the word 'peltast' was at times synonymous with 'mercenary', referring to troops for hire in general rather than any specific type.

Peltasts and troops of a similar sort were extremely useful in an army that had to do more than engage a phalanx in a prearranged battle. The Persian empire fielded peltasts of its own, or at least troops much like them in terms of equipment and role. In addition to their skirmishing, peltasts could also be used to chase off enemy light troops.

The possession of a sword and shield gave peltasts an advantage over other light infantry and allowed them to deal with a range of circumstances.

THRACIAN PELTAST
Named for their small shield, the *pelta*, peltasts supported the phalanx by skirmishing with their javelins. Upon occasion, peltasts harassed unsupported hoplite formations to destruction without being brought to close action.

In addition, there was occasionally some crossover between peltasts and hoplites. Some sources mention what may be peltasts armed with thrusting spears rather than javelins, or might be a form of light hoplite infantry fielded as an experiment or out of necessity.

The very lightest troops were termed *psiloi*, though they had various other names as well. *Psiloi* had no protection; indeed, some went to battle completely naked. Their role was to harass the enemy with javelins, slings and bows, and sometimes by simply throwing stones. *Psiloi* were not well regarded and were often considered irrelevant to the business of defeating the enemy phalanx.

Psiloi were used for screening and to cover the flanks. They were untrained and not organized beyond a general direction to occupy a part of the battlefield and make a nuisance of themselves. However, some city-states did employ archers and other missile troops in a slightly more organized manner, attempting to concentrate firepower rather than have the *psiloi* fight as individuals. This was never particularly successful, and light troops never attained any real status.

Cavalry was also rare and of little consequence. The scouting role was of little importance in formalized warfare, and cavalry could do little against a well formed phalanx. However, once one side broke, cavalry and *psiloi* could pursue fleeting hoplites faster than they could run, justifying their existence by inflicting casualties after the hoplites of the phalanx had broken the enemy.

Battle of Leuctra, 371 BC

Although Sparta was the dominant power in Greece at this time, Thebes was growing in stature and had taken control of former Spartan territories in Boeotia. The city-states there preferred Spartan rule to Theban, and requested aid which was granted. A Spartan army marched towards Thebes.

Thebes managed to muster about 6500 hoplites to meet the threat, with 1000 peltasts and 1500 cavalry in support. Many of these troops were raised in Boeotia and were not considered very reliable,

Leuctra 371 BC

The battle of Leuctra is often considered to be the earliest known example of the oblique order of battle. The Thebans used their massed hoplites to break the Spartan right before the rest of their force could be overwhelmed by the stronger Spartans.

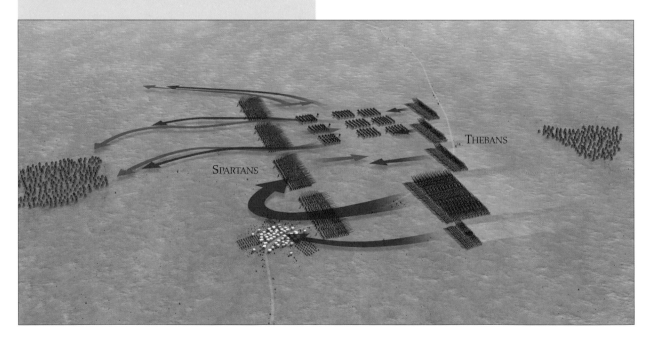

especially if things went badly. The Spartan army numbered 10,000 hoplites, with a thousand each of cavalry and light infantry in support.

The Thebans found themselves in a difficult position, as they had to meet the Spartan challenge or face revolts across their territory. Their army might simply desert before battle was joined. In addition, the Spartans had a reputation as warriors second to none. However, there was nothing for it but to offer battle and fight it out before too many Boeotians decided to desert. With no real prospect of defeating twice their number of the world's best hoplites in a straight phalanx battle, the Thebans opted for a novel tactic. Instead of a uniform line matching the length of the enemy, and therefore stretched dangerously thin, the Thebans deployed most of their hoplites on the left of their line, in a massive phalanx some 50 men deep rather than the usual 12. This phalanx was headed by the élite Sacred Band.

The rest of the line was extremely weak, and to protect it, units were echeloned back in a curve. This created a 'refused' right flank. The Theban strategy was to try to avoid defeat on the right long enough for the super-phalanx to win on the left.

The Spartans attempted to encircle the Theban force, ensuring that a defeat would be even more costly for their enemies. However, the Theban horse routed its Spartan opponents and sent them reeling back through the hoplites. This caused great disorder and, perhaps worse, concern among the Spartans. Often, many of the Spartan's opponents fled before the phalanxes even clashed, or were half-defeated before they had even reached the battlefield by the Spartans' reputation for invincibility. Yet here was an opponent who not only challenged the Spartans but who had the temerity to do so successfully. And worse was to come – the left-flank Theban phalanx advanced and smashed into the thinner Spartan line.

The Theban assault fell on the right of the Spartan line, the position of honour and the location of the best troops in the army. These were the personal bodyguards of the Spartan king. Vastly outnumbered, they were steamrollered by the Thebans, who smashed the Spartan right wing in short order.

▲ Philip II of Macedon, father of Alexander the Great, neutralized many potential enemies by diplomacy, and crushed the rest with his highly effective army.

With their right wing utterly defeated, their king dead and most of their army unable to even get into contact with the enemy, the Spartan army lost heart and began to retire. The Theban cavalry pursued and inflicted some additional losses.

A stand-off then ensued for a few days, as both sides buried their dead. Although the Spartans still possessed a powerful army, they did not want to face the Thebans and their strange tactics a second time. The arrival of Theban allies from Pherae sealed the matter. The Spartans asked for a truce and permission to retire. This was granted and the Spartan army marched home, where it had to deal with a wave of revolts.

The myth of invincibility that had defeated many of Sparta's opponents before battle was joined was shattered at Leuctra. Sparta had rarely been defeated before, and had never had a king killed in battle against fellow Greeks. Had the Thebans fought in the

▲ **The so-called Alexander Sarcophagus depicts the great general chasing his enemies from the field. Alexander's style of headlong, heroic leadership was highly effective, but cost him several wounds.**

conventional manner the outcome would have certainly been different, and this lesson was not lost on at least one observer. He was Philip, soon to become King Philip II of Macedon, one of the great innovators in the history of Greek warfare.

THE RISE OF MACEDONIA

Located to the north of Greece, Macedon was ruled by a single king and thus far more unified than the Greek city-states. Once his dominion over Macedon was complete, King Philip II of Macedon began to expand into Thessaly and Thrace. This occupied Macedonian forces until 342 BC, and once these conquests were completed, Philip II began looking southwards with a view to invasion and conquest.

Macedonian expansion was carried out using a mix of diplomacy, bribery and military force. Unable to defeat the powerful Macedonian army individually, many city-states decided not to risk resistance as part of an alliance, instead accepting inducements to

remain neutral or to become friendly towards Macedon.

In the end, resistance did materialize, in the form of an alliance led by Athens and Thebes. In 338 BC, the forces of Macedon met the allies in battle at Chaeronea. Although the Macedonians were better trained and hardened by earlier campaigns, the allies fought them to a standstill for some time.

Philip II then ordered his right wing to retire, drawing the Greek forces facing them into a pursuit that disrupted their formation. The more disciplined Macedonians then counter-attacked and drove the Athenians from the field.

This left the Theban contingent unbroken but badly outnumbered. After a hard fight they were overwhelmed. The Theban army included an élite force of 300 men called the Sacred Band. Their casualties were huge – 254 were killed and none of the survivors escaped unwounded.

Philip's son Alexander was present at the battle. According to some sources he led a successful cavalry attack that broke the Theban line, but this has not been proven conclusively. Whatever the case, Alexander won glory and was charged with overseeing negotiations for a Greek surrender.

Although the armies of Athens and Thebes had been completely shattered, Macedon had also taken heavy losses. To replace all the men that had been killed or wounded, Philip made an arrangement with the defeated city-states. Rather than being sacked and occupied, they would retain their own government and become part of an alliance designed to prevent conflict between the city-states of Greece. This alliance, called the Corinthian League, was to be overseen by

Macedonian officials but was not oppressive. The city-states would in return contribute troops to fight for Macedon.

By the standards of the time these were extremely generous terms, and the defeated allies quickly agreed. The Corinthian League, sometimes called the Hellenic League, lasted longer than any previous alliance between city-states and was a powerful factor in establishing the concept of Greece as a nation rather than a geographic region where many small states were located.

THE CAMPAIGNS OF ALEXANDER

Philip II of Macedon was assassinated in 336 BC and his son Alexander took the throne. His reign began with a ruthless purge of potential rivals and opponents, securing his position against internal challenges for the foreseeable future.

The external position was less easily dealt with. Revolts broke out in Greece, Thessaly and Thrace when news broke of Philip's death. Ignoring advice to take a diplomatic approach, Alexander lunged southwards with his cavalry, quickly defeating the Thessalians and co-opting their forces for his campaign.

Advancing rapidly through Greece, Alexander received the surrender and submission of the rebels. He then turned north to deal with the Thracian revolt. Despite the rebels' good position on high ground, Alexander attacked using archers to support the advance of his infantry. After defeating this force he pushed on to the Danube, which was crossed using rafts. While the northern revolt was being pacified, a new revolt broke out in Greece. Thebes, the main force behind the rebellion, was totally destroyed and its population sold into slavery. These savage reprisals subdued the other rebel cities.

With his flanks and rear secure, Alexander turned his attention to the invasion of Persia. An army numbering over 40,000 was assembled, with contingents from Macedon and the Greek city-states as

▼ **Alexander's forced crossing of the River Granicus almost cost him his life. Only the swift intervention of one of his close companions prevented the untimely conclusion of the Alexandrian legend.**

well as mercenary formations. Crossing into Persian territory in 334 BC, the Macedonian army was confronted by an army that had been raised by the satraps of the region.

Battle of Granicus

The Persians took up positions behind the River Granicus. An assault crossing was an extremely hazardous operation but, disregarding advice to seek a crossing place elsewhere and fight a conventional battle, Alexander ordered an attack.

Feinting with his left, Alexander drew the Persians' reserves onto their right flank, then threw his heavy cavalry into action against the Persian centre. The rest of the Macedonian army made a general advance, but for a time the heavy cavalry was unsupported. Despite coming very close to being killed, Alexander managed to lead his cavalry in routing their opposite numbers.

This permitted the Macedonian heavy infantry to charge the lighter and less well trained Persian troops opposite them, breaking them. A body of some 20,000 mercenary hoplites from Greece, fighting on the Persian side, remained on the field as the rest of the army fled. They attempted to negotiate with Alexander but were cut down, with the survivors sold into slavery.

Success at the Granicus allowed the Macedonian army to advance through Asia Minor. Many of the cities there were Greek colonies, permitting Alexander to portray himself as a liberator as well as commander, but more importantly the region could be used as a supply base for further advances into Persian territory.

In 333 BC, as the Macedonian army continued its advance through Asia Minor, a vast Persian army was assembled under the personal command of King Darius. This army then marched on Issus, succeeding in establishing itself behind the Macedonians. The Persians then began pushing south down the coast.

With their supply line cut, the Macedonians had no choice but to turn northwards and march towards the Persian force. The two armies met on the narrow coastal plain, allowing Alexander to secure his left flank on the Gulf of Issus and his right on high ground inland. This helped reduce the advantage of numbers held by the Persians.

Persian cavalry made a charge along the shore, engaging the Macedonian cavalry on Alexander's left flank and pushing them back. However, the Macedonians managed to avoid total defeat and

COMPANION CAVALRYMAN
The main striking arm of the Macedonian army was the heavy cavalry rather than the infantry. Alexander commanded his Companions personally, using them as a hammer to smash the enemy line.

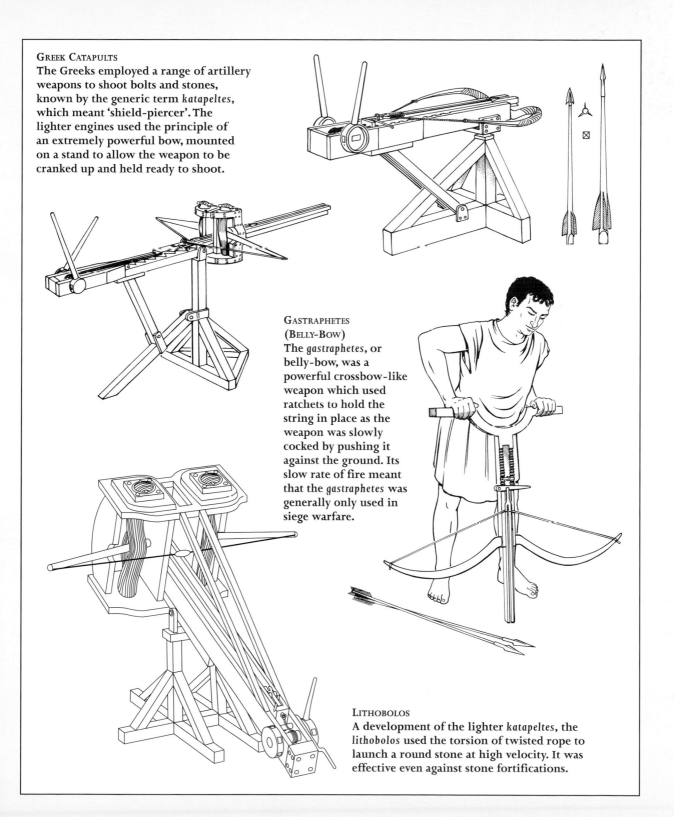

GREEK CATAPULTS

The Greeks employed a range of artillery weapons to shoot bolts and stones, known by the generic term *katapeltes*, which meant 'shield-piercer'. The lighter engines used the principle of an extremely powerful bow, mounted on a stand to allow the weapon to be cranked up and held ready to shoot.

GASTRAPHETES (BELLY-BOW)

The *gastraphetes*, or belly-bow, was a powerful crossbow-like weapon which used ratchets to hold the string in place as the weapon was slowly cocked by pushing it against the ground. Its slow rate of fire meant that the *gastraphetes* was generally only used in siege warfare.

LITHOBOLOS

A development of the lighter *katapeltes*, the *lithobolos* used the torsion of twisted rope to launch a round stone at high velocity. It was effective even against stone fortifications.

SIEGE OF TYRE

In ancient sieges, the advantage lay on the defenders' side. Artillery that could break walls had not yet been invented, and gravity-propelled missiles helped the defenders drive away enemies who tried to bring a ram up to the wall. The defenders were, however, vulnerable to enemy missiles shot from bows or early catapults. Against these, large shields or screens were mounted defensively on the wall. Alexander's mole, an artificial causeway, was gradually built out to Tyre, allowing the Macedonians to bring two great siege towers against the island city's walls.

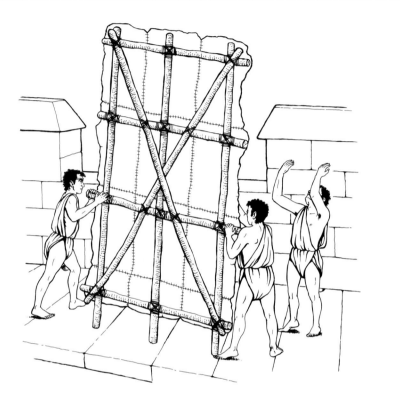

kept their opponents occupied while events unfolded elsewhere on the battlefield.

A Macedonian infantry assault broke open the Persian line, permitting the heavy cavalry to charge and rout the personal troops of Darius. As the King fled, the cavalry then attacked the rear of the Greek mercenary phalanx that had been fighting for the Persians, scattering it. The Persian army collapsed rapidly, and was pursued from the field. Darius escaped, but casualties among his forces were extremely high.

Siege of Tyre

After defeating the Persian army at Issus, Alexander's Macedonians pushed on southwards, down the coast. The intention was to take the coastal cities and thereby deprive the powerful Persian fleet of its bases. This would help protect the Macedonian supply line and prevent a force being landed by sea behind the advancing army.

Tyre, foremost of the city-states of Phoenicia, was of great strategic importance. The city had a component on the mainland and a newer section on an island a few hundred metres off the coast. This island had good natural harbours and was a base for the Persian fleet. Much of the population had been evacuated to Carthage in anticipation of invasion, and the landward city was abandoned by the time the Macedonian army arrived.

The Macedonians lacked a fleet strong enough to attack the island city, so they set about building a causeway, or mole, out of rubble from the landward city. This was built in the shallowest part of the waters between the island and the mainland, but it was still a significant engineering feat.

The mole allowed the Macedonians to position artillery within range of the city's walls, but it could not

be extended right up to the walls as the water was too deep close to the island. The defenders countered this move by sending a fireship against the causeway, burning two powerful siege towers positioned there, and followed up with an amphibious assault.

It was clear that the Macedonians could not take Tyre without a strong naval force. This was obtained by various means. The fleets of some formerly Persian city-states came over to Alexander's side, and forces from Cyprus came to join him along with vessels from Greece itself. This permitted a close blockade of the island's harbours to be implemented. Some of the Macedonian ships were fitted with battering rams, permitting them to become floating siege engines. Other vessels were refitted to carry cranes, in order to remove large blocks of stone that prevented the ram-carrying ships from approaching the walls.

The siege was a brilliant exercise in engineering, and although the defenders fought tenaciously and

TYRE 332 BC

Overcoming the extremely strong defences of Tyre required several innovations. After constructing a mole through shallow water to allow the siting of artillery close to the city, Alexander's forces used floating rams to breach the walls.

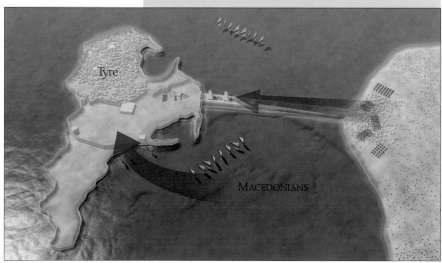

counter-attacked when they could, the walls were eventually breached. The city was then taken by storm. Most of the population was put to death as punishment for holding out so long, and as a reprisal for the execution of some captured Macedonians sailors.

Egypt and Gaugamela

After overrunning and pacifying the coastal region, Alexander mounted an expedition into Egypt where he was handed control without opposition. Then in 331 BC he turned inland against the heartland of the Persian empire. Darius gathered another huge army and marched to meet him at Gaugamela.

GAUGAMELA 331 BC

Alexander's tactics at Gaugamela had much in common with those of Epaminondas at Leuctra. Part of his force was disposed to allow a shot at victory while the rest of the army was tasked with staving off defeat for just long enough.

The Persian army included contingents from all over the empire, including the famous Immortals and a contingent of Greek mercenaries. There were also large numbers of scythed chariots. Darius had high hopes for these, and chose a suitably flat area to offer battle. Some historians record that the Persians spent some time levelling the ground and removing obstacles, making the ground more suitable for a massed chariot assault.

Seeing the vast numbers arrayed against them, Alexander's generals advised him to make a night attack. As usual, he ignored them. As a result, when the battle opened the Persians were tired, having stood to arms all night in the expectation of an assault.

The Macedonians' battle line was far shorter than that of the Persians, and it was obvious that the flanks would be enveloped. Rather than thin the line to increase its length, Alexander drew up his phalangites in a double row, such that the rear ranks could turn to face a flanking attack.

The Macedonian phalanx advanced against the Persian centre. Although outnumbered, their longer

spears gave them an advantage over their opponents, who were on the whole less well trained. Meanwhile, the Persians threw a large force of cavalry and some infantry at the Macedonian left flank.

The Persian chariots also made their attack, but this was disrupted by javelinmen and then defeated by specially devised tactics. The Macedonians opened lanes between their front ranks, channelling the chariots into the gaps. Once they were brought to a halt by the wall of spearpoints presented by the rear ranks, the chariots were then quickly eliminated from the flanks.

Alexander's strategy was to try to pull as much of the Persian cavalry as possible to the flanks, then strike directly at the heart of the enemy army, Darius himself. This worked almost too well, with the Macedonian flanks coming under severe pressure. However, the Macedonian heavy cavalry made its charge, backed up by as much of the infantry as could be disengaged in time to take part in the attack, and punched a hole through the Persian line.

The Persian left flank began to fall back to avoid being encircled, and Darius found himself in similar danger in the centre as his royal guard and élite Greek mercenary units were overrun. He was forced into a hurried retreat which precipitated a general collapse of most of the Persian line.

Alexander was unable to pursue immediately, as his own left flank was in severe danger of being annihilated. Wheeling left, the main Macedonian force came to the assistance of the embattled flank and drove off the enemy confronting them. With no more enemies on the field, a pursuit was possible and this force was harried to rapid destruction. Meanwhile, Darius had managed to escape with a remnant of his best troops. The Persian left flank, retreating in good order, caught up with him and he outlined his plans for the future. These were rejected by his senior officers, who kept him as a prisoner for a time and eventually murdered him.

With Darius dead and the Macedonians obviously capable of overrunning the rest of the empire, most of the remaining satraps transferred their loyalty to Alexander. It was necessary to mop up some resistance

but the Persian empire had essentially ceased to exist at this point. It was now part of Alexander's Macedonian empire. Having made himself master of Persia, Alexander decreed that the term of service for his Greek troops was over. They were free to return home if they wished, or they could re-enlist in the Macedonian army as mercenaries rather than units contributed as a form of tribute. This army then marched eastwards, overrunning the remaining Persian territories and imposing Macedonian rule.

Alexander encouraged his Greek followers to marry into local communities and did much to promote tolerance between ethnic groups, though all under his rule as emperor, of course. He installed some of his followers as overlords in conquered areas; in others he allowed the existing system to remain in place.

India and Hydaspes

By 326 BC, Alexander's army had reached the fringes of India, and some of the local lords he encountered

▲ Macedonian spearmen fight the Indian war elephants at the River Hydaspes, 326 BC, as imagined by a modern painter. Alexander neutralized the elephants by avoiding a direct confrontation with the beasts, instead using his cavalry to shatter the supporting troops and then routing the elephants with a close order phalanx.

accepted his authority. Others decided to fight, resulting in a hard campaign in which Alexander was wounded more than once. The army was becoming increasingly disaffected by this point, and plots against the life of Alexander were uncovered.

The last major battle of Alexander's career took place at the River Hydaspes, where the Indian king Porus offered battle. Porus' army included archers armed with powerful bows, large six-man chariots and over 200 war elephants.

After deploying decoy forces to try to confuse the Indians, the Macedonians brushed aside a cavalry and chariot force sent to stop them crossing the river and

HYDASPES 326 BC

Using decoy forces to draw off some of the enemy strength, Alexander's army crossed the River Hydaspes and attacked before the Indians were fully deployed. Clever tactics neutralized the Indian war elephants, which might otherwise have caused havoc among Alexander's cavalry.

took up positions facing the enemy. The decoy forces worked well, drawing off a part of the Indian force, but the Macedonians were still outnumbered. However, the Indians had been caught by surprise and were still deploying.

The Macedonian heavy cavalry was ineffective against war elephants, as the sight, sound and smell of the beasts would frighten any horse not specially trained to operate with or against them. Alexander used the mobility of his cavalry to avoid contact with the elephants and attacked the Indian cavalry instead, routing it. The elephants were dealt with using a combination of intense javelin fire and the long spears of the phalangites. Although pressed hard, the Macedonian infantry eventually managed to drive off the elephants, some of which stampeded through their own troops. The phalangites then advanced in close order. Most of the Indian army took the hint and surrendered or fled. Those that did not were killed.

King Porus surrendered to Alexander, who had been impressed with his courage in battle and in defeat. Alexander spared Porus' life, allowing him to

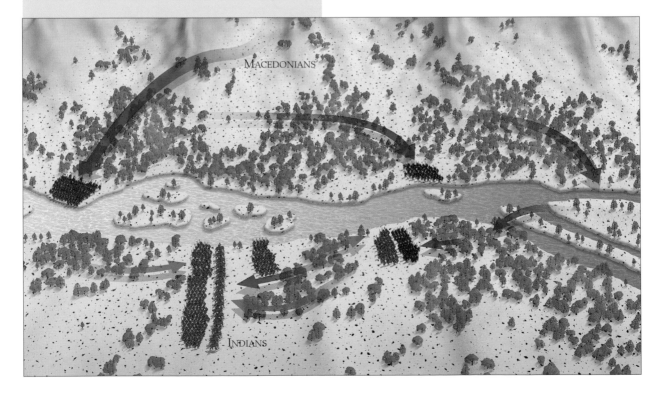

retain his throne under a new loyalty sworn to Alexander's empire.

After the Hydaspes, Alexander pushed further east and made further conquests against relatively slight resistance. However, faced with the prospect of campaigns against stronger Indian kingdoms the army refused to go any further. As mutinies go it was a fairly civil affair, but Alexander was unable to persuade his men to change their minds. The conquering army thus turned southwards, beginning a homeward march that took it through new territories. Further conquests followed, which proved acceptable to Alexander's men as long as the general direction was towards home.

Finally, the army returned to Persia, where Alexander died, in Babylon. It is not clear whether he died of disease, poisoning, alcoholism, the effects of wounds, or a combination of all of these.

Equipment and Organization

The forces of the Greek city-states were somewhat one-dimensional, relying entirely on their hoplites. Macedonian armies, on the other hand, used combined-arms tactics to a greater extent, employing light and heavy infantry with cavalry support.

Light infantry covered the flanks of the main heavy infantry force and deployed in front of it as a screen. Javelinmen in particular were highly useful in countering war elephants, and could harass an enemy infantry force until it began to break up. Their main function, however, was to protect the heavier troops and prevent them from being struck in the flank.

Although there were some similarities, the heavy infantry of the Macedonian army were not hoplites. Their weapon was the *sarissa*, an 18-foot (5.4m) long spear or pike, and they used a smaller shield than a *hoplon*.

MACEDONIAN SPIERA
The *spiera* was the standard unit of Macedonian pikemen. Comprised of 256 men, a *spiera* normally fought eight men deep with a frontage of 32 men, or in a deeper formation 16 deep with a frontage of 16 men. The unit's commander fought at the head of the rightmost file.

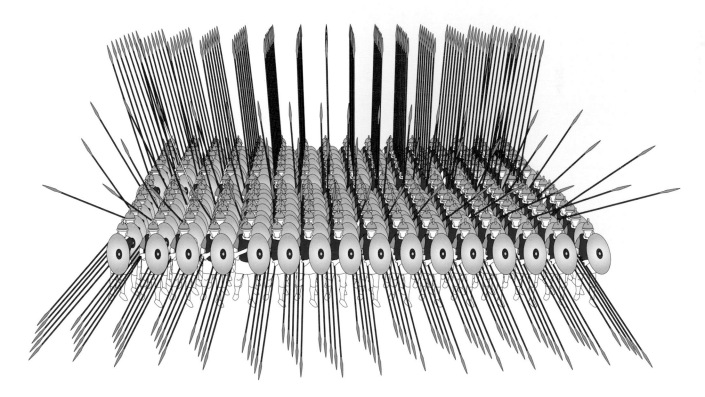

Within a *spiera* there were four 64-man sub-units called *tetrachies* that manoeuvred as blocks to form a *spiera* with the correct frontage and depth. Doing so while holding a long *sarissa* required a high standard of drill and discipline if the formation were not to dissolve into chaos.

Four *tetrachies*

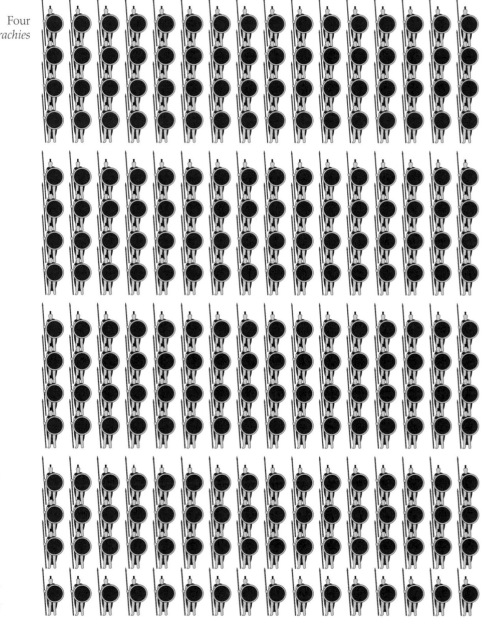

The *sarissa* required considerable strength and skill to use effectively but its length gave the phalangites of Macedon several advantages. Most obviously, they could outreach their opponents and begin inflicting casualties before enemy hoplites or other spearmen were within striking distance. The length of the pike also allowed more ranks of phalangites to present their weapon points, making the Macedonian phalanx deadlier than their rivals.

Within a phalanx, Macedonian infantry were formed in units called *spiera*. This gave Macedonian phalangites a reasonable degree of tactical flexibility. Adjacent *spiera* could be echeloned back, each covering the flank of the neighbouring unit whilst creating a refused flank. Units could also separate to go around obstructions or to create a second line.

Hypaspists

An élite force of infantry known as *hypaspists* was also deployed. More lightly equipped than the men of the phalanx, *hypaspists* were armed more like the hoplites of the city-states, with a shorter spear than the *sarissa*. They were unusual in that they were a high-prestige unit despite not being the most heavily (i.e. expensively) armed soldiers of the infantry.

The *hypaspists* were useful for their mobility and agility on the battlefield, which allowed them to be rapidly redeployed to cover a weakness or exploit an advantage. They could disperse to avoid a threat but were sufficiently well trained as to be able to recombine into an effective formation.

This use of high-quality but relatively light infantry was one main difference between the Macedonian way of making war and that of the city-states. A more flexible phalanx was another, along with more organized use of light troops.

▶ **The length of the *sarissa* enabled the Macedonian phalanx to present several spearpoints towards each enemy soldier, making it difficult for him to get close enough to fight.**

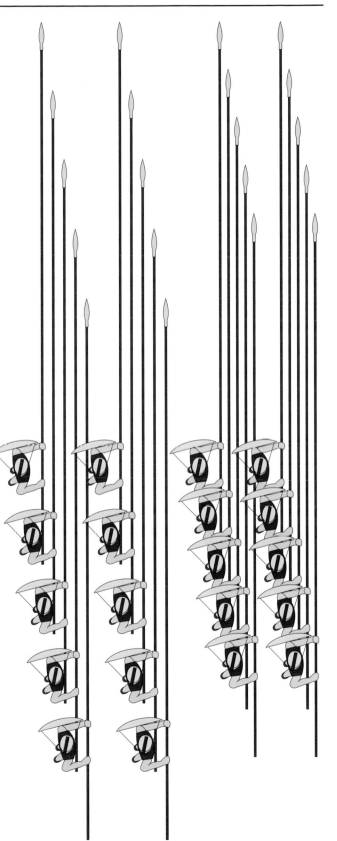

The infantry, though well regarded, was not the main striking arm as it had been in the Greek city-states. Its primary role was to grip the enemy line and pin it so that the élite of the army, the heavy cavalry, could make a decisive attack.

The heavy cavalry were the main battle-winning force of the Macedonian army. In Alexander's day, his Companions were the élite of the army. They were Alexander's friends, bodyguards and personal battlefield command all in one.

Although the heavy cavalry did not use stirrups, they were still able to use long spears in combat and to charge with great force. Protected by body armour and a helmet, they were highly disciplined and responsive to commands. On more than one occasion, Alexander was able to rally his cavalry after a charge and reorganize them to attack a new target. They were also able to break off combat and fall back to receive new orders, a significant advantage which proved decisive at Gaugamela.

The Macedonian heavy cavalry were supported by horsemen supplied by allies. These included additional spear-armed heavy cavalry contingents and lighter-armed skirmishing cavalry. At Hydaspes, Dahae horse archers assisted the flanking movement of Alexander's Companion cavalry, shooting arrows into the enemy cavalry to disrupt their formation before the Companions charged home.

The tactical flexibility of the Macedonian army was worthless, however, without highly disciplined troops capable of understanding and carrying out orders whilst retaining their formations. It also required a highly skilled commander to issue those orders. Alexander was such a commander, as well as being a heroic leader in the classical Greek tradition. Several times he was almost killed leading a charge on horseback or on foot.

ALEXANDRIAN ELEPHANT
The Macedonian army adopted the war elephant after encountering enemies that used them. War elephants were not the most reliable of forces, being prone to run amok if frightened. One vulnerable spot was the mahout who controlled the elephant from his perch on its neck.

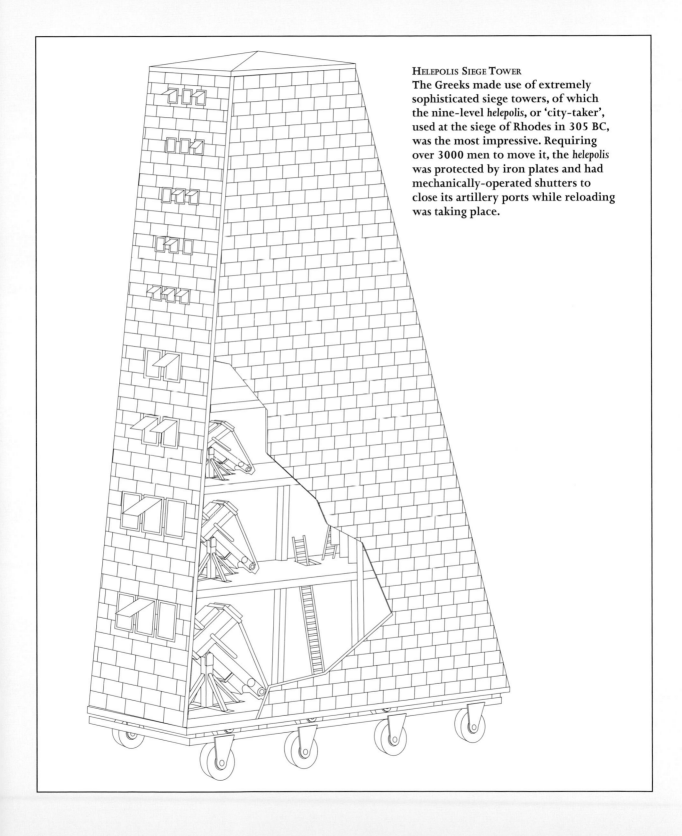

HELEPOLIS SIEGE TOWER
The Greeks made use of extremely sophisticated siege towers, of which the nine-level *helepolis*, or 'city-taker', used at the siege of Rhodes in 305 BC, was the most impressive. Requiring over 3000 men to move it, the *helepolis* was protected by iron plates and had mechanically-operated shutters to close its artillery ports while reloading was taking place.

Such reckless courage inspired his men but risked defeat if the commander was injured or killed, or if he fled the field. In contrast to Alexander's heroism, the Persian collapse at Gaugamela has been attributed to the flight of Darius from the field, though some sources state that the king only retired after his army was soundly beaten.

Alexander's successors inherited the Macedonian military system and, indeed, elements of his army. The basic system was adapted to incorporate new units such as war elephants. This flexibility was a key asset of the Macedonian system. Whereas the Greeks of the city-states evolved a military system that was ideally suited to fighting a particular enemy – another city-state, using the same military system – the Macedonians evolved a system designed to let them defeat whatever they encountered, and which permitted adaptation as lessons were learned and new opponents encountered.

THE SUCCESSOR STATES

Alexander the Great died in 323 BC. He left no clear heir and after a period of intense political infighting between his generals, as well as actual conflict, clear factions began to emerge. In Macedon itself Cassander ruled, while Egypt was controlled by Ptolemy I. Thrace fell to Lysimachus and Anatolia to Antigonus. In Mesopotamia, Seleuchus was ruler.

The Successor States fought among themselves for control of Alexander's former territories. The successful leaders founded dynasties which ruled for many years, creating states such as Seleucid Persia and Ptolemaic Egypt which were a fusion of local and Macedonian culture.

None of Alexander's successors managed to re-unite his territories and over time the new states they led began to become established as powers in their own right rather than being united fragments of a former empire. Alliances between the Successor States were made and broken as each sought advantages or at least to avoid defeat.

None of the Successors was willing to see an enemy or rival gain too much power, so if one state was threatened with destruction its former enemies might well fall on the victor, bringing about another round of conflict.

In 301 BC, the most powerful of the successors was Antigonus of Anatolia. Allied with his son Demetrius, who ruled Macedon, Antigonus was making gradual gains against the other Successors and had a real chance to re-unite Alexander's empire. However, an alliance between the other Successors emerged to oppose them.

The forces of the allies met those of the Antigonids at Ipsus in Phyrigia. Both sides fielded a mixed force of infantry, cavalry and elephants. The Antigonids had an advantage in cavalry and the allies in elephants, while the infantry of both sides was roughly equal.

The Antigonid phalanx was deployed in greater depth than its opponents, with most of the cavalry on its right flank. The allies, on the other hand, deployed their cavalry evenly between the flanks, with the phalanx and war elephants in the centre, with yet more elephants in reserve.

Both sides used a screen of light infantry, which opened the battle with the usual skirmishing. A charge by elephants from both sides then ensued, and the Antigonid cavalry attacked on the right flank. Initially successful, this attack was halted by the allies' reserve of elephants.

The allies gradually got the upper hand, reducing the powerful Antigonid phalanx with missile fire until it began to break. Antigonus was killed while personally trying to rally the phalanx, triggering a general collapse. Although Demetrius escaped, the Antigonid faction was greatly diminished and there was never any real chance of a unified empire after Ipsus.

Ptolemy secured his hold on Egypt and founded a dynasty that ruled there until deposed by Roman military power, while Seleuchus defeated both Cassander and Lysimachus in 281 BC. He was assassinated soon after, but the Seleucid dynasty continued to rule Persia.

The days of Greek dominance had come to an end, though this was not immediately apparent. In time, the armies of Rome would overrun Ptolemaic Egypt, Greece, and parts of Persia using a new and superior military system.

SELEUCID INFANTRYMAN
During its later history, the Seleucid Persian army fielded a force of about 5000 infantry equipped and trained much like Roman legionaries. This came about as a result of contact with the emerging Roman Republic.

SELEUCID ELEPHANT
Elephants were obtained from Indian allies and were given armour to protect them in battle. In 162 BC a treaty with Rome required that much of the Persian elephant herd be destroyed, suggesting that the Romans considered armoured elephants to be a highly dangerous weapons system.

SELEUCID SKIRMISHER
The Persians made extensive use of cheaply equipped skirmishers, whose origins can probably be traced to the peltasts of Alexander's Macedonian army. Skirmishers were recruited from various tribes within Persian territory and as mercenaries from overseas.

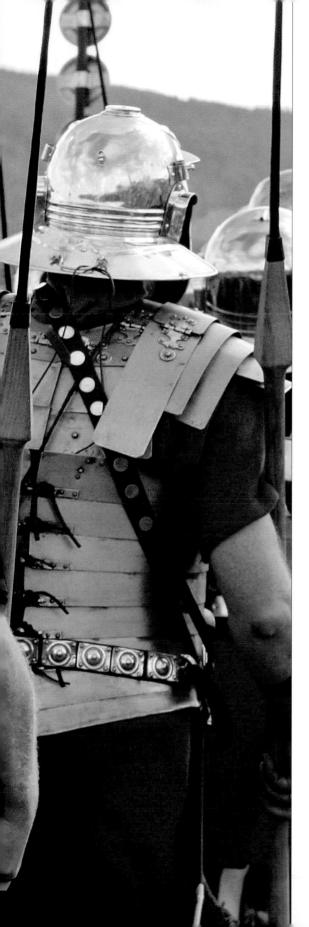

CHAPTER 4

Warriors of Ancient Rome

From a militia raised at need to defend a single city, the Roman army evolved into the most effective military force of the ancient world. Well trained and highly organized, the legions of Rome could defeat almost any foe in any terrain. It was not until a series of civil wars weakened the Empire that the army lost control of the frontiers and the collapse began.

Rome was probably founded around 750 BC. Originally a kingdom, Rome became a republic around 500 BC, although initially only nobles could be elected to high office. This gradually changed, but for the entire history of the Roman Republic and Empire politics, social standing and warfare were inextricably bound up together. In Rome, eligibility for military service was a condition of citizenship, and military forces were raised as and when needed. What were effectively militia units were led by whoever raised them, or his appointed commander, and organization was somewhat ad hoc. However, at some point in Roman history – it is not clear exactly when – a more formal system was introduced.

◀ Re-enactors equipped in the classical Roman manner, with armour and helmets designed primarily to defeat the overhead sword stroke of the typical barbarian warrior.

The population was divided into five military classes, with all males who owned property eligible to serve. Every man was required to possess military equipment suitable for his class, and to respond to the call when his service was needed. The term for the military of Rome was the *legio*, which meant, roughly, 'the multitude'. In theory, the whole male population could be called upon to fight at need, in much the same manner as the citizen-soldiers of the Greek city-states.

In keeping with Rome's Greek origins, the majority of her troops were infantry, equipped much like hoplites. They fought with a long spear and were protected by a shield. The most prestigious class bore swords and wore a breastplate and helmet. Men of the second and third classes were similarly equipped but had less or no armour, using a slightly larger shield instead. Men of the fourth class were cheaply equipped with spears, javelins and possibly a small shield. They had no armour. Nor did the fifth class, who were slingers.

◄ **The earliest armies of Rome were equipped in the manner of a Greek hoplite, with greaves and a stabbing spear, as shown in this stone carving of an early Roman warrior.**

Small numbers of cavalry were contributed by the upper social classes, who also provided the commanders and officers that led the army. The cavalry was not a battle-winning force, largely due to insufficient numbers. Its role was primarily that of pursuing a defeated enemy, though cavalrymen could be used as a mobile reserve, fighting dismounted in support of the infantry.

The standard battle formation was a Greek-style phalanx, with cavalry and light troops in support. This was an inflexible and ponderous formation, and was not well suited to the terrain it fought over. Roman phalanxes were defeated several times by more mobile opponents.

Italy's terrain differed considerably from that of Greece, and more importantly the politico-military environment was quite different. Where Greece was a land of city-states whose rulers sought formal battles as a means of settling disputes, Italy was dominated by tribes that lived in hilly country and were inclined to fight long wars of raid and counter-raid. This environment required a departure from the Greek hoplite style of warfare.

WARS OF THE EARLY REPUBLIC

Roman forces campaigned against nearby tribes, towns and cities, conquering them or forcing treaties upon them where diplomacy and the offer of alliance did not work. The result was the gradual emergence of Rome as the foremost of a group of allied cities, whose forces could be called upon at need.

The first great challenge to Roman survival began around 390 BC, when Gallic tribes began raiding into Italy. A Roman army of some 15,000 or so was mustered to meet them, but was decisively beaten at the battle of the Allia River. Soon afterward, Rome itself was overrun and plundered.

The sacking of Rome was a traumatic event for the Republic, and prompted major military reforms. However, it did not seriously cripple the economic or political growth of the Republic, and soon Rome was expanding once again.

One major obstacle to Roman expansion was a powerful tribe whose territory lay nearby, the Samnites. War with the Samnites began in 343 BC and

SAMNITE BELT
The Samnites were long-standing enemies of Rome. They were entirely capable of producing equipment to rival that of Rome, including decorative belts for their warriors.

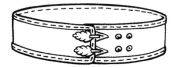

SAMNITE HELMET
The Samnite helmet with its hinged cheekpieces gave good protection. Decorative crests and feathers made the wearer seem taller and more threatening.

SAMNITE WARRIOR
Protected by a large shield and Greek-style armour, the Samnite warrior was a formidable foe. The Samnites favoured skirmishes and raids, withdrawing into rough terrain when threatened by Roman phalanxes.

SAMNITE GREAVES
Shaped like the muscles of the leg for comfort as well as strength, a warrior's greaves protected him from a spear that might slide under the shield rim.

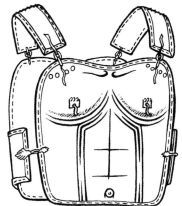

SAMNITE CUIRASS
The Greek-style 'muscle' cuirass gave good protection from a frontal or rear attack with a thrusting weapon, but was less effective against downward cutting actions.

by 341 BC Rome had gained the upper hand. However, revolt among the Latin cities diverted Roman attention and it was not until 327 BC that the Romans could begin to seek a decisive outcome.

This renewed conflict, known as the Second Samnite War, ran from 326 BC to 304 BC. War was used as a tool of diplomacy; after each Roman victory the Samnites were offered less favourable peace terms. The final settlement was not acceptable to the Samnites, who revolted in 298 BC. Initial defeats for Rome prompted other states to join the war, but within 16 years the Roman Republic had defeated all of them.

Victory over the Samnites cemented Rome's position as a major power in Italy, but there were other powers in the region. These included the Greek colonies in southern Italy. Although Greek power had waned, it remained a formidable military and sea power.

War with Greece

Fearing that they were likely targets for Roman expansion, the Greek colonies in Italy asked for support from King Pyrrhus of Epirus. Between Pyrrhus and the colonies, the Greeks fielded over 40,000 men. This force was primarily made up of infantry, fighting in their traditional tight phalanx. Although less flexible and manoeuvrable than the legions of Rome, the Greek phalanx was difficult to break and was well supported by cavalry. Pyrrhus also fielded war elephants, which the Romans had never seen before.

To counter the elephants the Romans used incendiary weapons and ox-drawn wagons fitted with spikes, as well as the simple expedient of withdrawing into terrain where the elephants could not operate. Pyrrhus' elephants proved, as elephants usually did, to be an unreliable weapon. At the battle of Beneventum in 275 BC they stampeded into the Greek phalanx and severely disrupted it.

> **"**ITALY, AND YOUR CROSSING INTO IT, IS THE FIRST STEP IN THE ACQUIREMENT OF UNIVERSAL EMPIRE, TO WHICH NO ONE HAS A BETTER CLAIM THAN YOURSELF. AND NOW IS THE MOMENT TO ACT WHEN THE ROMANS HAVE SUFFERED A REVERSE.**"**
>
> **DEMETRIUS OF PHARUS**

Although repeatedly defeated, the Roman forces inflicted heavy losses on the Greek army, leading to the concept of a 'Pyrrhic victory', i.e. one won at an unacceptable cost. Although the Greeks kept winning battles, they could not achieve a decisive result and their allies were beginning to defect. With no prospect of winning the campaign, Pyrrhus withdrew from Italy.

Rome quickly overran the Greek colonies in Italy. Last to fall was Rhegium, in 270 BC. This established Rome as master of all Italy south of the River Po. More importantly, it was the beginning of Rome's rise to international power. She had shown that her armies could defeat a first-class military power such as Epirus and thus gained much political credibility.

THE PUNIC WARS

The Latin word 'Punic', meaning inhabitant of Carthage, gave a name to the three wars between Rome and Carthage. The First Punic War (264–241 BC) was largely a maritime conflict over control of Sicily. Rome quickly built a fleet to challenge Carthaginian naval supremacy, but inexperience resulted in heavy defeats. Unable to take on Carthaginian vessels on their own terms, the Romans decided to change the rules.

A device known as a *corvus* was fitted to Roman galleys. This was essentially a hinged boarding bridge that could be dropped onto an enemy ship, facilitating a boarding action. Roman infantry were extremely good at fighting in any terrain, and by turning a sea fight into what was effectively a land battle fought in a very restricted area, the Romans played to their greatest strengths.

The war ended with the destruction of most of the Carthaginian fleet off the Aegetes Islands. Carthage sued for peace, though a 'cold war' continued. Victory gave Rome control of the island of Sicily in addition to a large tribute. Internal Carthaginian troubles after the war allowed Rome to annex Sardinia and Corsica.

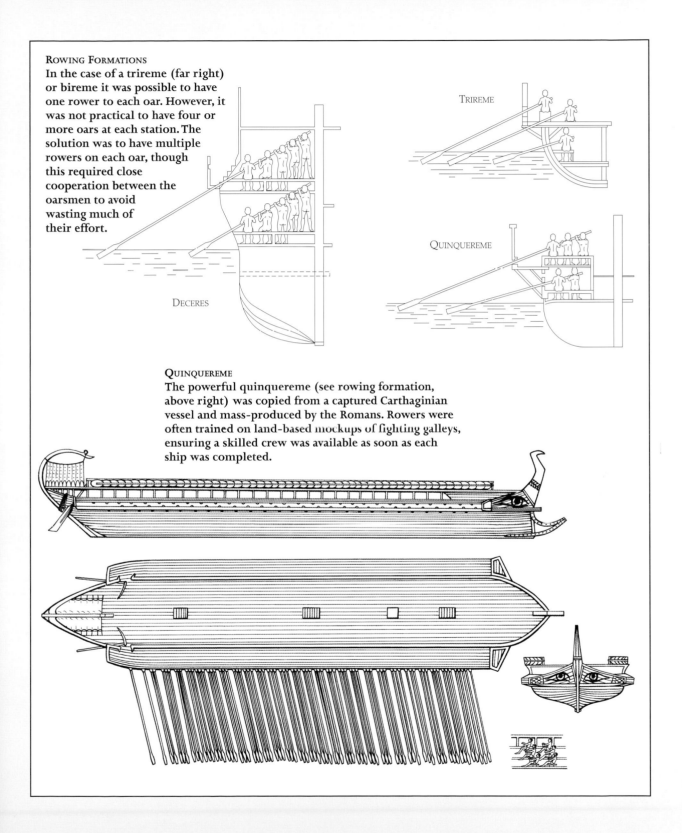

ROWING FORMATIONS
In the case of a trireme (far right) or bireme it was possible to have one rower to each oar. However, it was not practical to have four or more oars at each station. The solution was to have multiple rowers on each oar, though this required close cooperation between the oarsmen to avoid wasting much of their effort.

TRIREME

QUINQUEREME

DECERES

QUINQUEREME
The powerful quinquereme (see rowing formation, above right) was copied from a captured Carthaginian vessel and mass-produced by the Romans. Rowers were often trained on land-based mockups of fighting galleys, ensuring a skilled crew was available as soon as each ship was completed.

In the next few years, Rome beat off Gallic incursions and continued to grow in power. The Celtic peoples of Cisalpine Gaul, the region of Italy north of the River Po, had long been enemies of Rome, albeit on an intermittent basis. In 225 BC, Roman troops marched into the area and conquered it within five years, making the region a Roman territory. This headed off a potential alliance between Gaul and Carthage but did not prevent a second Punic war.

Carthage had been expanding its holdings in Hispania for some time, and had recovered from the setbacks of the First Punic War. In 219 BC, Carthaginian troops attacked Saguntum, a city in Hispania that was friendly to Rome. This created a diplomatic incident that under other circumstances might have come to nothing; Saguntum had provoked the Carthaginian attack and Rome had no firm treaty requiring her to assist any city in the region. But in this case, there was

sufficient bad blood between Rome and Carthage that full-scale war became inevitable.

The Carthaginian commander, Hannibal Barca, attempted a strategic masterstroke by marching his army from Hispania through southern Gaul and into Italy by way of the Alps. Any crossing of the Alps by an army was a formidable undertaking. Doing so with war elephants was a quite remarkable achievement.

As Hannibal advanced towards Italy overland, Roman forces were being moved into Hispania by sea. There, they found that the local cities were not particularly well inclined towards either side and set about winning over some allies. In this they were unwittingly assisted by Hanno, a nephew of Hannibal. Hanno decided to take on the Romans with the forces he had available, which were heavily outnumbered. Victory garnered considerable local support for Rome and enabled an offensive campaign to be launched on land and at sea.

Roman success in Hispania drew in Carthaginian reinforcements which could otherwise have assisted the invasion of Italy. Attempting to force the issue, Hasdrubal Barca, brother of Hannibal, attacked the Roman army at Dertosa. His plan was to envelop both flanks with his cavalry, which came close to working. The fighting power of the Roman legions permitted them to

CARTHAGINIAN INFANTRYMAN
This Carthaginian infantryman's shield is supported by a neck strap as well as the usual arm loops. By turning his shoulder towards a threat, the soldier can present his shield as a sort of mobile barricade.

break through the enemy line, though both sides suffered heavy losses.

Although Roman forces were unable to achieve a decisive victory in Hispania they assisted the campaign elsewhere by tying up Carthaginian troops. Meanwhile, a naval war was being fought, mainly in the seas around Sicily. A Carthaginian attempt at a surprise attack in 218 BC against Lilybaeum was compromised, leading to defeat at the hands of a Roman galley squadron. An expedition to retake Sardinia was defeated on land by the garrison, which had recently been reinforced.

In Italy, however, things did not go well for Rome. Rebellions broke out among the Gallic tribes of Cisalpine Gaul. This distracted Roman attention and drew off troops due to be sent to Hispania. The rebellion was still ongoing when Hannibal arrived in the region.

A Roman force was sent to intercept Hannibal, resulting in a clash between the Roman and Carthaginian cavalry at Ticinus. The Romans pulled back across the River Trebia without suffering severe losses, but the political consequences of this fairly minor defeat were severe. More tribes rose up against Roman rule, increasing the size of Hannibal's army.

Troops mustering in Sicily for an invasion of Africa were hurriedly recalled and sent north. This finally allowed the Romans to face the invaders with approximately equal strength, although the Carthaginian cavalry was more effective than its Roman equivalent.

After a period of skirmishing, the Roman army was drawn into battle at the River Trebia. This was a disaster for Rome; troops who had been given no breakfast were forced to cross an icy river before entering combat. Fighting at greatly reduced effectiveness, they were then struck in the rear by a Carthaginian detachment. Half the Roman force was lost.

Rome was forced to abandon Cisalpine Gaul and fall back southwards, allowing the Carthaginians to increase the size of their army by recruiting among the local tribes while the Romans hurriedly threw together new forces. The Romans were in a weak position and in 217 BC, Hannibal marched south and succeeded in drawing the Romans into an ambush at Lake Trasimene. Caught between the enemy and the lake, the Roman force was annihilated.

TREBIA 218 BC

Hungry and half-frozen from wading through the river, the Romans were attacked in the flanks and rear by Carthaginian cavalry and elephants. Although part of the Roman force was routed, the central units formed a defensive square and fought their way clear, saving at least part of the army.

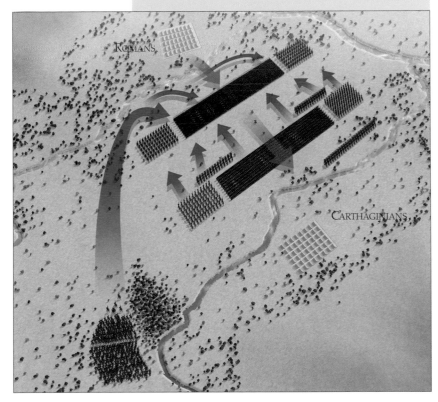

The way to Rome was open, but Hannibal chose to march into southern Italy instead, seeking to influence the cities there to change sides. There was every chance that this would happen, so in Rome, drastic measures were taken. Quintus Fabius Maximus was appointed Dictator, giving him complete authority over all military matters.

Hannibal's army was too powerful to risk a straightforward confrontation, so Fabius embarked upon what has become known as a 'Fabian' strategy. He shadowed the Carthaginians, harassing them whenever he could, but avoided an open battle that could result in the destruction the only army capable of protecting Rome. This strategy prevented defeat, but it could not win the war.

Defeat at Cannae

In 216 BC Fabius was removed from command and more aggressive consuls took over the army.

Responding to Hannibal's seizure of the supply depot at Cannae, they advanced with a huge force to dislodge the Carthaginians. This was exactly what Hannibal wanted; his move to Cannae was calculated to draw the Roman army out.

The resulting battle of Cannae was a tremendous defeat for Rome. Hannibal deployed his force with a weak centre, which the Romans predictably drove back. As they did so, the Carthaginian cavalry defeated its Roman opposite numbers on the flanks and began hooking into the rear. As the Carthaginian centre bent further back, the stronger wings of the infantry closed in on the Roman flanks. At last, with a reinforced centre in front of them, cavalry in the rear and an infantry assault on the flanks the Romans collapsed and were massacred.

Several Italian cities revolted upon hearing of the defeat at Cannae, but others stood by their alliance with Rome, which was still able to field powerful

▲ An early sixteenth-century painting of Hannibal arriving in Italy with his army and war elephants. Although those elephants that survived the march did not live long, bringing them at all was an impressive achievement.

armies. These were directed against Hannibal's Italian and overseas allies. In Sicily, Syracuse declared for Carthage and was besieged by Roman forces in 214 BC, while a second campaign in Hispania was launched to restore Roman fortunes there.

In Hispania, the Roman army had been defeated in 211 BC and was holding out in the north but unable to carry out offensive operations. In 210 BC, an army led by Scipio Africanus landed in Hispania and captured Cartagena (New Carthage) a year later. His campaign was successful, but he could not prevent Hasdrubal from marching towards Italy with reinforcements to assist his brother.

Scipio's campaign in Hispania came to a climax in 206 BC, finally driving the Carthaginians out. In the meantime Roman forces chipped away at Hannibal's alliance in Italy, capturing some cities and inflicting a string of minor defeats on the Carthaginian army.

Hannibal's force was still a threat to Rome in 204 BC, even as Scipio landed in Africa and began advancing on Carthage itself. Hannibal was recalled to defend Carthage, and an attempt was made to negotiate a peace settlement. This failed, and the political situation in Carthage became increasingly unsettled.

Hannibal himself had grave misgivings about the troops he was to command. Some were veterans, but many were almost untrained. Nevertheless, the Carthaginian stand at Zama in the year 202 BC was close run. The Carthaginian infantry made good gains before being hit in the rear by Roman cavalry which was rallying from its pursuit of the Carthaginian horse. The Carthaginian army collapsed and Carthage had no choice but to accept harsh Roman peace terms.

CANNAE 216 BC

By exploiting what should have been his enemy's main advantage – the formidable fighting power of Roman heavy infantry – Hannibal was able to draw the Roman centre into his own formation while he crushed the flanks. Assailed on all sides, the main Roman force was then overwhelmed.

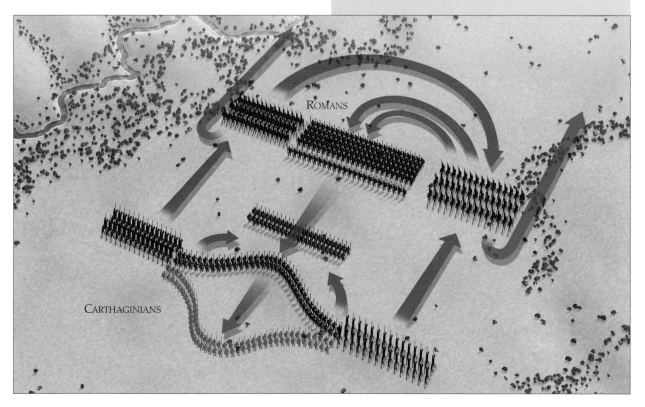

ROMANS

CARTHAGINIANS

Carthage survived as a client state of Rome until 149 BC. In the intervening years she suffered raids from Numidia and eventually raised an army to defend herself in defiance of her surrender terms. This provided those Romans who favoured the complete destruction of Carthage with an excuse. A series of increasingly unreasonable demands were made until finally Carthage refused to comply.

A punitive expedition was launched, which was initially repelled. Carthage was then besieged from 149–146 BC. After the fall of the city it was entirely destroyed, though it is likely that the surrounding fields were not, as legend suggests, sowed with salt. Salt was very expensive in the Ancient World and in any case, within a few years the region was exporting large quantities of grain to Rome.

War with Carthage removed one of Rome's main rivals for domination of the Mediterranean. As well as this, it also provided the impetus for Rome to become a major sea power in its own right. In fact, control of the Mediterranean was one of the most important

factors in the growth of the later Roman Republic and the Empire that followed it.

WAR WITH MACEDON

The First Macedonian War was a minor affair running from 215–205 BC. Ostensibly to suppress piracy, Roman troops landed on the eastern shores of the Aegean and conducted a campaign of harassment against Greek forces there. The aim was to prevent further involvement of Macedonian forces on mainland Italy, and in this the campaign was

CYNOSCEPHALAE 197 BC

The Macedonian phalanx initially pushed the Romans back, but lost its cohesion due to rough ground and hard fighting. As the phalanx broke up the legionaries outfought their opponents in a close-quarters battle and launched a flanking attack on the Macedonian centre.

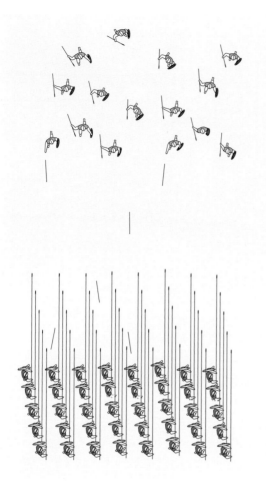

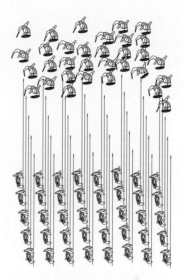

LEGION VS PHALANX
Faced with a dense hedge of spearpoints, legionaries throw their *pila* in the hope of causing gaps in the phalangites' formation. If the Romans can fight their way into the formation they will almost certainly win, but if the phalanx maintains its tight formation, the legionaries are at a massive disadvantage against the long spears of their opponents.

successful. Rome was assisted by Greek allies, notably the Aetolian League.

The Second Macedonian War broke out in 200 BC and lasted for four years. It arose from an accusation by some Greek states that Macedon had made a treaty with Persia. This threatened Roman interests in the region, so a campaign was launched against Macedon.

After a period of indecisive skirmishing, Roman and Macedonian troops met in battle at Cynoscephalae in 197 BC. Here, the superior command structure and flexibility of the legion showed its worth. Both forces were somewhat disordered as a result of operating in difficult terrain, but this hampered the Macedonians far more than their Roman opponents.

The Macedonians had an advantage at first contact due to their long pikes, but once the two formations were closely engaged, they found the Romans difficult opponents. Nevertheless the legions came under severe pressure, especially in the centre and on the left flank. The Roman commander was there, and in another army his preoccupation with the situation in front of him might have seriously slowed down or even paralysed the army's overall command structure.

In the Roman army, however, initiative was encouraged. With no clear orders from above, the officers of the Roman right flank launched an attack with their handful of war elephants, severely disrupting the Macedonians' formation. Into this chaotic situation they made a headlong assault with legionary infantry. Meanwhile all the reserves that could be rallied were directed to make a flanking attack on the enemy.

▲ **Roman legionaries and light troops confront the Macedonian phalanx at the battle of Pydna, 168 BC. The difference in reach between the Roman *gladius* and the Macedonians' long spears is clearly evident, yet it was the Roman force that triumphed.**

Victory at Cynoscephalae owed as much to the ability of small Roman units to rally and quickly return themselves to the control of their superiors as it did to the fighting power or the skills of the commander in charge of battlefield operations. The victory effectively ended the war, resulting in a treaty that converted many of Macedon's vassal city-states into Roman allies and bound Macedon itself not to interfere in outside affairs.

Ironically, given that the war had been fought to prevent a Macedonian-Persian alliance, the Aetolian League then made a pact with Persia against Rome. This was mainly out of dissatisfaction over the meagre territories given to the states of the League in return for their assistance. Persian troops landed in Greece, but were defeated at Thermopylae in 191 BC and Magnesia in 190 BC. Persia sued for peace and was forced to pay a huge indemnity to Rome.

After almost two decades of peace, Macedon once again began trying to regain its power and prestige. This threatened Roman interests in the region, as

Rome wanted Greece divided and thus unable to present much of a threat. A Roman army entered Macedonian territory but was unable to achieve much until a new commander, Paullus, was appointed. Paullus improved the morale and training of his force, and implemented a policy of issuing warning orders ahead of his commands to undertake manoeuvres. As a result, his subordinates could ensure their commands were ready and avoid the army becoming disrupted by an unexpected manoeuvre.

The decisive clash occurred at Pydna in 168 BC, again pitting the legion against the phalanx. Luring the phalangites into rough ground that disrupted their formation, the legionaries outfought their opponents at close quarters and inflicted a strategic defeat. Macedon was broken up into four republics after the war, and soon afterward these were dissolved, Macedon becoming a Roman province.

LEGIONARY TACTICS

The raw material from which the Roman legions were recruited was no different from that of any other fighting force. Romans were no stronger, braver or more hardy than any other people, but what they had in their favour was a great talent for organization.

Thus where the soldiers of other states might be taught how to handle their weapons and perhaps undertake some unit-level drill, Roman troops were subjected to a carefully planned training regime designed to turn out good soldiers as well as skilled fighters. Units could undertake complex evolutions without becoming completely disordered. One of the key factors of the Roman fighting system was the ability of troops to rally and place themselves quickly back under the control of their officers, ensuring that the force remained effective even in the midst of a hard-fought battle.

Legionaries were trained to dig and build as well as fight. Their practice of constructing a fortified camp every night on the march may have been tiresome, but it prevented a force from being overrun by a sudden attack and probably prevented several strategically significant disasters in the long history of the Empire. The ability to construct temporary bridges also improved strategic mobility and allowed the Roman army to strike where it was not expected.

The Roman gift for organization also provided an excellent logistics system, which in turn allowed more troops to be fielded for critical campaigns, and permitted them to stay in the field longer than their opponents. These advantages all added up to a force that could field more men, move faster, recover more quickly after a setback and was partially immune to unexpected disasters. However, this would mean nothing if the troops themselves were ineffective as combat soldiers.

Roman troops were trained to a high standard as individual fighters, but also to support and assist one another. They could form dense formations at need, such as when interlocked shields were needed to protect against arrows, but normally ensured that each man had sufficient space to wield his weapons and undertake some tactical movement.

The standard tactic was to hurl heavy javelins just before contact and then charge home with the sword, with each man not only fighting his nearest opponent but watching out for an opportunity to assist his comrades. There was nothing unsporting about stabbing an enemy engaged with the next legionary along the line if the opportunity presented itself.

The Roman army also understood that a man can only remain effective in combat for a few minutes.

EARLY LEGIONARY FORMATION
Roman forces used a formation known as a quincunx. Screened by the light infantry velites, the main force formed three lines, with gaps equal to the frontage of a maniple. This allowed the light infantry to move to the rear and reinforcements to come forward, replacing tiring or defeated maniples.

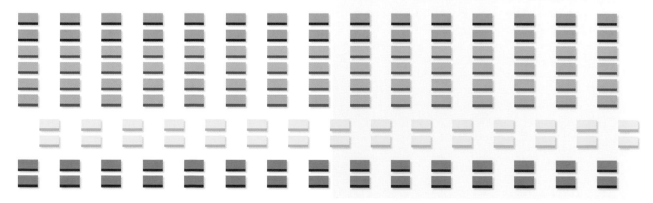

Drills for replacing wounded or tired men in the front line were constantly practised, allowing the legion as a whole to retain its fighting effectiveness in a long engagement. Those pulled out of the line could re-enter combat once they had rested, or could form a reserve to deal with problems or exploit an opportunity elsewhere.

The legionary system produced a professional army whose high standards were rarely even approached until the modern period. But far too often the army was divided against itself fighting civil wars against equally well trained and equipped soldiers rather than dealing with external troubles. It was not any deficiency in the army that allowed the Empire to be overrun, but in the political system that commanded it.

Battle of Pydna (168 BC)

Macedon's alliance with Rome began to unravel from 179 BC onwards, and in 172 BC a Roman force marched into Macedonia. To oppose the invasion, King Perseus of Macedon gathered about 39,000 infantry and 4000 cavalry. His infantry were mainly phalangites, armed with long pikes and trained to fight in a dense formation that presented several pike points against each enemy soldier.

The Romans fielded a consular army of two Roman and two Italian legions plus supporting troops, which included 34 war elephants. With this force, totalling around 37,000 infantry and 2000 cavalry, the Romans achieved some successes. There was no decisive victory however, so a new commander, Lucius Aemilius Paullus, was appointed, and a period of preparation and training undertaken before hostilities resumed.

The two armies met near the city of Pydna in 168 BC, with the Romans deploying from the march against a Macedonian force that was ready in position and waiting for them. Paullus launched his war elephants against the Macedonian left wing, where they did considerable damage. However, the legionaries in the centre could not penetrate the phalanx. Their attacks, though delivered with great determination, were beaten off by the wall of lethal spearpoints they faced and the phalangites began to press forward.

This brought the phalanx into rough terrain, where it lost some of its cohesion. Gaps opened up in the wall of pikes, and the legionaries advanced into them. Once at close quarters the Romans

PYDNA 168 BC

The Macedonians crossed the river to launch an attack, but their left flank was routed by Roman elephants. The remainder of the Macedonian phalanx became disrupted by rough ground, allowing small units of Romans to fight their way in. The phalanx eventually broke up and was routed.

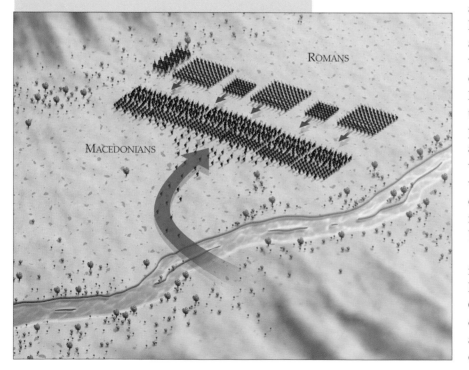

ROMANS

MACEDONIANS

had a considerable advantage. Even when the phalangites dropped their spears and drew swords or daggers, they were fighting the Romans in the Roman manner rather than their own, which was exactly what the Romans wanted.

On the initiative of junior officers, the maniples of the Roman legions began to exploit the situation, breaking up the phalanx and attacking it from the flanks. It was not long before the enormous phalanx, some 21,000 men strong at the start of the battle, collapsed and began to rout.

Some sub-units fought a stubborn rearguard action, but most of the Macedonian army scattered. Among those who fled was the commander, Perseus. He surrendered soon afterward and his kingdom was divided up into four republics which were then recombined into the first Roman province in Greece.

Equipment and Organization

In the early years of the Roman Republic, the military was reformed into a more effective force. The former 'multitude' was divided into two legions, one associated with each of the two elected Consuls that ruled Rome. Later, the concept of a consular army was introduced. Such an army was composed of two Roman legions plus supporting forces.

Legions were raised and disbanded as necessary, except for *legio I–IV*, which made up the two consular armies. Additional legions were raised when the need arose, and additional forces were obtained from allies. The allied city-states of Italy were required to contribute one legion to a campaign for every one that Rome put into the field.

Starting as a militia or citizen-soldier system, the process of raising legions evolved into something like conscription. Romans called to service became part of the army until they were no longer needed. Once a man had joined a legion, he served with it until it was disbanded or he was discharged.

The main advantage of such a system was that a legion gained experience and could be trained up to a high standard if it was in being for any length of time. A man could not be called upon to serve for more than 16 years, but this was a very long time to be away from

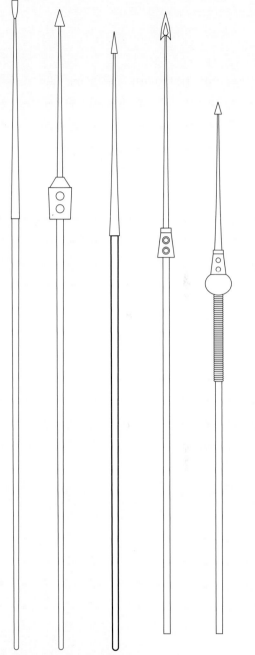

PILA
Of the various designs of Roman army *pila*, the classic had a heavy head and slender shaft, which enabled it to punch through a shield and injure the user. Even if this failed, the *pilum* could not easily be pulled out of a shield and weighed it down, rendering it useless.

a farm or business. In practice, the term of service was much shorter in most cases, though a man might be called up again to serve with a newly-raised legion for a new campaign.

The backbone of the early Republican legion was the heavy infantry, raised from those social classes that could afford the necessary equipment. This consisted of body armour, helmet and shield plus a dagger, sword and the *pilum*, a heavy javelin.

The infantry were divided into three groups according to their experience. A young man with little experience fought with the *hastatii*. Older (and presumably, steadier) men in the prime of life, i.e. in their mid-thirties or younger, were known as *principes*. Together, the *hastatii* and *principes* formed the first two lines in battle.

The most experienced men fought in the third line. They were known as *triarii* and were equipped with spears rather than *pila*. Their function was to form a steady reserve to cover the retirement of the first

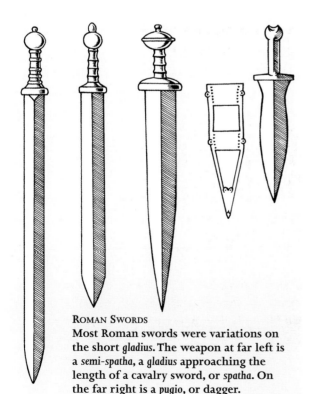

ROMAN SWORDS
Most Roman swords were variations on the short *gladius*. The weapon at far left is a *semi-spatha*, a *gladius* approaching the length of a cavalry sword, or *spatha*. On the far right is a *pugio*, or dagger.

lines if they were beaten, or to advance and tip the balance in favour of the Romans if the outcome of a battle was unclear. The *triarii* were also a source of moral support to hard-pressed men in the front lines – the *triarii*, who had passed the test of battle, were watching the younger men earn their stripes in front of them.

Each of these three lines were subdivided into ten maniples. A maniple of *hastatii* or *principes* was formed of two 60-man centuries whilst the *triarii* used half-strength centuries. A legion at full strength thus contained 1200 *hastatii* and 1200 *principes* plus 600 *triarii* making up its heavy infantry contingent.

As the name might suggest, a 'century' was originally a unit of 100 men, but over time this evolved into a smaller century which was then doubled up into a maniple. The centuries of a maniple were termed the Prior and Posterior centuries. The Prior century took position on the right of the Posterior one, and the Prior centurion was in overall command of the maniple.

The maniples of a battle line were deployed in a 'chequerboard' pattern, with the maniples of the front line of *hastatii* separated by a gap equal to the frontage of the maniple of *principes* behind. The third line of *triarii* maniples were arranged directly behind the front line. This was an extremely flexible formation, allowing units room to move at need but still capable of forming a solid front.

The legion also contained a force of 1200 light infantry, or *velites*. These were drawn from the poorer classes who could not afford the standard legionary gear. They functioned as scouts and flank guards as well as securing terrain features that did not merit detaching a maniple. In battle, the *velites* formed a screen in front of the heavy infantry, harassing the enemy with javelins and then falling back through the gaps in the 'chequerboard' of maniples to avoid being caught between the two forces as they clashed.

A legion also contained a cavalry contingent numbering ten units of 30 men. Gear for the heavy cavalry was expensive and thus only available to the upper echelons of society. In addition to a suitable mount, a cavalryman had to provide himself with a sword, spear, helmet, body armour and a shield. Numbers were sometimes made up with lighter-equipped cavalrymen, who harassed the enemy and supported their heavier brethren. The cavalry often fought dismounted, in much the same manner as their predecessors in the kingdom of Rome had done.

THE REFORMS OF MARIUS

The chief flaw with the military system of the early Republic was that an army had to be recruited from scratch whenever a crisis appeared. Some of the men called for service might have served before, but the army as a whole lost experience as soon as a legion was disbanded after a war.

In addition, it was becoming difficult to recruit sufficient men to meet the needs of Rome's greatly expanded territories. Although not an empire in name, Rome controlled a very large area, much of it overseas, and the troops to defend it had to be recruited from a fairly small population base.

By 107 BC, continuing troubles with Gallic tribes and a war in North Africa had created a need for more troops than could be raised using the existing system. There was an additional problem, too. The segment of Roman society eligible for military

HASTATUS
Equipped with pila and gladius the hastatii formed the front line of the legion and engaged the enemy first. If necessary, they swapped position with the similarly equipped but more experienced principes, resting until the time came to re-engage.

TRIARII
The triarii were highly experienced men, somewhat older than the hastatii or principes. They acted as a final reserve and were equipped with long spears rather than the pilum.
'To fall back upon the triarii' was a Roman figure of speech referring to a last resort in desperate circumstances as well as a battle tactic for an equally dire situation.

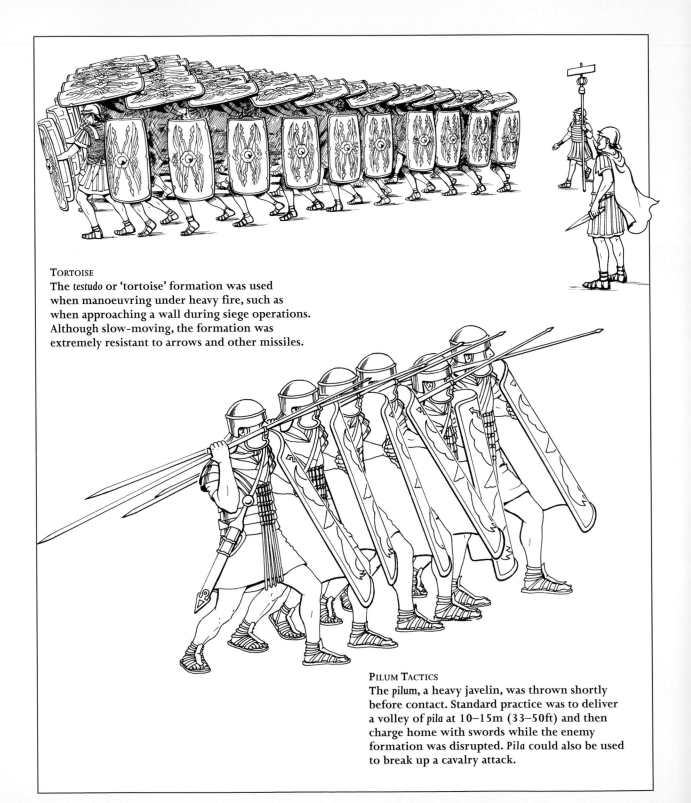

TORTOISE

The *testudo* or 'tortoise' formation was used when manoeuvring under heavy fire, such as when approaching a wall during siege operations. Although slow-moving, the formation was extremely resistant to arrows and other missiles.

PILUM TACTICS

The *pilum*, a heavy javelin, was thrown shortly before contact. Standard practice was to deliver a volley of *pila* at 10–15m (33–50ft) and then charge home with swords while the enemy formation was disrupted. *Pila* could also be used to break up a cavalry attack.

▲ **The Cimbri tribe, originally of Germanic origins, inflicted several major defeats on the Roman army and inspired terror throughout Roman territories. They were defeated by a reformed army under Gaius Marius.**

service was economically significant, and the absence of these men for long periods from their businesses and farms was damaging the Roman economy.

With the majority of available troops campaigning northwards against the Gauls, the Consul Gaius Marius faced a difficult task. He had been assigned the duty of bringing the North African war against King Jugurtha to a satisfactory conclusion. To do this he needed troops, and there were none to be had. Marius pushed through a reform of the Roman military system that had far-reaching consequences. He opened recruitment to the lowest classes of society and made the state responsible for arming and outfitting troops.

Enlistment was an attractive option for many poorer Romans. It offered steady employment, a guarantee that the soldier would be fed and paid, and a grant of land upon retirement. For citizens of allied states, service in the Roman army was to be rewarded

Roman citizenship, which was seen as very desirable status by many.

Marius did not just raise an army with his reforms; he invented a new military system. Soldiers were no longer citizens armed at their own expense and serving for the duration of a crisis. Now the Roman army would remain in being as a standing force, manned by long-service professionals in units that retained their identity from one campaign to the next.

A standing army permitted ongoing training and drill, increasing the fitness, skill and discipline of the legions to a level unheard-of elsewhere in the Ancient World. A standard system of training was implemented throughout the army. Among these was the practice of hacking at a wooden post with a double-weight wooden sword and burdened by a weighted shield. This built strength and endurance as well as technique, and remained a standard training method long after the fall of Rome.

The system of land grants had an additional benefit. Since retiring soldiers were granted land in frontier territories, they provided a reserve for the defence of the region and more importantly, exerted social and political influence. Thus conquered territories were subjected to Romanizing influences and gradually changed their culture.

However, the move away from a citizen army did create one major problem. The army was loyal to its commanders first and foremost, and when those commanders found themselves at odds with their political masters, the army became a tool in internal politics. The many civil wars that wracked the Roman Republic and Empire were made possible, to some degree at least, by Marius' reforms.

Standardized Legions

After the Marian reforms, the legions were standardized in organization and composition. The smallest sub-unit was an eight-man squad which shared a tent and cookpot on the march and in camp. From this basic building block, the centuries and cohorts were constructed.

The standard tactical unit was a century, which was expected to be able to fight and march as a self-contained force. The troops of a century carried all the weaponry and gear they needed to function in the field, plus several days' rations. Additional equipment was carried by a baggage train that accompanied the legion, but each legionary had a sufficiently heavy load that the nickname 'Marius' Mules' was soon applied to them.

A century was standardized at 80 men, with the legion's ten cohorts each containing six centuries, i.e. 480 men to a cohort. The first cohort of a legion was later reorganized, with five double-sized centuries (160 men each) for a total of 800 men in the first cohort. Armies could be formed at need by assigning two or more legions and supporting troops.

After Marius' reforms, a gradual shift continued. Legions from anywhere in Italy came to be considered Roman legions rather than allied formations, ceding their supporting role to formations of *auxilia*. A legion contained heavy infantry equipped in a standard manner, while the *auxilia* were supporting troops. These included light infantry, cavalry and any other forces that were deemed necessary to make up a fighting force.

The Marian system was used until the latter years of the Empire. By this time the situation had changed considerably, and it became common to raise a unit called a legion but numbering around 1000 men and equipped differently to the heavy infantry of the classical legion.

ROMAN COHORT
A cohort of six centuries; two each of *hastatii* and *principes* with the half-strength centuries of *triarii* at the rear. Each century has lightly-equipped *velites* attached and is commanded by a centurion assisted by a senior soldier called an *optio*.

Marius was successful in Africa, but not against the Gauls. By 105 BC, five Roman armies had been defeated by the Gauls and rebellions were occurring as a result of damaged Roman prestige. Taking command in Gaul in 102 BC, Marius marched his army to the Rhône and made camp until the Gauls arrived.

Aware of the enemy's fearsome reputation and the nervousness of his own men, Marius at first declined to give battle, remaining safely in his fortified camp while the tribesmen hurled challenges at his legionaries. After ravaging the local countryside, they grew impatient. Some launched an uncoordinated attack on the Roman camp, which was easily defeated.

This was what Marius had wanted. His troops had become used to the tall, loud barbarians and were no longer so awed by them. They had faced their enemy in battle and won, albeit a minor victory. Now Marius felt that his men could face the Gauls without being half-defeated by their reputation.

In due course, the Gauls marched off in the direction of Italy. The Romans followed but refused

battle, building a fortified camp each night in good defensive terrain. Marius intended to seek battle at a time of his choosing, but at Aquae Sextiae a skirmish between water-gathering parties escalated into a large-scale skirmish which the Romans won. Marius formed up his now-confident army for a decisive action the next day.

Using his cavalry to provoke the Gauls into charging, Marius waited with his men in their chosen position at the top of a slope. As the Gauls laboured upward, they were met with a volley of javelins. The Romans then charged downhill with Marius in the front rank. The Gauls were driven back down the hill

AQUAE SEXTAE 102 BC

Provoking the Gauls into a rash uphill charge, the main Roman force delivered a volley of *pila* before charging into the enemy. Meanwhile a concealed force attacked the Gauls' flanks and rear, causing a complete rout.

but managed to form a battle line on the plains. At this point a detached Roman force attacked their rear, causing a rapid collapse.

Victory at Aquae Sextiae removed part of the threat to Rome, but significant forces of Gauls still threatened northern Italy. Marius marched his army homeward and joined the campaign to eliminate the threat. His now experienced troops were able to inflict a decisive defeat on the courageous but poorly organized Gauls, restoring Roman prestige and ensuring that there was no further barbarian threat to Rome for some years.

WARS OF THE LATE REPUBLIC

From 100 BC onwards, several Roman allies within Italy became increasingly disaffected with what they saw as rather paltry rewards for their participation in the recent conflicts. In 91 BC, a group of Italian cities revolted and created an alliance among themselves. Thus began the Social War, which was unusual in that it pitted almost identical forces against one another.

The standardization of training, tactics and equipment instigated by Marius now ensured that Rome had no advantage over the rebels, who could field large numbers of veteran troops. Rome faced a problem she had encountered before – the defection of her remaining allies if she was seen to be losing the fight. However, despite setbacks and some defections, Rome and her Latin allies managed to avoid defeat for the first half of the war.

A decisive victory in the north in 89 BC allowed Roman forces in the south to go on the offensive, defeating an army of their old foes, the Samnites. This persuaded some former allies to rejoin the Roman side, though the Samnites themselves fought on.

The Social War was ended by negotiation and reforms that settled some of the grievances of the

> " ... IT IS AS RELEVANT TO THE GLORY OF THE ROMAN EMPIRE AS OF ONE MAN TO MENTION AT THIS POINT ALL THE NAMES AND TRIUMPHS OF POMPEY THE GREAT, FOR THEY EQUALLED IN BRILLIANCE THE EXPLOITS OF ALEXANDER THE GREAT... "
>
> PLINY

rebels as well as rewarding those that had remained loyal to Rome. However, this would have been useless had the armies of Rome not demonstrated that they could defeat the rebels eventually, or at least drag out the war for longer than any of the combatants was willing to accept.

Mithridatic Wars

Over the following decades, Roman forces dealt with slave revolts and piracy. They campaigned in Gaul and Hispania as well as launching major campaigns of conquest. These brought the Balkans and Thrace within Roman control, but also resulted in a series of wars with the Kingdom of Pontus.

Named for King Mithridates of Pontus, the First and Second Mithridatic wars were inconclusive, but the third and final was a huge conflict which ran from 73–63 BC. Roman attention was distracted by a major revolt in Hispania led by a renegade Roman governor, who sent advisors to help train Mithridates' army.

Mithridates defeated Roman forces at the battle of Chalcedon close to the entrance to the Bosporus. From there he marched on the strategic port of Cyzicus, which he needed as a supply base for further operations. The port held out until Roman forces could arrive by sea, changing the strategic position in their favour.

Cyzicus was located on an island linked to the mainland by a causeway, and Mithridates' force was mainly deployed on the island in siegeworks. The Romans established themselves on the mainland, across Mithridates' supply line. This forced Mithridates to begin reducing his force involved in the siege, and also to launch increasingly desperate attempts to take the city before his supplies ran out. These failed, and many of the troops attempting to relocate elsewhere fell into Roman hands.

Mithridates abandoned his siege of Cyzicus and was repeatedly attacked during his retreat. His main army was gradually reduced to insignificance whilst other Roman forces defeated his allies and detachments. The Romans then invaded Pontus and besieged several of its cities, trying to force a decisive field battle. This did not succeed until 72 or 71 BC – the date is unclear. A new army raised by Mithridates was defeated, causing morale to collapse within the Pontic forces.

Mithridates sought the protection of his son-in-law, who ruled Armenia. After pausing to impose a suitable governmental apparatus on Pontus, making it a Roman province, the Roman army advanced into Armenia, probably in 69 BC. This was the first contact Rome had had with Armenia and, more significantly, Parthia. The latter was to become a long-time opponent of Rome.

The armies of Armenia were decisively defeated at Tigranocerta but this did not bring the war to an end. Neither did an attempt to besiege the capital at Artaxata, and soon the campaign turned against Rome, when Pontus was invaded by Mithridates at the head of an army raised mostly in Armenia.

Attacking at Zela, Mithridates' army inflicted a heavy defeat on the Roman forces stationed in Pontus. News of this caused morale in the Roman army marching back from Armenia to collapse, with many units refusing to obey orders.

The Roman response was swift and decisive; having already established himself as a commander and statesman, most recently in a stunningly successful campaign against Sicilian pirates, Gnaeus Pompeius Magnus (Pompey the Great) was given control of the war. He was also assigned additional powers to make alliances and peace treaties without the need for Senatorial approval.

Forming an alliance with Parthia, Pompey offered Mithridates a peace settlement, which was rebuffed. Mithridates made a stand at the fortress of Dasteira, but was forced to retreat after several weeks of conflict. His camp was attacked during the retreat by Pompey's legions. Mithridates fled, finding refuge in the Crimea. There, he held out in a remnant of his kingdom until 63 BC when his son overthrew him. Mithridates died soon afterward, probably by suicide.

Meanwhile, Pompey embarked on a campaign of conquest that took him into Armenia and what is now Georgia. He had reached Syria by the time he heard of Mithridates' demise, and returned to Rome in triumph in 61 BC.

By the end of the Mithridatic Wars, large new territories had been gained and vast treasures

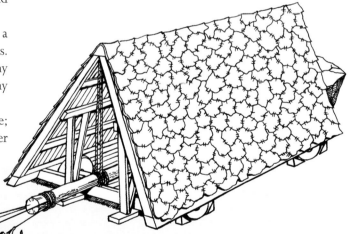

ROMAN RAM
The frame and roof protecting a Roman ram was given the same name as an infantry formation – *testudo* **or 'tortoise'. According to Roman law, once the first ram hit a city wall, the defenders could no longer expect any mercy.**

◀ Siege tower, Alesia, 52 BC. The Romans were extremely adept at siege warfare, routinely undertaking large-scale projects such as siege ramps. The designs of their siege engines and towers were largely copied from Greek technology, refined by experience in the field.

captured. The wars also marked the end for Seleucid Persia. Only Egypt, of all Alexander the Great's Successor States, remained free of Roman overlordship. Rome was not yet formally an empire, but her territory in the east had almost reached its greatest extent.

The Campaigns of Julius Caesar

As a means to gain the wealth and military glory he needed to further his political ambitions, Gaius Julius Caesar engineered a conflict with the Helvetii people in 58 BC, who were engaged in a tribal migration. Ensuring that the Helvetii came into conflict with tribes who were Roman allies, Caesar provided himself with an excuse to crush them.

Commanding six legions, Caesar followed the Helvetii. He made good use of reconnaissance in a manner not unlike that used by modern armies. Mounted patrols maintained contact with the tribesmen but avoided action, and were followed up by scouts who ensured that the route of the main force was free from obstructions and ambushes.

Caesar's army was attacked by the Helvetii near Bibracte. Warned by his cavalry scouts, Caesar drew up his force in the classic three lines on a hill. The Helvetii attacked uphill at the waiting Roman lines, and were met in the same manner as at Aquae Sextiae. A volley of javelins at 15 metres (16 yards) broke up the Gallic formations, and the first Roman line charged into the resulting chaos. A late-arriving force of Gauls presented a threat to the Roman flank, but this was countered by wheeling the third line of cohorts to meet the new threat while the first and second lines continued their advance. In the end, after five hours of conflict, the Helvetii were decisively defeated.

Caesar then received requests for aid from more of the Gallic tribes and began a new campaign. This time the enemy was Ariovistus, a Gallic king who, ironically,

had recently been named Friend of Rome. Winning a second major victory in the same year might have been enough for some commanders, but not so Julius Caesar.

Caesar embarked upon a series of campaigns against the Gauls, Germans and even the Britons.

▲ Arguably the most famous of great Romans, Julius Caesar was Dictator, but never Emperor. Had he lived longer, his immense talent and ambition might have brought about the Roman Empire a little earlier.

Some of these conflicts were deliberately engineered. Others resulted from the previous one, as nearby tribes became alarmed at the defeat of their neighbours. Eventually the Gauls, a people traditionally divided among many tribes, began to organize themselves against the might of Caesar. Vercingetorix of the Arverni emerged as the overall leader, and managed to field a force that was well organized by Gallic standards. In 52 BC, a significant number of tribes rose against Rome and her allies.

Caesar's forces were caught off-guard by the uprising, and were ill-supplied and in some areas rather weak. Nevertheless their aggressive and confident response won them the initiative and persuaded many unaligned tribes to stay out of the fighting. Roman allies were reassured and continued to provide support in the form of grain and fodder.

In addition to the very considerable fighting power of the legions, the Roman force had other advantages. Better supply arrangements allowed the Romans to remain concentrated where their opponents had to disperse to find food. Deception operations were also mounted in order to gain an advantage, such as disguising parties of slaves and camp followers as legionaries and sending them marching off to deceive enemy scouts.

The Gauls were gradually worn down and their towns captured by siege, until finally the main Gallic army took refuge at the town of Alesia. Unable to launch a direct attack with any certainty of success, the Romans began a siege. A wall was thrown around the town to prevent a breakout, and a second ring of fortifications, facing outwards, was built to protect the besieging troops and to prevent relief from reaching the town.

ALESIA 52 BC

Caesar's army built a double wall around Alesia, protecting themselves against external attack as well as keeping the Gauls bottled up under siege. Although hard-pressed at times, the Romans managed to hold their walls against breakout attempts and a relief army, until at last the Gauls were forced to surrender.

GAULS

ROMANS

▲ According to some accounts, the Gallic leader Vercingetorix rode out to surrender on his magnificent charger, dismounting to lay his weapons before Caesar's feet. Caesar's own account of the event is less grand.

After a period of siege and increasingly desperate attempts to break out, the Gauls admitted defeat and surrendered. This did not entirely end the Gallic revolt. A smaller rising the following year was easily put down. A mix of savage reprisals and politically expedient leniency restored stability to the region.

Caesar and Civil War

This freed Caesar to return to Rome with his glorious reputation. However, he had many enemies who would be able to strike at him once he gave up command of his army. This presented a problem, as his authority to command the army ended at the border between Cisalpine Gaul and Italia, marked by the Rubicon stream. If Caesar brought his troops with him into Italia, he would be in open defiance of the law. If he did not, he was at the mercy of his opponents. In 49 BC, Caesar chose to march part of his army into Italia, bringing about a state of civil war. This pitted Caesar against the Senate's chosen champion, Pompey the Great, who realized that Rome could not be held against Caesar's veterans. Needing time to train an army to the necessary standard, Pompey relocated to Macedonia while Caesar gained control of all of Italy within two months.

Caesar meanwhile marched westwards into Hispania. This campaign was one of manoeuvre rather than head-on clashes, as Caesar wanted to avoid heavy casualties on both sides. This strategy paid off when the enemy legions were finally compelled to surrender, as Caesar was able to incorporate them into his army.

Finally, in 48 BC, Caesar landed in Macedonia with seven legions to oppose Pompey's nine. Pompey's fleet cut off his supply line, leaving Caesar without reinforcements and short of food. The latter was somewhat remedied by a bold raid that seized one of Pompey's supply stockpiles, but for some months Caesar's forces were in a perilous position.

Reinforced by four more legions under Mark Antony, Caesar was able to take the offensive at last. An attempt to take Dyrrachium resulted in a confrontation between the two armies that became a race to build fortifications protecting key points. Caesar attempted to besiege Pompey; Pompey built forts to prevent the Caesarian siege lines from encircling his position.

Skirmishing went on throughout the construction period, increasing in intensity as Caesar's troops attempted to close their ring of fortifications around Pompey's force. Both sides suffered setbacks, but it was the Caesarian force that came off worst. Caesar broke off the siege and moved his army inland. Pompey followed, and the two armies clashed at Pharsalus on the banks of the River Enipeus.

Caesar formed up with his left flank secured by the river and the right held by his cavalry, supported by light infantry. Pompey hoped that his cavalry, which vastly outnumbered that of Caesar, would be decisive. His plan was to face Caesar's infantry with his own legions while the cavalry, supported by slingers and light infantry, drove off Caesar's cavalry and then fell on the enemy flank and rear. This was the obvious tactic, given the circumstances, and Caesar was ready for it. The tactical flexibility of the cohort system enabled Caesar to pull one cohort from the third line of each of his legions and create a fourth line that covered his vulnerable flank. This was concealed behind the cavalry and could not be seen by Pompey.

Caesar's infantry advanced to attack Pompey's legions, which stood their ground rather than advancing in the usual Roman manner. Meanwhile the Pompeian cavalry attacked, falling into some disorder as they did so. Although the Caesarean cavalry was pushed back, the fourth line of infantry was able to charge the disordered Pompeian cavalry. Infantry attacks against cavalry are very rare in all of history – successful ones even more so – but this time the circumstances were exactly right.

Caesar's infantry attack resulted in a bitter fight, with numbers and dense formations helping Pompey's force hold their own against the experienced Caesareans. The matter was decided by a flanking

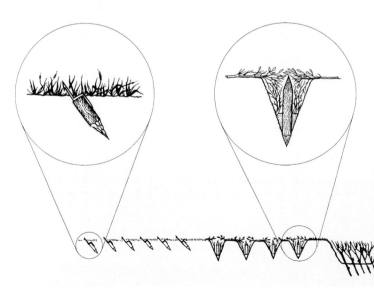

Siegeworks at Alesia
The siegeworks were protected by earth and timber fortifications which were further strengthened by a double ditch in front. Any attack was delayed even before reaching the ditch, by forked branches emplaced as obstacles (abatis), iron barbs fixed in planted stakes so that they pointed outwards (stimulus) and by pits with sharpened stakes ('lilies') in the bottom. However, the defences served only as force-multipliers for the Roman legionaries, not a replacement for them.

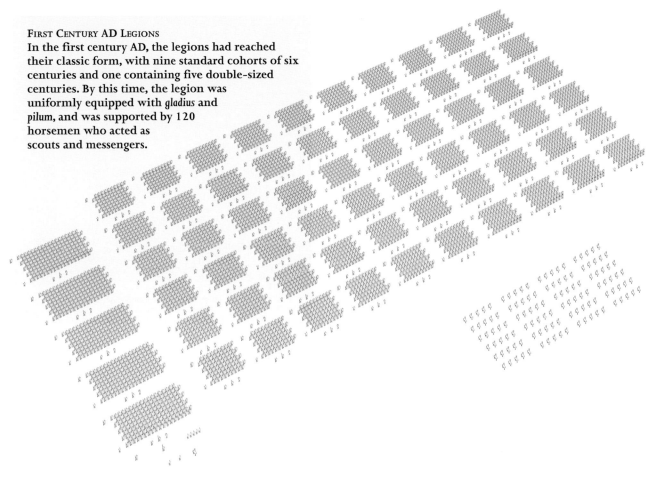

FIRST CENTURY AD LEGIONS
In the first century AD, the legions had reached their classic form, with nine standard cohorts of six centuries and one containing five double-sized centuries. By this time, the legion was uniformly equipped with *gladius* and *pilum*, and was supported by 120 horsemen who acted as scouts and messengers.

attack by the Caesarean fourth line, freed to manoeuvre now that the Pompeian cavalry had fled the field. Caesar's third line moved up to join the fighting, Pompey fled as his army collapsed, and eventually reached Egypt where he was murdered by members of the Egyptian court who sought Caesar's favour.

After dealing with an invasion of Pontus by Pharnaces, son of Mithridates, Caesar set about eliminating his remaining opponents. Although his campaigns were at times ill-prepared to the point of recklessness, Caesar's veteran legions delivered victory after victory until at last he had defeated all his opponents and was undisputed master of Rome.

As Dictator for Life, Caesar displayed considerable clemency, even appointing former enemies to high office. However, he was assassinated by a group of men with varying motives in 44 BC at a meeting of the Senate, bringing about the events that ended the Roman Republic and replaced it with an Empire.

THE END OF THE REPUBLIC

The assassination of Julius Caesar resulted in a period of political turmoil that developed into a new civil war between the assassins, who styled themselves the *Liberatores*, and those who wanted to avenge the murder of Caesar. The two chief *Liberatores*, Brutus and Cassius, secured for themselves a powerbase in the eastern provinces and gained the assistance of neighbouring powers, including Parthia. Meanwhile the pro-Caesar faction, led by Mark Antony, Caesar's heir Octavian, and Marcus Aemilius Lepidus, remained in Rome with control of the western provinces.

Antony and Octavian led an army into Macedonia in 42 BC. The two sides clashed at Philippi, with

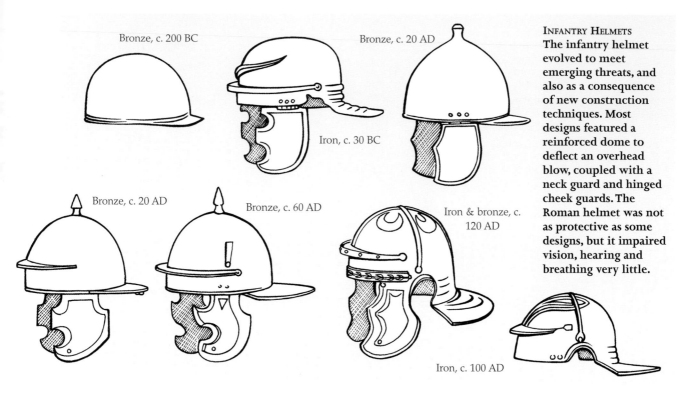

Bronze, c. 200 BC

Bronze, c. 20 AD

Iron, c. 30 BC

Bronze, c. 20 AD

Bronze, c. 60 AD

Iron & bronze, c. 120 AD

Iron, c. 100 AD

INFANTRY HELMETS
The infantry helmet evolved to meet emerging threats, and also as a consequence of new construction techniques. Most designs featured a reinforced dome to deflect an overhead blow, coupled with a neck guard and hinged cheek guards. The Roman helmet was not as protective as some designs, but it impaired vision, hearing and breathing very little.

roughly equal forces. The first battle of Philippi was a close-fought draw, though Cassius committed suicide upon hearing a false report that Brutus had been defeated. Brutus assumed overall command but morale, always a problem for the *Liberatores*, now fell further. Brutus tried to improve matters by offering a donative (essentially a pay bonus, or a bribe) to his troops in addition to those they had already received.

There then ensued a period of fortification and counter-fortification, while Brutus hoped that his fleet's control of the sea would cut off the enemy supply line. Before his blockade could take effect, Brutus' mercenaries and some of his allies began to desert, forcing him to attack while he still had an army. The second battle of Philippi was another close-fought affair between very similar armies.

Brutus' army was eventually broken and fled for the safety of its camp, but found the entrances held by Octavian's troops. Brutus took what troops he could rally into the hills but fell into despair and killed himself soon after. His remaining troops were captured and enrolled into service with the victors, as was not uncommon in Roman civil wars.

Although some of the *Liberatores*' leaders remained at large, the power of their faction was broken at Philippi. However, this was not the end of the troubles facing Rome. Antony and Octavian found themselves at war for a time as a result of internal disputes, and on the eastern frontier Parthian troops had invaded the eastern Roman territories. Conflict with Parthia had been going on intermittently for many years, and had not usually gone well for Rome.

The infantry-dominated Roman army was not well prepared to deal with the Parthian mode of combat, which combined horse archery with heavily armoured cavalry. At the battle of Carrhae in 53 BC, the Romans suffered their worst defeat in centuries, and Parthia again proved a difficult opponent. The lost territory was eventually retaken by forces under Mark Antony, but a Roman incursion into Parthian lands was forced to withdraw after its siege train was ambushed en route and destroyed.

SHIPBOARD WEAPONS
Right: *Ballistae* **made excellent shipboard weapons. Their main drawback on land, lack of mobility, was irrelevant at sea as they were part of the ship and moved with it. Below: Warships of increasing size were built by the Roman navy. The vessel depicted is a 'sixteen', with two banks of oars crewed by 16 men at each station.**

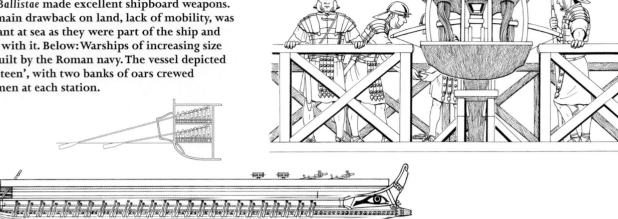

Antony's army was severely depleted, and the paltry reinforcements sent by Octavian were nowhere near enough to replace his casualties. On the other hand, Cleopatra of Egypt was able to furnish enough troops, and Antony was on very good terms with her – good enough that she had borne three children by him. Their famous affair and political alliance led to more infighting, and eventual outright war between Rome and Egypt in 31 BC.

Octavian gained the upper hand on land and at sea, while Antony's forces were weakened by desertion. Eventually Antony's fleet became blockaded in the bay of Actium and were forced to attempt a breakout against superior forces. Part of Antony's fleet escaped with help from Cleopatra's forces but their power was effectively broken. Defeated again in battle at Alexandria, Antony and Cleopatra both committed suicide.

This left Octavian to become master of Rome. He was granted the title Augustus in 27 BC and

ACTIUM 31 BC

Blockaded on land and at sea, Mark Antony's force attempted a naval breakout. As his left wing became involved in heavy combat, the enemy fleet made an outflanking manoeuvre. This permitted Cleopatra's fleet to escape into open water. Antony's fleet was largely destroyed, though Antony himself escaped.

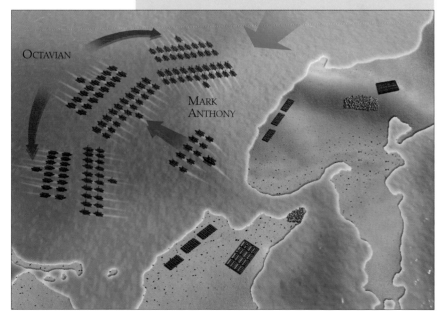

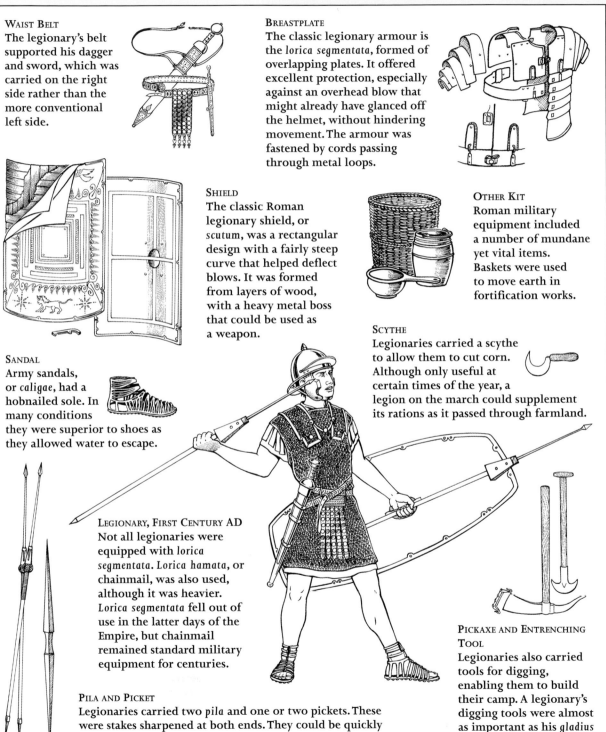

WAIST BELT
The legionary's belt supported his dagger and sword, which was carried on the right side rather than the more conventional left side.

BREASTPLATE
The classic legionary armour is the *lorica segmentata*, formed of overlapping plates. It offered excellent protection, especially against an overhead blow that might already have glanced off the helmet, without hindering movement. The armour was fastened by cords passing through metal loops.

SHIELD
The classic Roman legionary shield, or *scutum*, was a rectangular design with a fairly steep curve that helped deflect blows. It was formed from layers of wood, with a heavy metal boss that could be used as a weapon.

OTHER KIT
Roman military equipment included a number of mundane yet vital items. Baskets were used to move earth in fortification works.

SANDAL
Army sandals, or *caligae*, had a hobnailed sole. In many conditions they were superior to shoes as they allowed water to escape.

SCYTHE
Legionaries carried a scythe to allow them to cut corn. Although only useful at certain times of the year, a legion on the march could supplement its rations as it passed through farmland.

LEGIONARY, FIRST CENTURY AD
Not all legionaries were equipped with *lorica segmentata*. *Lorica hamata*, or chainmail, was also used, although it was heavier. *Lorica segmentata* fell out of use in the latter days of the Empire, but chainmail remained standard military equipment for centuries.

PILA AND PICKET
Legionaries carried two *pila* and one or two pickets. These were stakes sharpened at both ends. They could be quickly emplaced to assist in fortifying a camp.

PICKAXE AND ENTRENCHING TOOL
Legionaries also carried tools for digging, enabling them to build their camp. A legionary's digging tools were almost as important as his *gladius* or *scutum*.

gradually increased his power and prestige through civic projects such as road-building. Other titles and honours followed and were used by subsequent Roman emperors.

Under the leadership of Augustus, Roman armies campaigned in Ilyria, Pannonia, Hispania, and Galatia, adding yet more territory to that controlled by Rome. In addition to direct control of regions, buffer states were set up to protect against invasion. These included conquered territories in the Alps and client kingdoms in the east.

Several lasting changes were made during Augustus' reign. Perhaps most importantly, the system of taxation in the provinces was reformed to provide a stable and predictable stream of revenue. The road system was begun, allowing faster communications and troop movement. Rome gained professional fire and police services as well as the Praetorian Guard, which started out as a bodyguard unit but eventually became a political force in its own right.

Not everything went well for the Romans under Augustus, however. A major expedition into Germania was lured into an ambush in the Teutoberger Wald in AD 9, with the loss of three legions and their supporting troops. This brought to an end Roman expansion into Germania; thereafter the frontier was at the Rhine. Augustus died in AD 14. His title and powers passed to his stepson Tiberius, beginning the long line of Roman emperors.

THE EARLY EMPIRE

The first task facing Roman forces was the pacification of the northern frontier. A show of strength was necessary to deter attacks by Germanic tribes. An expedition in AD 15–16 crossed into Germania and inflicted defeats on the tribes there, then withdrew after locating and burying the remains of the legions lost in the Teutoberger Wald.

Britain was invaded in AD 43, with the conquest following a typically Roman pattern. The Romans sought local allies who were often happy to assist in the subjugation of their rivals, and gradually the frontier was pushed north and west from the landing points on the English Channel.

War with Parthia flared up again in AD 58, as a result of a disputed succession in Armenia. Unlike previous clashes with Parthia, this time the Romans were successful and installed their favoured candidate on the Armenian throne. They were assisted by a series of revolts among the Parthian nobility. However, once the Parthians had set their own house in order they

EARLY IMPERIAL LEGION FORMATION
It is not clear exactly when the first cohort of each legion was reorganized to contain five double centuries. The change was probably gradual and may have occurred during Caesar's era. The first cohort was not only larger than the others, it was also an élite formation containing the best men in the legion.

went on the offensive and defeated a Roman army at Rhandeia. A peace settlement was reached in AD 64 but intermittent conflict between the Roman Empire and Parthia continued for many years afterward.

Roman rule in the province of Judea had always been troubled, and in AD 66 a new rising took place. The Jewish rebels were initially successful, and when Roman forces responded in the usual manner with an aggressive advance they were defeated at the pass of Beth-horon.

Succession wars

The Roman response was hampered by a dispute over succession to the Roman Imperial throne after the death in AD 68 of Emperor Nero. In what has become known as the Year of Four Emperors, Roman forces fought one another in support of their preferred candidate. The winner was Vespasian, who founded the Flavian dynasty. More importantly perhaps, he demonstrated that a general who had the support of the army could make himself emperor by force alone.

In Judea, Roman forces gradually regained control of the province, laying siege to the capital at Jerusalem and finally eliminating the last Zealot holdouts in the fortress of Masada. Gradually, the internal and external troubles were calmed and a period of relative stability began. With it came new heights of power.

ROMAN SIEGE WARFARE

The Romans were extremely good at adopting and adapting successful techniques used by others. Many of their siege engines were based on Greek designs, while their techniques had their origins in far more ancient conflicts.

In addition to archery, Roman troops used *ballistae* to wear down the enemy and to cover parties conducting siegeworks. *Ballistae* were light engines like a very large crossbow, shooting a stone or javelin in a fairly flat arc. *Ballistae* were deployed with the army and sometimes used in field battles. From the first century AD, each century of a legion theoretically had a *ballista* for support, though actual numbers varied according to availability. A lighter version of the *ballista*, the Scorpion, was also deployed, often atop siege towers.

A crank-operated self-loading Scorpion existed, but it proved to be of limited use. Heavier projectiles were hurled in a high arc by the *onager*, named after a wild ass as it had a pronounced 'kicking' action when fired. *Onagri* could inflict personnel casualties or break down light obstacles, and were sometimes used to deliver incendiary projectiles.

These artillery weapons were used to support siege operations which were little different from those used by previous armies, though the Roman's organizational skills brought their art to a high pitch. Walls were undermined by tunnelling or smashed with rams, which were often mounted on siege towers.

A siege tower could be used to mount more than one weapon. It was not uncommon to have archery or *ballista* platforms plus a ram or drawbridge to allow troops easy access to a wall. However, getting the tower to the wall was a difficult proposition, especially where the wall was built on high ground or with a ditch in front. Siege ramps were used for this purpose.

The construction of a ramp was a considerable feat of engineering, especially if it had to be conducted under fire. The Roman genius for organization was a considerable asset in such works, which proceeded swiftly and efficiently despite the best efforts of the defenders to destroy the work going on below.

It was a convention of Roman siege warfare that a garrison could surrender honourably when the first ram touched the fortifications. In most cases, a breach was inevitable at this point, and a garrison that resisted further was liable to be massacred in retaliation for making the besiegers suffer the torment and casualties of an assault.

Once a breach was made or a tower dropped a drawbridge onto the wall, it was stormed by legionaries whose short swords were ideal for close-quarters fighting. The time for technique and engineering skill was passed at this point; now it was a contest between the defenders' desperation and the professional fighting power of the Roman legionary.

Battle for Jerusalem (AD 70)

Judea came to the brink of rebellion several times during the occupation, and in AD 66, a full-scale revolt

ONAGER

The *onager* was named after a wild ass, for the kicking motion it made when fired. It launched a heavy projectile in a high arc.

SIEGE TOWER

Roman siege towers were built as large as they needed to be for the task at hand. The one used to storm Masada was 30m (99ft) high, though smaller towers were usually sufficient. Roman towers mounted a variety of weapons including rams and artillery, as well as bridges to reach the enemy wall tops.

ARCHER

In a siege, archery was extremely important in softening up the enemy and covering the work of the siege engineers. Archers were recruited mainly from the eastern provinces. They were not part of the legions but were supporting *auxilia*.

GIANT BALLISTA

Ballistae were built in various sizes. The larger, more powerful engines possessed greater range and hitting power but took a long time to construct and to prepare for each shot. Thus large engines were only practical in a protracted siege or in fixed defensive positions.

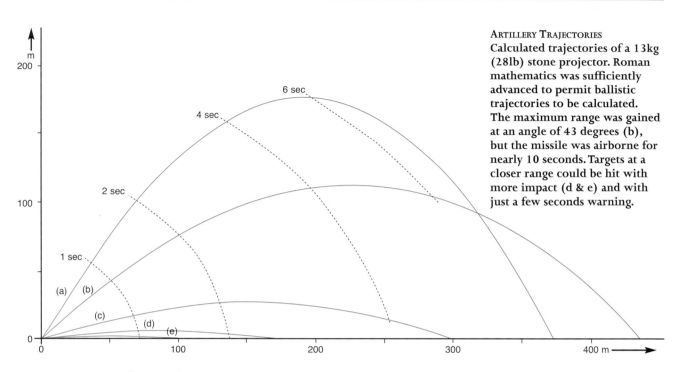

ARTILLERY TRAJECTORIES
Calculated trajectories of a 13kg (28lb) stone projector. Roman mathematics was sufficiently advanced to permit ballistic trajectories to be calculated. The maximum range was gained at an angle of 43 degrees (b), but the missile was airborne for nearly 10 seconds. Targets at a closer range could be hit with more impact (d & e) and with just a few seconds warning.

broke out. After suffering defeats early on, and distracted by a civil war from AD 68–69, the Romans more or less pacified the province by AD 70.

The capital, Jerusalem, remained in rebel hands. Jerusalem had been a hard target when a Roman army under Pompey stormed it in 63 BC and was unlikely to be any easier to attack and destroy this time around. In addition to the population, some 24,000 or so rebel Jews had taken refuge in Jerusalem, which was protected by stout fortifications and divided into districts by internal walls.

The Roman army outside Jerusalem numbered about 35,000 men under the leadership of Titus Flavius. The latter conducted a personal reconnaissance of the city's defences and was almost killed by a party of Jews who sallied out from the defences. A major attack was also launched on the Roman army as it began to establish itself before the city. This was very nearly successful, but after winning a narrow victory the Romans began their siege preparations. These were typically thorough. A secure fortified camp was built and artillery positions set up. From here, Roman engines shot at the defenders, who replied with *ballistae* captured from the garrison.

Covered by their artillery, Roman forces began building a set of siege ramps up to the city walls. The defenders sallied out to try to destroy the Roman engines and hampered the siegeworks with missile fire, but the ramps reached the walls and began to batter at them.

Once the wall was breached, storming parties entered and quickly drove off the defenders, allowing the Romans to advance through the streets. It was then necessary to breach two more internal walls in order to approach the rebels' stronghold in the Great Temple. Skirmishing in the streets, ambushes of work parties and occasional sorties in strength held up the Roman advance for a time but finally the stronghold was under attack.

It took 17 days to build siege ramps up to the walls of the Great Temple, during which time the rebels made a serious attempt to storm the Roman camp. Some Roman troops deserted as morale among the besiegers began to suffer. In response, Titus Flavius ordered a defensive wall to be built, cutting off food supplies from the city and protecting his own forces. Another set of ramps were built, taking 21 days, and finally the walls were breached.

Repeated storming attempts were made, culminating in a bloody day-long hand-to-hand fight. The Romans were then forced to fight their way through the whole temple against desperate resistance. At some point during the battle, the temple caught fire and the surviving rebels retreated to their final refuge, the Old City.

More ramps were built and the Old City was stormed, but by this point the defenders were demoralized and on the brink of starvation. Resistance collapsed and with it the rebellion came to an end, although a band of Zealots still held the fortress of Masada and would require a truly prodigious feat of siege engineering to remove them – the construction of a siege ramp 100m (328ft) high, up which a siege tower some 30m (98ft) tall was pushed to breach the walls.

JERUSALEM AD 70

Roman forces fought their way through successive walls to clear each section of the city in turn. Although the Jews put up a determined resistance, counter-attacking vigorously when they could, their last strongholds in the Great Temple and Old City were finally stormed, bringing the revolt to an end.

THE ZENITH OF THE EMPIRE

In AD 101, the Emperor Trajan invaded Dacia. The Dacian king Decebalus had united his people for the first time in decades and was recruiting soldiers, most especially deserters from the Roman legions. With these forces he had raided Roman territory and inflicted sufficiently serious defeats on Roman forces that Rome was at that time paying them tribute.

Trajan led nine legions into Dacia, plus supporting troops including detachments from other legions. Some of Trajan's force was concentrated, but several smaller contingents were also deployed with subsidiary objectives in mind.

The Dacians fortified the passes into their territory and garrisoned them with infantry, while cataphract cavalry were obtained from allies in Sarmatia. Meanwhile, the Romans built a pontoon bridge across the Danube and fortified it to protect their logistics and communications.

The Dacians fought as typical barbarian infantry, wearing little armour in battle and wielding swords, javelins and bows. Their most formidable weapon was called the *falx*, a long-hafted weapon with a curved, sickle-like blade which could reach under a shield. This was one reason for the adoption of greaves to protect the legs.

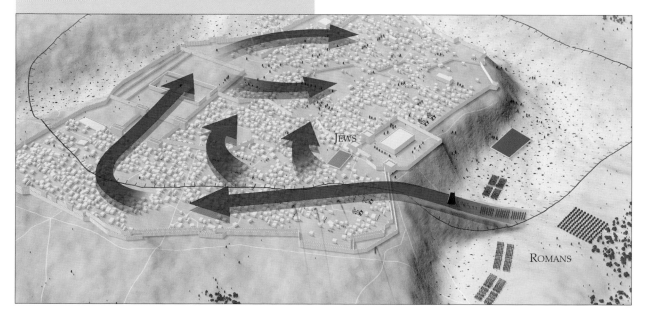

JEWS

ROMANS

Roman practice at the time was to use a front line of auxiliary troops, with the legions behind. One reason for this was the superior drill and discipline of legionary infantry, which made them more responsive to orders. Legionaries made a better reserve force than auxiliary infantry, and in addition, the practice saved Roman lives.

Trajan's army was successful in battle at Tapae and continued its advance, burning Dacian settlements as they went. The Dacians, meanwhile, sent forces across the Danube to attack Roman garrisons, forcing Trajan to hunt down the raiding forces before continuing the campaign.

The campaign was a difficult one, but in AD 102 the Dacians surrendered. Among the terms was a requirement to reduce the Dacian army and hand over Roman deserters rather than recruiting them, but Decebalus soon broke this agreement. The war began again in AD 105.

Using a combination of force and negotiation to obtain the surrender of local leaders, Trajan gradually weakened Decebalus' position, and in AD 106 his army launched a major offensive. This time the Danube was crossed via a massive stone bridge specially built by army engineers. Advancing to the Dacian capital at Sarmizegethusa Regia, Trajan's army laid siege. Decebalus himself committed suicide rather than surrender. This brought the war to an end, with Dacia becoming a Roman province.

In AD 114, war broke out with Parthia, once again as a result of disputed succession in Armenia. Trajan assembled a force of 17 out of 30 legions that existed at that time, plus supporting troops, and stockpiled enormous quantities of supplies. His invasion went well, capturing Armenia, Mesopotamia and much of Parthia including the capital, Ctesiphon. However, revolts broke out all over the new territories in AD 116, which along with a rebellion in Egypt, required Roman troops to rush around like a fire brigade.

Trajan was succeeded by Hadrian in AD 117, who was not territorially ambitious. More interested in stability than expansion, Hadrian launched no campaigns of conquest but worked to ensure that the frontiers were guarded by well-trained legions led by astute officers. Hadrian ordered the construction of a wall across northern Britain, essentially abandoning any hope of subjugating the lands further north.

Elsewhere on the frontiers, Hadrian ordered that bases and fortifications, previously of timber construction, be rebuilt in stone. This gave the Roman army more secure bases to operate from but also made its dispositions permanent. The previous structures were intended to be used until the frontier moved outward again; Hadrian's new fortifications were a statement that the Empire had reached its greatest size and was now concerned mainly with keeping what it had.

The Empire enjoyed a period of stability and prosperity, sometimes known as that of the 'Five Good Emperors' for the reason that the succession passed smoothly and internal disputes were uncommon. One reason for this was the practice of adopting a successor rather than simply passing on the crown to the eldest child. Candidates for succession had proven themselves in economic, political and military affairs and were well suited to rule the Empire. Not coincidentally, this period is also known as the *Pax Romana* in honour of the peace that Roman rule brought to the territories of the Empire.

BEGINNINGS OF DECLINE

During the *Pax Romana* there were troubles within the Empire and on the frontiers, of course, but these were largely contained by effective military forces based close to potential crisis points. Thus, although the Germanic tribes were active in raiding across the frontier during the reign of Marcus Aurelius, the Empire was not seriously threatened. However, in AD 180 Marcus Aurelius was succeeded by his son Commodus, who became insane and caused considerable damage to the Empire before being assassinated to get him out of the way.

Commodus was followed by Septimus Severus, first of the Severan Dynasty. Severus increased the role of the army in politics as a consequence of using it as a political powerbase, and by the time of Alexander Severus, who was assassinated in AD 235, the army was often beyond the control of the Emperor.

AQUILIFER, LATE FIRST CENTURY AD
An aquilifer was a senior signifer bearing the eagle standard of a Roman legion. The name comes from the type of standard, *aquila*, meaning 'eagle'. This was the universal standard used from 104 BC; earlier, the wolf, boar, bull and horse were also used. The eagle standard was the most important possession of the legion and its loss was a terrible disgrace for the unit.

AUXILARY, LATE FIRST CENTURY AD
In the frontier wars fought by Rome in the mid- and later Imperial period, auxilary infantry became ever more important in guarding the outposts of the empire. They were not as well armed or trained as the traditional legionary, but became more common as the Empire struggled to find good recruits.

CENTURION, FIRST CENTURY AD
A centurion of the early Imperial Roman army. The centurion's position was at the front-right corner of his century, a position of considerable danger in battle. As a result of this policy of leading by example, casualties tended to be high.

In the next 50 years (AD 284–325) there were no less than 25 Emperors. Political infighting became more important than the defence of the Empire, though the frontiers were held and the Empire survived. Factions within the army acted as powerbrokers or supported their favoured candidates in return for bribes or other concessions.

This period of internal turmoil became known as the Crisis of the Third Century and severely weakened the Empire. Yet the frontiers held and revolts were put down, as once again the soldiers of Rome enabled the tottering Empire to regain its balance.

War on the Frontiers

The Emperor Diocletian, who took the throne in AD 284, considered that the Empire was too large to govern and split it in two. The Western Empire was ruled from Rome, while the capital of the Eastern Empire was chosen as Byzantium, a former Greek colony and trading city. Byzantium became known as Constantinople after the death of Emperor Constantine, but perversely the Eastern Empire became known as the Byzantine Empire after the fall of the Western one.

Two emperors now ruled the Roman Empire, one in the east and one in the west, and from AD 293 each was given a subordinate emperor with the title of Caesar to assist them. This system broke down in AD 306, when Constantine the Great was proclaimed as Emperor by the army upon the death of his father.

A civil war ensued, and at its end the Empire again had one ruler, Constantine. However, this was a very unsettled period and upon the death of Constantine, Imperial power was divided among his three sons, who fought among themselves. When the dust settled, only Constantius remained, but his supposedly unified empire was looking increasingly ramshackle. A senior general named Silvanus, sent to deal with problems in Gaul, was proclaimed as emperor by his army, demonstrating the dangers of trusting anyone with an army large enough to be an effective political instrument.

However, military problems still had to be dealt with. The Franks had captured Colonia Aggrippinensis (modern Cologne) and another Germanic tribe, the Alamanni, had begun large-scale raiding into the Empire. The benefits of settling veterans on the frontier were demonstrated when the Alamanni laid siege to Augustodunum (modern Autun in France).

CAVALRYMAN, EARLY SECOND CENTURY AD
A Roman cavalryman of the Imperial period. Protected by chain mail and a helmet, cavalry used an oval shield and longer sword (called a *spatha*) rather than the *scutum* and *gladius* of the legionaries. The long spear was normally used as a lance but could also be thrown.

The defence of the town was led by these retired veterans, who used their old soldiering skills to hold out long enough for relief to arrive.

Once Silvanus had been removed by assassination, Constantius turned to his kinsman Julian in the hope that blood ties would engender loyalty. Julian was sent to Gaul with an army that contained the usual legionary and auxiliary infantry plus cataphract cavalry (which was becoming more common in the Roman army), horse archers and light field artillery in the form of *ballistae*. With these troops at his disposal, Julian launched a punitive campaign against the Alamanni, driving the tribesmen away from the towns they had overrun.

Finally the Alamanni massed against the Romans, fielding perhaps 35,000 men. The core of the army was the household troops of the tribal leaders, who were well-equipped and experienced fighters. The Alamanni formed a rough line with sub-units forming a roughly triangular shape. This was mainly due to the most aggressive warriors elbowing their way to the front line.

Against them, Julian had 10,000 infantry. His 3000 cavalry were placed on the right wing where the terrain was better. They were opposed by all the Germanic cavalry, interspersed with small bands of light infantry. These got the better of their Roman opponents, routing them although some rallied and returned to the fight.

The infantry fight was long and desperate, with the first Roman line penetrated and the second severely threatened. Eventually, however, the Romans were able to outlast their opponents and the Alamanni broke. In the wake of the victory, Julian's soldiers acclaimed him as Augustus – emperor – but he quickly put a stop to this, demanding an oath of loyalty to the current Emperor from his men.

Further operations against the Alamanni followed, along with the rebuilding of border defences. This was a sign that the Romans meant to stay in force, which promoted the Alamanni to sue for peace. The Franks were still active, however, and Julian was required to turn his force against their raiding parties until they, too, were pacified.

LIGHTWEIGHT BALLISTAE
Lightweight *ballistae* were added to the legions during the Imperial period. The Roman army made less use of archery than many contemporary forces, but the deployment of light battlefield artillery made up for this deficit.

Julian succeeded in restoring the frontier to relative calm by AD 360, though in the meantime, northern Britain was being overrun by tribes from beyond the northern frontier. Small forces were detached to assist the garrison, while a rather larger contingent was demanded to assist Emperor Constantius against the Persians. This provoked Julian's troops into proclaiming him Augustus once more. This time he accepted, and refused the order to transfer his troops. It is noteworthy that Julian was carried shoulder-high on a shield by some of his men, in the manner of a Germanic chieftain.

In the event, Constantius died the following year (AD 361) and Julian became Emperor. In AD 363 he campaigned against the Persians at the head of the largest Roman army of the century. Although the Persian capital was reached, it could not be taken. Emperor Julian was killed in action during the retreat, forcing his hurriedly-chosen successor to agree a less-than-favourable peace with Persia.

One factor in the defeat of Julian's army was lack of experience with large forces. The Roman army of the time mainly operated in small units to deal with raids on the borders. No commander had been able to gain experience of large military operations, and elementary mistakes were inevitable.

THE FALL OF THE WESTERN ROMAN EMPIRE

The arrival of the Huns on the eastern fringes of Europe was a major factor in the final collapse of the Roman Empire. Displaced tribes began to move west into Roman territory. This increased the pressure on Rome's weakening borders. Attempts were made to take advantage of the situation by allowing tribes to settle in Roman territories as *foederati*. Essentially this meant that they received land and support from the Empire in return for protecting the borders. However, many *foederati* were unreliable either as a result of their own nature or due to Roman mistreatment.

The Goths, allowed to settle on the Roman border, were pushed into rebellion this way, and crushed a Roman army sent against them at Adrianople in AD 378. Losses against the Goths included Emperor Valens but more importantly a significant part of the Roman army. This weakened the Imperial frontiers at a time when they were under greater pressure than ever before. The Eastern Empire survived

the disasters that followed, continuing into the Medieval period as the Byzantine Empire, but the Western Empire was overrun by a succession of barbarian invasions.

Germanic tribes including Alans, Goths, Suebi and Vandals marched through Gaul from AD 405 onwards, plundering as they went. Some settled while others pushed onwards towards Hispania. The Vandals crossed into North Africa and set up their own kingdom there. Rome itself was sacked by the Visigoths in AD 410 and by the Vandals in AD 455. The last Western Roman Emperor, Romulus Augustus, was deposed in AD 476 by the Ostrogoths, who set up their own kingdom in Italy. This event is normally taken as marking the end of the Western Roman Empire.

The last significant attempt to reclaim the western territories was launched in AD 533 by the Emperor Justinian, who sent his general, Belisarius, to drive out the Vandals from North Africa and Italia. This campaign was successful, but Justinian's suspicious of his talented subordinate, coupled with an outbreak of plague that weakened the Empire at this critical time, prevented the gains made by Belisarius from becoming permanent.

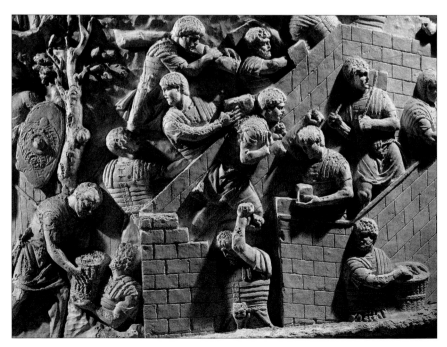

▶ **A relief from a copy of Trajan's Column showing Roman soldiers building fortifications. Emperor Trajan commemorated his own deeds in the carvings on the column.**

It is not clear when the Eastern Roman Empire began styling itself as the Byzantine Empire, nor when hopes of retaking the Western one finally faded, but by the mid-600s, the Byzantines had problems closer to home.

Tactics and Organization

The army of the later Roman Empire was considerably different from that of earlier years. The main division within the army was between the *limetani* and the *comitatenses*. *Limetani* forces were stationed on the frontiers, conducting garrison and patrol duties while the *comitatenses* were field forces that in theory acted as a mobile reserve to deal with anything the local *limetani* could not.

Political considerations had reduced the number of legions under any one person's command. Some provinces had at one time supported as many as four legions, but this was judged too large a force to permit a subordinate to command. Force levels had been reduced or provinces subdivided and the forces assigned to them parcelled out between the new regions.

Units were also smaller. Whereas the classic legion had contained nearly 5000 heavy infantrymen, most now fielded around 1000. As time went on, legions of troops other than heavy infantry were fielded, such as cavalry or light infantry formations. Auxiliary units were also smaller than they had been, often numbering no more than 500 men in a cavalry formation, and perhaps double that for infantry.

A blanket grant of citizenship to everyone within the Empire had removed the main incentive for service. Thus the legions recruited much of their strength from outside the Empire. These 'barbarian' troops were equipped and trained in the Roman manner, but the army had lost its edge over the years. Standards of drill and effectiveness had slipped and the main advantage over barbarian infantry had largely been lost.

The Roman army of the late Imperial period was well suited to small-scale operations along the frontiers, keeping back barbarian raids, but much less effective in dealing with major threats or fighting the pitched battles it has so capably dealt with in the past. Command and control were hamstrung by political considerations, which required that powerful armies not be placed in the hands of ambitious men, however competent they might be.

LEGIONARY, SECOND CENTURY AD
Burdened by his armour, weapons, rations, tools and camp gear, the legionary was still capable of rapid marches, arriving at his destination fit to fight or build a camp. This required not only fitness but also discipline. After the fall of the Roman Empire, this was largely lost, until the modern era.

CHAPTER 5

Warriors of the Post-Roman Era

The northern frontiers of the Roman Empire were home to various 'barbarian' peoples. Some, such as the Gauls and Britons, were conquered and to a greater or lesser extent Romanized during the heyday of the Empire. Others, such as the Germanic tribes who lived beyond the Rhine, remained independent although contact with Rome did result in some cultural and military influences.

The arrival of the Huns in Eastern Europe pushed many of these tribes westwards, creating a 'domino effect' as one tribe displaced the next. This was one cause of the collapse of the crumbling Roman frontier, and the chaos of the Migration Period (AD 300–700) reshaped the map of Europe forever.

Some tribes undertook lengthy migrations, moving from Germania to Hispania and even North Africa. By the end of the period, many modern regional populations were in place, and some of today's states can trace their origins back to the tribes that settled at the end of their great journeys. For example,

◄ Events in the lives of important Roman citizens were often commemorated after death. This sarcophagus from AD 260 depicts Roman troops battling Ostrogoths.

Lombardy in Italy is named for the Lombards, originally a Germanic people.

THE GOTHS

The Goths were a Germanic people who rose to rule a number of other tribes in a powerful kingdom which was overrun by the Huns in AD 370. This forced large numbers of Goths to migrate into Roman territory while others remained in their ancestral lands under the rule of the Huns.

One major group of Goths, later to be known as the Visigoths, moved into Roman territory in the Balkans. They were permitted to settle along the Danube in return for helping defend the frontier against the Huns. This agreement quickly broke down, and the Visigoths found themselves at war with the Roman Empire. Defeating a Roman army at the battle of Adrianople in AD 378, the Visigoths obtained a peace settlement with the Empire that allowed them to settle in Roman territory. This was an uncomfortable arrangement, beset by skirmishes and incidents, and after 15 years full-scale war broke out.

Under their king Alaric I, the Visigoths advanced into Italia and succeeded in sacking Rome. The Western Roman capital was at that time at Ravenna, but all the same this act had great symbolic significance. The Visigoths then settled in Gaul as part of a new agreement with Rome. The Visigothic kingdom in Gaul grew into a major force in Europe. It controlled Iberia

GOTH CAVALRY
The Goths and other barbarians made increasing use of horses in war, but only the richest individuals could afford to ride into battle. Barbarian cavalry simply transplanted foot combat onto horseback, often using exactly the same weapons.

◀ A nineteenth-century painting showing the death of Totila, king of the Ostrogoths, at the battle of Taginae in AD 552. Totila led a spirited but doomed attack against a superior Byzantine force.

was Theodoric, who would become the greatest leader of his people.

Theodoric and the Ostrogoths had a difficult relationship with the Empire – at times friendly and at others hostile. Theodoric himself was granted Roman titles, and as an officer of the Empire, as well as king of his own people, was sent to recover Italy for the Empire. The Ostrogoths captured Ravenna and made it their capital in AD 493, gradually coming to dominate the former heartland of the Roman Empire. At its height, the Ostrogothic kingdom encompassed Italy, Sicily and Dalmatia.

As an officer of the Eastern Roman Empire, the Ostrogothic king Theodoric was acceptable to the post-Roman people of Italia, who lived peaceably alongside the new Ostrogothic arrivals. The Ostrogothic king ruled both groups, but each lived by its own laws and customs. However, it was not long before the Byzantine Emperor decided that Italia should be properly reincorporated into the Empire.

The Ostrogothic capital at Ravenna fell in AD 540, and after some negotiations the Ostrogothic kingdom rejoined the Empire. Within five years, it had rebelled and was at war with Byzantium once again. The Ostrogothic leader, Totila, was defeated and killed in AD 552 at the battle of Taginae. The Byzantine forces deployed with a dense formation of allied Germanic troops in the centre, flanked by Byzantine regulars on

in addition to its Gallic territories, forcing the Vandals to continue their migration into North Africa. However, its power began to wane in the early 500s as the Frankish kingdom became the main power in the region. The Visigoths still controlled Hispania, but they began to suffer incursions by Moors from North Africa. As Hispania was gradually overrun, some Visigoths migrated into the Frankish kingdom. Others became vassals of the new Muslim rulers.

The other main group of Goths has become known as the Ostrogoths (East Goths), who remained in their old lands under Hunnic rule. Eventually, after the death of the Huns' great leader Attila, the Ostrogoths defeated a Hun army under Ellac, Attila's successor, and established their independence. The Ostrogoths then began to migrate westwards into the Balkans where they came into contact with the Eastern Roman Empire. Children from senior Ostrogothic families were raised and educated in Constantinople as hostages, as was the custom of the time. Among them

GALLIC WARRIOR, 50 BC
The typical barbarian warrior was lightly equipped with sword and stabbing spear, relying on a wooden shield and possibly a helmet for protection. The small shield was entirely adequate to deal with hand weapons but offered relatively little protection against arrows.

each side. Large bodies of archers were positioned on the flanks. Outnumbered, the Ostrogoths launched a cavalry charge at the centre of the Byzantine line. The charge was shot to pieces by Byzantine archers, after which the Byzantines gradually gained the upper hand. The Ostrogoths fought on until evening, but were finally routed.

After Taginae, the Ostrogoths put up relatively little resistance and were gradually overrun. After a failed revolt they abandoned Italy, settling in what is now Austria. There, the Ostrogoths quietly faded from history.

BARBARIAN INFANTRY WARFARE

Most tribal warriors were volunteers or subject to fairly loose controls, and could begin to drift away if a campaign went on too long or took them too far from home. Maintaining an army in being required a mix of charismatic leadership and visible success that would inspire warriors to continue rather than slip away. In any case, it was necessary for warriors to return to their farms and workshops to avoid economic disaster.

Even without these factors, barbarian armies were rarely organized enough to support a large logistics train of the sort required to keep an army properly supplied. Thus while vast numbers of warriors could be concentrated for a battle, they had to disperse again quickly in order to feed themselves.

Most commonly, barbarian warfare tended to be fairly small-scale in nature, characterized by raids and clashes between small forces. While bloody, such conflicts rarely caused long-term changes in the local power structure. Larger-scale raids, especially against civilized areas where there was a great deal of plunder to be had, were more difficult to organize but could produce handsome rewards. Not just in terms of plunder; cities could be induced to pay tribute in return for not being raided, enabling a tribe with a warlike reputation to operate what amounted to a protection racket on a vast scale.

Large-scale changes were usually achieved by long periods of raiding and conflict rather than a single great battle. This was one of the causes of the collapse of the Roman Empire, as tribes along the border gradually chipped away at declining Roman strength until they broke through the defended frontiers.

The great migrations were also caused by long-term factors rather than any single battle. Events such as the wholesale movement of an entire people required the realization that remaining in the present locality would eventually lead to conquest or extinction. There might be no single catastrophic defeat, just a gradual increase of losses to raids and the growing certainty that utter defeat was just a matter of time.

Barbarian combat was highly individualistic. Men fought as informal warbands centred on a charismatic or noble leader, or as a group of warriors from the same village. There was, for the most part, little attempt to create homogenously equipped units. Instead, a unit was formed along social lines, with its members fighting with whatever weapons they possessed.

However, most men were quite similarly equipped. The standard battlefield weapon for most men was a simple spear of no great length. A unit equipped with spears could form a basic but highly effective defensive formation at need, in the form of a shield wall. By overlapping their shields and locking them together, the warriors created a defensive rampart for themselves, over which they stabbed with their spears. A shield wall was not a manoeuvrable formation, but it did offer good protection on the defensive. Offensively, the warriors could open out a little,

advancing to stab with their spears and bash their opponents back with their shields. A shield was not just a defensive barrier; it could be used to send an opponent staggering, making him easy prey for a spear thrust.

The fairly short spears of Germanic warriors were reasonably effective at close quarters, but many men

▼ **This seventh-century Frankish funeral carving denotes the warrior's high status by his possession of a sword. A lower-ranked individual would not have been able to afford one.**

resorted to hand weapons instead. Daggers and hand axes required relatively little room to manoeuvre, but the typical Germanic sword was fairly long and intended for cutting rather than stabbing. This required a certain amount of space around the warrior,

GERMANIC TRIBAL CHIEFTAIN
Despite being labelled 'barbarians', the Germanic tribes were capable of manufacturing richly decorated clothing and high-quality weaponry. This Germanic chieftain possesses both as symbols of his status.

necessitating an open formation of soldiers once hand-to-hand combat had begun.

Tactically, barbarian armies were not capable of great sophistication. Flank attacks, ambushes and similar stratagems were possible, but once battle was joined the matter tended to be one of small groups fighting whatever was in front of them until one side or the other gave way.

This lack of subtlety was to some extent counter-balanced by ferocity and high morale engendered by heroic leadership and the practice of fighting alongside friends and neighbours. Men knew that their actions on the battlefield would be spoken of back home, and were willing to risk death or maiming to ensure that they could hold their head up among their peers long after the battle was over.

Battle of Adrianople (AD 378)

Gothic tribespeople, forced from their homes by the Huns, found themselves under attack by Roman forces as they wandered through the territory of the Empire. Roman troops were defeated at Marcianople in AD 376. An indecisive engagement at Ad Salices in AD 377 followed.

The Empire saw the Goths, who had captured large quantities of military equipment after these battles, as a serious threat. The Eastern Emperor, Valens, advanced with an army of about 15,000 men to meet the Goths near Adrianople.

The Goths had about 10,000 fighting men available when Valens' army approached. The Goths, who were encumbered by their goods and families, assumed a defensive deployment. Their wagons were drawn up in a circle to create a defensive fort, which was guarded by some of the infantry. The remainder were formed up on a ridge nearby.

There were few Gothic cavalry present at the beginning of the battle. However, approximately 10,000 of them were nearby foraging and began to hurry back when news of the battle started to filter through. Unaware of this, the Roman force formed up as a double line of heavy infantry in the centre and cavalry on the flanks. A screen of skirmishers covered the advance.

The Romans halted, and negotiations were opened between the two armies. During this pause the Roman right wing cavalry advanced and launched an attack. This may have been due to a lack of discipline; the units present were a mix of veteran and low-quality units. Whatever the reason, the attack hit the Gothic flank but was easily beaten off.

This brought on a general engagement, with the Romans hoping to defeat their opponents in the classic manner using a frontal infantry assault. The Roman left wing cavalry, although not properly deployed from the march, launched an attack which went well at first. The Gothic infantry were pushed back to their wagons and were struggling to hold the perimeter when salvation arrived.

The Gothic cavalry, rushing back to help, hit the Roman left wing and drove it from the field. Encouraged, Gothic infantry began to advance and pushed the Romans back. As the infantry battle raged, Gothic cavalry fell on the flank and routed many units. The Roman reserves, unengaged until this point, broke and fled.

Valens was left commanding two highly experienced legions – which at that time numbered about 1000 men each – and was able to hold out for a time. These units possibly saved some of their comrades by occupying the Goths' attention, although many Romans were cut down by cavalry as they fled. Valens' two legions were slaughtered almost to a man,

ADRIANOPLE AD 378

Poor reconnaissance led the Romans to believe that they were facing 10,000 Goths with few cavalry. The Roman attack was successful until an additional 10,000 Goths, all of them mounted, attacked on the flank. Most of the Roman army was routed, and Emperor Valens was killed.

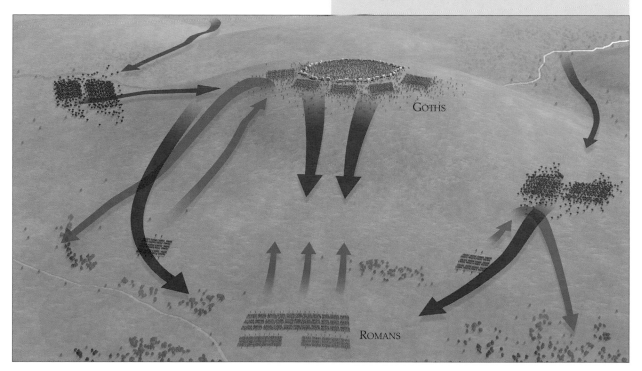

and the Emperor was killed. The Goths then tried to storm Adrianople the next day, but were rebuffed with heavy losses. After a period of indecisive conflict a new peace treaty was agreed, whereby the Goths would receive land in return for defending the Roman frontier.

THE FRANKS

A Germanic tribal confederation began to form around AD 230, which ultimately became the Frankish people. As the Roman Empire collapsed and the frontiers were no longer strongly defended, the Franks moved westwards into Gaul and gradually overran most of the region. Although many Franks raided the declining Roman Empire, others defended it. As a result, when Roman government collapsed in Gaul around AD 260, Frankish soldiers and nobles were instrumental in bringing the province back under control. Frankish forces continued to dominate the ostensibly Roman military presence in the province.

The Frankish army of the time was trained and equipped in the same manner as Roman troops. However, a throwing axe (the *francisca*) was often used instead of the Roman *pilum*. A short spear known as an *angon* was also favoured by the Franks; this could be thrown or used for stabbing.

The Franks were briefly united under Clovis I, who drove the Visigoths from Gaul, but it was not until AD 751 that the Franks became a major power under the Carolingian dynasty. The Carolingian Empire rose to dominate much of Western Europe.

Over time, the Frankish military moved from being a post-Roman infantry force to a primarily cavalry one, with nobles providing their retainers with mail coats, long spears and warhorses. The Franks also placed great emphasis on the ability to hold or take fortified places, using siege techniques and artillery engines they had adopted from the Romans.

THE VANDALS

The Vandals may have originated in Scandinavia, moving south across the Baltic into Germania around 200–100 BC. They raided into the Roman territories on the Danube for many years before coming to an

FRANKISH WARRIOR
Frankish infantry were equipped in the same manner as the 'barbarized' Roman legions of the same period. Rather than the pilum they favoured throwing axes or a short spear that could be thrown or wielded in the hand.

agreement with Rome. The Vandals were permitted to settle on the frontier in the hope of creating a buffer state for the Empire.

The Vandals were pushed westwards by Hunnic invasions from AD 400 onwards, fighting their way

▶ A seventeenth-century depiction of battle between Roman and barbarian troops, giving a good indication of the chaos of the battlefield.

through Gaul to settle in Hispania. Having established themselves, the Vandals then set about conquering North Africa. This gave them a base from which their ships could raid all over the Mediterranean. Their main settlements were along the coast of what is today Tunisia and Algeria.

The Vandals conquered Carthage in AD 493 and made it their capital. At the peak of their power they dominated the western Mediterranean, ruling the Balearics, Corsica, Sardinia and Sicily. They were also drawn into Imperial politics by requests for assistance from Roman factions. This resulted in a Vandal army marching through Italia, sacking Rome itself.

The power of the Vandals eventually began to decline. This made them a target for the Eastern Roman

AD DECIMUM AD 533

Intercepting the Byzantines at the 'ten mile post', after which the battle is named, the Vandals blocked the Byzantine advance and fell on their flank. The ability of the disciplined Byzantine troops to rally and counter-attack turned near-defeat into a decisive success.

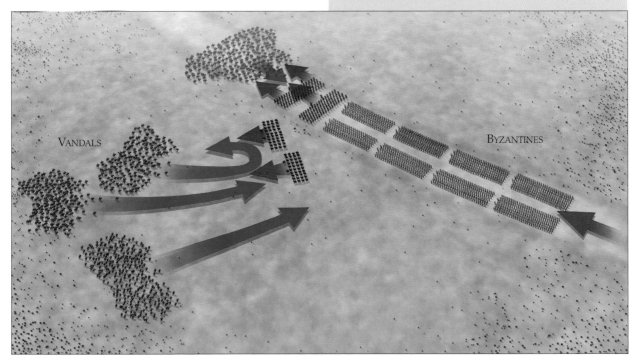

VANDALS

BYZANTINES

Emperor Justinian I, whose ambition was to reincorporate the western territories of the empire. A Byzantine army landed in North Africa in AD 533, advancing on Carthage.

The Vandals intercepted the expedition 16km (10 miles) from Carthage. Their plan was to block the Byzantine advance and then launch a flanking attack. However, the Byzantines beat off the flank attack and eventually forced the blocking position. Carthage was taken, and Vandal power was broken the following year at the battle of Ticameron.

Afterwards, the Byzantine force campaigned in Italy, temporarily returning it to the control of the Roman Empire, the capital of which was then Constantinople. The commanding general, Belisarius, was rewarded with a triumphal procession, the last such to be held. In other ways too, his campaign against the Vandals marked the passing of an era. The main instrument of victory was not infantry but heavily armoured cavalry, and this would become the pattern for the next several centuries.

Equipment and Organization

The early Goths, Franks and Vandals were settled farmers, with no tradition of horsemanship among the ordinary folk. Thus it was not really feasible to raise cavalry, even if this had seemed desirable.

Military organization was typical of such tribal peoples. Senior nobles could afford to maintain a small body of professional warriors. These men served in part as a status symbol, partly as a political tool in enforcing the noble's will and partly as a bodyguard force. Of course, in wartime they also formed the core of an army and could generate revenue by raiding. The bulk of any military force was made up of irregulars who owed their lords a period of military service as part of their social contract, or who offered to fight in the hope of gaining plunder and recognition.

A barbarian force of this nature tended to be made up of men who were enthusiastic and reasonably good at fighting, especially if they had gained experience in raiding or previous wars, but had little large-scale cohesion. The standard tactic was to get stuck in and fight until the enemy ran away or surrendered.

The arms and equipment of the barbarian warrior tended to be fairly basic. Many wore no armour at all, other perhaps than a helmet of leather or metal. Nobles and some professionals might be able to afford

ANCIENT BRITON
The ancient Britons fought in a typically 'barbarian' style, using long slashing swords that were unsuited to close-order formations. Individual skill and aggression could bring victory against fellow Britons, but the disciplined Roman forces were adept at defeating chaotic barbarian onslaughts.

metal body armour but the common warrior had to rely on his shield or else force his opponent onto the defensive by an aggressive assault. Hand axes and long daggers were common sidearms, with swords being expensive status symbols as well as useful battlefield weapons. Most warriors were armed with a spear as their main battlefield weapon, resorting to sidearms at close quarters or if the spear was lost. Some men were equipped with bows, but more commonly warriors threw spears or hand axes at their enemies. The Frankish throwing axe was said to be able to split a shield in two, depriving an enemy of its use even if he survived the impact. Barbarians in Roman service received equipment similar (or in many cases identical) to that in use by the Roman army at the time. However, by then, the days of the classical legion were long gone, and many Roman soldiers were fighting with a spear, shield and long sword – the 'Roman' equipment adopted by many Romanized barbarians thus differed little from their own war gear.

Cavalry gradually began to become more important in the barbarian armies as the years went by. However, Germanic cavalry did not adopt the horse-archer style of combat of the steppe peoples, but simply moved their own close-quarters hand-to-hand fighting style onto horseback. Thus the Germanic cavalryman was normally armed with a cutting sword, which was fairly long to allow him to reach an enemy, and/or a short spear similar to that used on foot. He might or might not have body armour, though helmets and shields were common and richer men protected themselves as well as they could afford.

Although the mode of combat gradually changed, the barbarian armies remained essentially feudal in nature. They were raised and led by nobles who owed allegiance to the next higher level of nobility. This created a command structure based on noble rank rather than military experience and training. As a result, command and control tended to be somewhat loose, and logistics virtually non-existent. Thus maintaining a barbarian army in the field for any length of

◀ A Roman sarcophagus depicting combat with naked Galatian barbarians. Such carvings were a form of propaganda, portraying the enemies of Rome as savages who needed civilizing.

time was a serious problem. The largest numbers fielded tended to be while a tribe was migrating, with families and stores not far behind the fighting men. The carts used to transport belongings could also form a useful mobile fortification at need as well as serving as a logistics base. Barbarian armies had to feed themselves by foraging much of the time, and were prone to pillage as they passed through a region. This made movement slow compared to the disciplined marches of the Roman army with its well-organized supply train, and could allow an enemy to defeat segments of the barbarian army by attacking foraging parties.

However, there was no way to change this without altering the structure of tribal society. An organized,

disciplined professional army along the Roman model was more effective in combat, but was simply not attainable by the societies that produced the great barbarian armies of the Migration Period.

THE HUNS

The origins of the Huns are not completely clear, but they are widely thought to have migrated westwards from a region north of China, perhaps as a result of pressure exerted by the ancestors of the Mongols. The Huns were a nomadic people for whom horsemanship was an integral part of daily life. Their forces could move fast in both tactical and strategic terms, and specialized in the use of archery from horseback.

The Huns, like other nomadic peoples, left little in the way of permanent records, so much of what is 'known' about them is in fact speculative or inferred from secondary sources. What is known is that around AD 370, horse people from the east arrived on the fringes of Europe and overran the tribes they encountered there. By AD 395 the Huns were making

HUNNIC HORSE ARCHERS
The Huns were extremely skilled horse archers, who learned to shoot accurately even at full gallop. This was quite a feat of horsemanship; without stirrups many riders would struggle just to stay on their mount. Developing this level of skill required constant practice and was beyond the capabilities of more settled peoples.

their presence felt along the Roman frontier. Their horse-archer tactics were very difficult to counter, and they were able to plunder several eastern provinces. However, the Huns at that time had no central leadership and could be bribed into departing or even serving Roman interests.

By far the greatest Hunnic leader was Attila (AD 406–53), who inherited leadership of the Huns along with his brother Bleda, around AD 434. Now much more unified and hence more powerful than before, the Huns were able to demand tribute from Roman cities and to sack those that declined to pay. A peace treaty with the Eastern Roman Empire broke down in AD 439 when the Eastern Emperor decided to stop paying the large tribute the Huns demanded.

The Huns' strategy against Rome was deliberately savage, since fear was one of their main weapons. Several towns and cities were destroyed and their population enslaved or put to the sword as the Huns advanced down the Danube. Finally they encountered a Roman army at Arcadiopolis. Rather than a huge set-piece battle, the Huns used their mobility to fight a series of small actions which resulted in the Roman force becoming cornered in the Cheronsus valley with no line of retreat. Defeat in the Cheronsus valley forced the Eastern Roman Emperor to sue for peace, promising even greater tribute. A treaty was agreed in AD 443. This temporarily secured the survival of the Eastern Roman Empire, but hostilities resumed when the tribute was not paid.

Meanwhile, in AD 446, Attila had become sole leader of the Huns after ordering his brother's murder. He advanced on Constantinople, defeating two numerous but poorly trained Roman armies. Unable to secure entry to the city, Attila accepted a new treaty – including a more affordable tribute – offered by the Romans. The Huns then moved west, beginning a campaign against the Western Roman Empire in AD 451. Few details are known about this campaign, but there is some evidence for the same sort of plunder and slaughter as accompanied the Huns' previous campaigns.

▲ Bronze plate depicting Attila as 'The Scourge of God'. Many believed that he had been sent by Heaven to punish their sins.

Attila's forces besieged the fortified city of Orleans, which was able to resist long enough for a relief force to arrive. The Huns began to retire but were caught. This was in part because a large section of the Hunnic army was composed of slow-moving infantry rather than the traditional mobile horse archers. The relief force was composed of Roman troops, which included a large number of 'barbarian' Germanic warriors from outside the Empire, and a contingent sent by the Visigothic king. The clash was extremely bloody and went on for almost a whole day. By nightfall the Huns had been driven back to their camp but were not beaten.

The Huns then waited in their camp for a few days, possibly hoping that their opponents would attack. The Visigoths wanted to, but the Roman commander was worried about the political ramifications of a Visigothic victory over the Huns. The Visigoths then departed – some sources claim the Romans sent them away – and the Huns were able to retreat.

Attila retired eastwards into what is now Hungary to recover from the defeat, then launched a campaign into Italy beginning in AD 452. However, the Romans were able to avoid defeat and with his army compromised by disease, Attila accepted a deal brokered by the Pope. The tribute on offer was comparatively small, but it was enough for the Huns to retire without losing face.

Attila died in AD 453, and although his sons tried to maintain their dominance they lacked Attila's skills and charisma. The Huns ceased to be a unified force and as a result ceased to be much of an influence on European events.

Equipment and Organization

Horsemanship was a way of life to the Huns, who even held discussions of important matters on horseback. The horses themselves were small and hardy steppe ponies which were fast for their size and could cover long distances without becoming unduly tired. Each warrior owned several mounts and would switch between them, further reducing fatigue. Warriors' mounts were almost always mares, which could be milked to provide riders with valuable sustenance.

The Huns were primarily horse archers, using a powerful recurve bow. The stirrup had not yet been invented, but the Huns were sufficiently skilled horsemen that they could shoot accurately even at the gallop. Their bow was not very effective against armour, but its barbed arrows were deadly against an unprotected opponent. Volume of fire ensured that armoured foes would be hit somewhere vulnerable sooner or later.

The bow was backed up by hand weapons for use in close combat. These sometimes included a spear and more often, a sword. However, Hunnic tactics were typical of horse-archer armies, in that close combat was avoided wherever possible. Individual warriors and small groups swarmed around the enemy, shooting into their formations and then retreating to avoid retaliation. The Hunnic mode of warfare was

CAMPAIGN AGAINST EASTERN ROME AD 443

Few cities were able to withstand the Huns as they pillaged their way through the Eastern Roman Empire. Adrianople, Constantinople and Heraclea were too well protected to be overrun, but nearby cities were sacked. After the defeat of a major army in the Cheronesus valley, the Empire sued for peace.

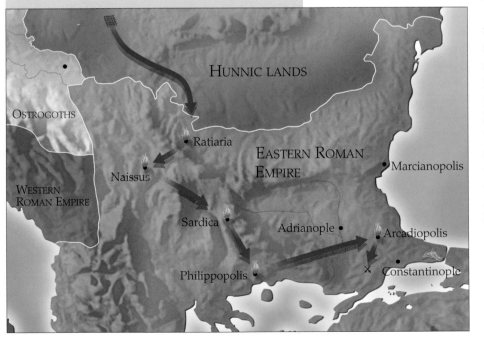

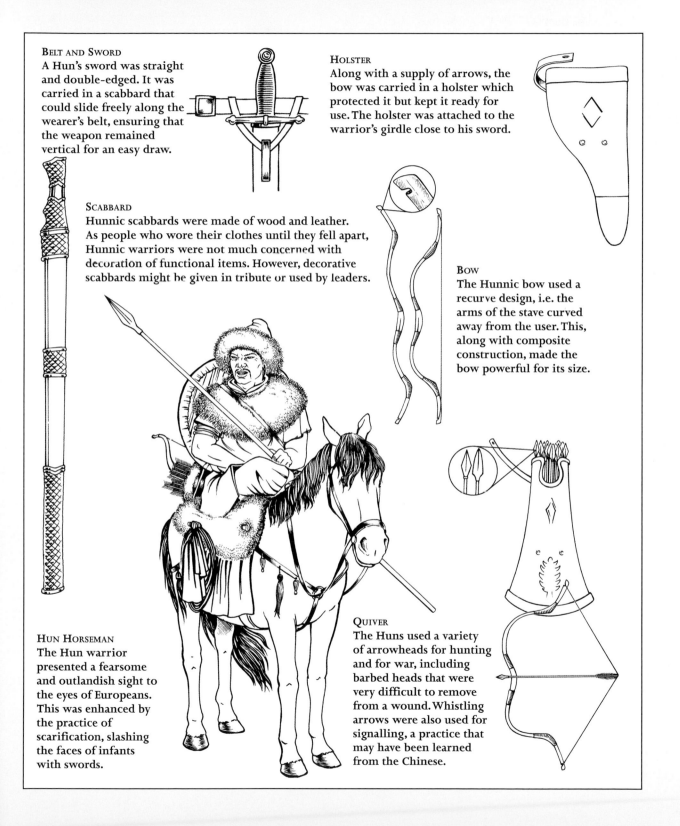

BELT AND SWORD
A Hun's sword was straight and double-edged. It was carried in a scabbard that could slide freely along the wearer's belt, ensuring that the weapon remained vertical for an easy draw.

HOLSTER
Along with a supply of arrows, the bow was carried in a holster which protected it but kept it ready for use. The holster was attached to the warrior's girdle close to his sword.

SCABBARD
Hunnic scabbards were made of wood and leather. As people who wore their clothes until they fell apart, Hunnic warriors were not much concerned with decoration of functional items. However, decorative scabbards might be given in tribute or used by leaders.

BOW
The Hunnic bow used a recurve design, i.e. the arms of the stave curved away from the user. This, along with composite construction, made the bow powerful for its size.

HUN HORSEMAN
The Hun warrior presented a fearsome and outlandish sight to the eyes of Europeans. This was enhanced by the practice of scarification, slashing the faces of infants with swords.

QUIVER
The Huns used a variety of arrowheads for hunting and for war, including barbed heads that were very difficult to remove from a wound. Whistling arrows were also used for signalling, a practice that may have been learned from the Chinese.

almost the complete opposite of that used by the Greek phalanx or Roman legion. Rather than seek a decisive clash, the Huns simply nibbled at their opponents until they were reduced to impotence. The appearance of hordes of warriors flitting about on horseback, shooting and then vanishing into their own dust, was a psychological weapon in its own right. If the enemy did not break from fear, then he would be worn down by archery until his formations collapsed.

Good mobility also allowed the Huns to harass an enemy force or to capture lightly-held areas by using a rapid approach to gain surprise. Defeat could be avoided by simply retiring at speed to rally and return when the situation was more favourable.

THE PARTHIANS AND THE SASSANIDS

The first mention of Parthia in history is as a territory of the Persian Empire, and Parthia remained a Persian province until a severe defeat suffered by Seleucid Persia presented an opportunity for revolt. Independence was gained in 247 BC, but soon afterwards, Parthia was conquered by the Parni, a people originating southeast of the Caspian Sea.

Parthia was reincorporated into Seleucid Persia from 209 BC but regained its independence under the Arsacid dynasty, descended from the leader of the Parni conquerors. A feudal system was implemented, under which Parthian nobles received land in conquered territories in return for their support. However, support for the Arsacids was not wholehearted among the Parthian nobility. Political infighting, rebellions and raids by tribal peoples along the borders wore down the strength of the Parthian Empire, while wars with Rome threatened it with total destruction.

◀ A Parthian relief showing a horse archer in action. Unlike the Huns, the Parthians supported their horse archers with heavily armoured cataphract cavalry.

Parthia gradually began to break up under internal pressures. It was conquered by forces loyal to Ardashir I, a Parthian vassal who rebelled and, taking advantage of the troubles besetting Parthia, gradually gained control of its territories. Ardashir's victory in AD 224 marked the end of the Arascid dynasty.

Ardashir succeeded in creating a new incarnation of the Persian Empire, and founded his own dynasty, which became known as the Sassanids. The Sassanids were the last rulers of pre-Islamic Persia and at their zenith were extremely powerful; they alone of all the empires and states bordering the Roman Empire were thought of as equals. In AD 230, Sassanid forces raided Roman territory and fought the punitive campaign launched in response to a standstill. A campaign of conquest into Roman Mesopotamia resulted in territory changing hands more than once, and this remained the pattern for many years to come.

Despite incursions by Arab tribes and other enemies along their borders, Sassanid forces were able to campaign – not always successfully – against Roman holdings to their east. In AD 259 a Sassanid army inflicted a massive defeat on a Roman force at Edessa. However, success in field battles was frequently reversed by the failure to capture walled cities. This robbed Persian campaigns of any real lasting success.

The period from around AD 380–500 was one of relative peace with Rome. There were two minor wars (AD 421–2 and 440) but Rome had its own problems and Sassanid Persia did not want to do anything to provoke further conflict with its declining but still powerful neighbour.

Among other troubles, Persia came under attack by the Huns from AD 483 and was forced to pay heavy tribute until the reign of Khosroe I (AD 531–79), who managed to repel the Huns and began to rebuild Persian fortunes. However, since AD 502, Persia had again begun to clash with Rome. The next century was characterized by a series of Romano-Persian wars,

interspersed with revolts and internal dissent which weakened the Persian empire.

By the early 600s, Persia was under attack by Arab tribes as well as the Eastern Roman Empire. Khosroe II managed to lay siege to Constantinople in AD 626 but was outflanked and suffered a major defeat at Nineveh in AD 627. This was the beginning of the end for Sassanid Persia. A series of coups in AD 628–32 led to 10 years of internal stability, but Persian forces were increasingly unable to deal with Arab incursions. Arab forces defeated a Persian army at al-Qadisiyyah in AD 636 and broke Persian strength at Nihawand in AD 642. The last Sassanid ruler of Persia was killed in AD 651, by which time the Islamic conquest of the region was complete.

Equipment and Organization

Parthian military forces were made up of feudal retinues plus mercenaries. Each great noble maintained a body of troops, and additional forces could be raised for a campaign. The system suffered from the usual vices of a feudal military – what forces could be raised depended greatly on who was in dispute with whom at the time. The military problem facing Parthia was considerable. In addition to the usual need for garrisons to protect trade and to maintain internal stability, Parthia was constantly threatened with invasion by organized militaries (Roman and Persian) from the west and by tribal incursions from the east.

A great deal of strategic mobility was required, enabling forces to transfer from one region to another as the need arise. It followed logically that the major Parthian forces were cavalry. Infantry were used as garrisons and might be included in an army if a suitable force was available nearby, but they were not considered militarily significant.

Two types of cavalry were deployed by the Parthians. Light horsemen wore no armour and were

> **"THERE CAN BE NO POWER WITHOUT AN ARMY, NO ARMY WITHOUT MONEY, NO MONEY WITHOUT AGRICULTURE, AND NO AGRICULTURE WITHOUT JUSTICE."**
>
> **ARDASHIR I, FOUNDER OF THE SASSANID DYNASTY**

armed with a short but powerful recurve bow plus a sword for close combat if it could not be avoided. The light cavalry fought in a typical horse-archer mode and were renowned for their skill. The term 'Parthian Shot' has passed into common use, meaning a barbed statement made metaphorically or literally over the shoulder whilst departing. The term comes from the Parthian tactic of turning around to shoot backwards whilst galloping ahead of a pursuing foe.

Whilst the light cavalry skirmished and softened up the enemy, the death-stroke was delivered by the heavily armoured cataphracts. Man and horse were protected by scale mail, made of small plates of metal. The cataphract's weapons included a bow and a heavy

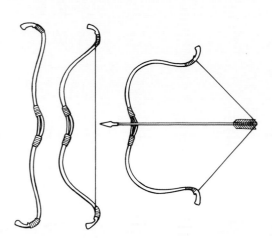

PARTHIAN HORSE ARCHER

The Parthian horse archer used a recurve bow similar to the Hunnic design, holding arrows in his left hand ready for use as this was quicker than reaching to a quiver. The archer could shoot at any point in the horse's stride, but at the top of the rise in a canter, with all four hooves off the ground, was the optimum moment for accuracy.

lance or spear plus a sidearm such as a sword or dagger. Heavy-cavalry archery was used to soften up an enemy or to wear down an infantry force, perhaps goading the enemy into breaking their formation for a reckless attack which the cataphracts could easily shatter.

The Parthian lance was long and heavy by contemporary standards. Despite the lack of stirrups, Parthian cataphracts are credited with the ability to pierce two men at once with a lance thrust. However, the preferred tactic was to use archery to reduce an enemy without suffering the inevitable losses of close combat, resorting to the lance only when it was time to finish off a beaten foe.

Camels were also sometimes used as archery platforms. The height and endurance of the beasts was an asset, as was their effect on horses that were not used to them. The strange noises and smells emanating from camels could frighten horses – and men too, if they had not heard of such strange-looking creatures before. Camels were also often used for logistics purposes, carrying food, water and spare arrows for the soldiers.

Parthian armies were not well suited to long campaigns, nor for sieges, but they were effective in allowing military power to be transferred from one region to another to meet a range of threats.

Sassanid Persian armies were fairly similar, as might be expected. Cataphracts were extensively used in the earlier years of the

HORSE ARCHER TACTICS
Against infantry, who could not close the distance rapidly, horse archers would shoot a number of volleys as they approached then turn away to the right with the bow hand facing the target. The most accurate shot was made at the point of closest approach. Cavalry could not be approached as close in case a sudden charge caught the horse archers.

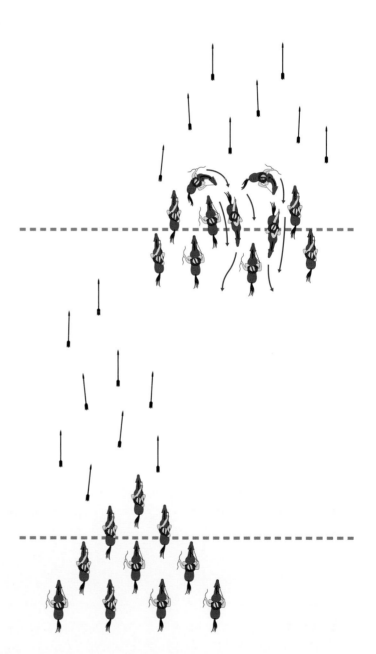

dynasty, though armoured cavalry were of lesser importance once contact with the Huns demonstrated what could be achieved by swarms of horse archers.

Horse archers were used extensively by the Sassanid Persians, along with light cavalry armed with javelins and shields. These were often recruited from allied Arabs or Huns. Skirmishing tactics were much the same as those used by other light-cavalry forces. The Sassanids made more use of infantry than the Parthians, though they were not well regarded. Spearmen, who wore no armour but were protected by a light wickerwork shield, were used along with unarmoured archers and slingers. The infantry were primarily useful in siegework and were considered expendable. The Persians also fielded elephants obtained from India. These fearsome but unreliable beasts were of unpredictable value in a battle. They might break an enemy line if all went well, but could be a liability against an enemy that had developed good anti-elephant tactics.

CAVALRY WARFARE

There were essentially two kinds of cavalry army. One might be described as 'Hunnic' in character, consisting almost entirely of horse archers. As noted elsewhere, a horse archer force relied mainly on missile fire, wearing down its enemies until their formations broke up before quickly retreating to safety to avoid retaliation.

Horse archery was a very difficult skill to learn, requiring years of practice. It was not really possible for settled peoples to create a horse-archer force, so most settled peoples created a different kind of cavalry army, one based around the use of hand weapons rather than bows.

VISIGOTH HEAVY CAVALRYMAN
The western barbarians gradually adopted the practice of protecting their war mounts with armour, much as eastern cataphracts had been doing for some time. This progression gradually led to the armoured knight of the Middle Ages.

At the beginning of the Migration Period, most armies were based on infantry, with cavalry as scouts and supporting troops. However, as time went on there was a move towards greater importance for cavalry, until eventually it became the main fighting force in almost every army.

The gradual shift from infantry to cavalry occurred for several reasons. There

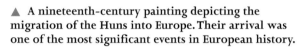
▲ A nineteenth-century painting depicting the migration of the Huns into Europe. Their arrival was one of the most significant events in European history.

were very real advantages to fighting on horseback, in addition to the prestige that went with possession of a war-horse. A horseman could wear more armour without tiring and was harder for enemies to reach and strike. In addition, horses provided mobility, and this became vital when fighting highly mobile enemies such as the 'horse barbarians' who invaded Europe at the beginning of the Migration Period, and also neighbouring tribes who had adopted the mounted style of combat. To some extent, the adoption of cavalry was a result of the arms race that was going on at the time – if a tribe's neighbours had cavalry, the tribe needed to gain a similar advantage or risk defeat.

It was not the invention of the stirrup that made heavy cavalry possible; armoured horsemen had charged their enemies with lances for centuries before the stirrup made its appearance. Many of the techniques used by pre-stirrup lancers and horse archers are now lost, as these skills fell out of use, but it is known that a lance charge could be delivered without stirrups. The couched lance, held tightly under the arm, is mainly associated with the medieval period. Earlier lancers used their weapons differently, and as a rule used relatively light spears which could nevertheless transfix a man through body armour. A cavalryman could use his weapon overhand to thrust

downwards, or under the arm. A skilled lancer could engage targets not only to his front but all around him, allowing cavalrymen to engage in what amounted to ride-by spearings of enemy troops. Thus there was a fair amount of subtlety possible with a lance, though aiming the point from a moving horse, with the shaft flexing with every step, was something of a challenge.

A lance could be broken or lost in combat, so a backup weapon was necessary. Swords were popular, largely because they were more convenient to carry than most other weapons and were effective, too. Cavalry swords needed a certain amount of reach, so even in the Roman army, which favoured a short sword for infantry, cavalry weapons were longer to allow the soldier to reach his target.

The massed charge of cavalry could sometimes cause enemy forces to break up and scatter out of fear alone. In this case, and after a victorious battle, cavalry were excellent for pursuit as they could move faster than a running man and maintain pursuit for long periods without tiring. This is another traditional cavalry role – exploiting a victory to give it strategic value.

Generally speaking, lighter cavalry were better for pursuit than heavy troops, and were also more useful as scouts and foragers. Thus the cavalry armies often included lighter horsemen to fill these roles. Lighter cavalry were sometimes equipped with bows or javelins to give missile support, and sometimes with hand weapons for shock effect. One tactic was to use heavy cavalry for the initial charge, then follow up with more lightly protected horsemen to add weight and momentum to the attack.

Some cavalry armies incorporated light and heavy cavalry, often obtaining horse archers by recruiting tribes who possessed the requisite skills as mercenaries or allies. This allowed a combined-arms approach to combat, with the lighter cavalry softening up the enemy with missile fire (and also undertaking scouting and similar tasks) while the heavy horse were tasked with delivering the shock action that would break an enemy force.

Alternatively, many armies that relied on heavy cavalry for their main striking power fielded infantry in support. These ranged from untrained levies handed a spear and herded along to the battlefield, to highly trained professional troops who could be relied upon to turn in a good performance when necessary.

The combined-arms approach had several advantages, notably flexibility. A balanced army could fight in terrain that cavalry would find too restrictive, and could react to changing circumstances. If the cavalry were driven off, they could retire and rally behind the support of their infantry – or flee and leave the infantry behind as a speed-bump to slow pursuit.

Battle of Carrhae (53 BC)

The Roman invasion of Parthia in 54–53 BC came about mainly as a result of the ambitions of Marcus Licinius Crassus, who wanted to win military glory to match that of his allies, Pompey and Caesar. Crassus had at his command seven legions (with their

> " EQUITES CATAPHRACTI, FERREA OMNI SPECIE (CATAPHRACT HORSEMEN, IRON IN THE WHOLE APPEARANCE). "
>
> SALLUST (86–34 BC)

supporting troops) and around 7000 cavalry, and after a long march through what is now Turkey his army entered Parthian territory. Almost immediately, several cities surrendered in the face of Crassus' considerable force. Burdened by large quantities of booty, the Romans garrisoned the cities they had taken and waited out the winter rains in comfortable quarters.

The Romans were extremely confident, having vanquished all manner of foes in the past. However, the Parthian mode of warfare was entirely new to the Romans, who knew very little about their new opponents. They could have found a useful ally in the King of Armenia, whose knowledge of Parthian affairs was accompanied by an army that could fight in the Parthian manner. However, the Parthian king, Orodes II, wisely sent troops into Armenia to keep the Armenians busy and thus took them out of the equation.

The Romans advanced across the desert towards Seleucia. They were met by the Parthians' regional force which was entirely composed of cavalry. Crassus ordered his army to form an extended line of battle and when it became obvious that there was absolutely nothing to secure his flanks on, he amended this order. The Roman force then redeployed into a hollow square. This formation has been used for centuries by infantry facing cavalry or when surrounded by large numbers of light troops. However, the Roman legionaries lacked missile weapons with much range. Their *pila* were normally thrown from 15m (16 yards) or so. If the Parthians charged the square, the Romans could fight in their accustomed manner. If not, they were little more than targets.

Having laboriously formed their flankless formation, the Romans resumed their march at a slow pace until the Parthian army came in sight. At this point 6000 of the 7000 cavalry in Crassus' force departed at speed. They were Arab mercenaries and while they were willing to take risks they were also aware that the Parthians were a formidable enemy. A

Roman defeat seemed imminent, and they did not want to be part of it.

The Parthian force consisted of about 1000 heavily armoured cataphracts supported by 10,000 horse archers. These surrounded the Roman square and began shooting into it. Within the Roman formation, about 1500 of the light troops had bows. These shot back as best they could, but they were vastly outmatched in terms of both numbers and power of their bows. Besides, the Roman archers were shooting at fast-moving horsemen while the Parthians could scarcely miss the giant square target in front of them.

The Romans tried to counter-attack, which at first seemed to go well. The Parthians fled, shooting backwards as they went. Once they had drawn the remaining Roman cavalry and its supporting infantry away from the main force, the 'fleeing' Parthians turned to fight and were joined by more of their comrades. As the counter-attacking force was being shot down, the cavalry did their best to cover their comrades' retreat to the main force. They managed to

get into contact but were overmatched by the Parthian cataphracts' armour and weapons. Five hundred of the 5500 who had taken part in the counter-attack were taken prisoner. The rest were killed.

While this was going on, Parthian horse archers continued to shoot into the main force, wearing it down. Groups of cataphracts began making local attacks, hitting a section of the square then pulling back when the fight seemed to be going against them. They could do this thanks to their superior mobility.

The Romans were saved from further slaughter by nightfall, and made off during the hours of darkness.

CARRHAE 53 BC

Surrounded by horse archers and under heavy fire, the primarily infantry Roman force to counter-attack. Once separated from the main body, the counter-attacking force was overwhelmed, after which the main Roman force was steadily worn down.

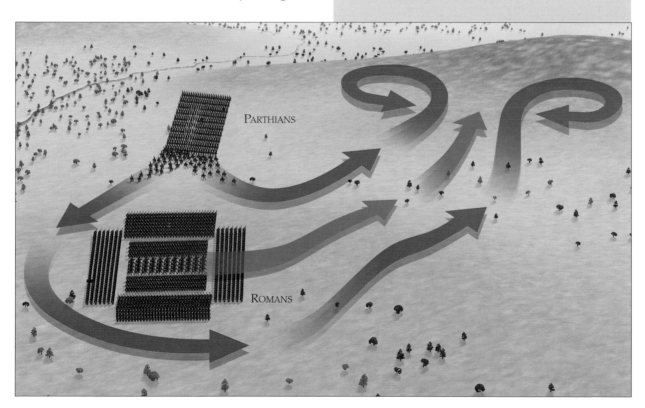

PARTHIANS

ROMANS

▲ Medieval illustration of the Battle of Carrhae. Crassus' ill-considered attempt to seek military glory in Parthia resulted in disaster and defeat at the hands of far more mobile troops.

They found refuge in the town of Carrhae, which had a Roman garrison. However, shortage of supplies forced a further retreat towards Armenia. Of the 42,000 Roman and allied troops that fought at Carrhae, only about 5000 escaped. The remainder were killed or captured in the battle or during attempts to retreat to safe territory.

THE BYZANTINE EMPIRE

The Byzantine Empire (also called the Eastern Roman Empire) eventually became resigned to the impossibility of regaining the Western one. Exactly when this occurred is open to much speculation, but

with Arab forces overrunning nearby lands from AD 634 onwards, attention became focussed closer to home.

Despite external threats and internal troubles, the Byzantine Empire remained a major power for centuries more. From 1025 onwards, a decline began but even then there were periods of resurgence. However, Byzantine fortunes gradually declined until 1453, when Constantinople fell to the Ottoman Turks. With the death of the last Byzantine ruler, Constantine XI, the Byzantine Empire finally came to an end, and with it the last vestiges of the Roman Empire.

The military system used by the Eastern Empire remained characteristically Roman long after it began styling itself the Byzantine Empire, and it was this military system, albeit deploying forces rather different from the classically Roman infantry legions, that preserved the empire though its long and turbulent history.

Equipment and Organization

The Byzantine Empire was divided into provinces, called *themes*, with a commander assigned to each to oversee its defences. This commander also had authority in some civil matters, ensuring that defence was never compromised by other considerations.

Troops were raised in each *theme* under a system of universal conscription. Once raised, troops were assigned to units of 300–400 men which formed the basic tactical unit and was the equivalent of the Roman cohort. Five to eight units made up a *turma* commanded by a general, with two or three *turmae* forming what amounted to a corps.

The *thematic* troops raised in the provinces were probably not regulars. More likely they were semi-professional militia or territorial troops who were paid a supplement over and above their normal earnings. They successfully resisted invasion on several occasions, but also rebelled from time to time, and were difficult to put down.

A body of professional troops was also maintained, termed *tagmata*. The *tagmata* started out as palace guard regiments of no combat value, but gradually evolved into a real fighting force with high standards of equipment and training. These units formed the backbone of Byzantine campaign forces from the eighth century AD onwards.

CATALAUNIAN FIELD AD 451

The Hunnic invasion of Europe was finally halted in a hard-fought 'soldiers' battle' at the Catalaunian Field. Although not a decisive defeat, the battle began a decline in Hunnic military fortunes from which the cavalry army could not recover.

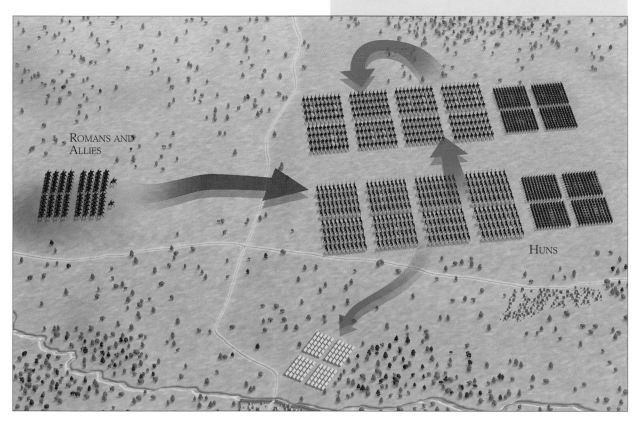

ROMANS AND ALLIES

HUNS

Units of cavalry and infantry were of the same size, and the Empire as a whole fielded about equal numbers of infantry and cavalry. Disciplined infantry equipped with long spears and backed up by archers were well regarded by the Byzantine military, perhaps as a result of the Roman legacy. The Byzantine army's excellent logistics system was another Roman legacy.

Unlike the classic Roman legions, it was the armoured cavalry that formed the main striking arm. The cataphracts used by Byzantine forces varied from time to time as new technologies and tactics were tried out. At times, shields were carried; at others, not. Armour that was extremely heavy on the front but much lighter at the back was also experimented with.

The role of the cataphracts never changed however. They were shock troops, with good mobility and excellent protection, intended to inflict defeat upon any enemy they encountered. Their heavy armour enabled them to survive in the midst of the most intense combat, and their discipline made it possible to rally even after a serious setback.

Some cataphracts carried bows and would give fire support to their comrades. Solid formations of infantry, steady enough to resist the charge, could be shot up from a distance. However, the main weapon of the heavy cavalry was the lance. Once the enemy were shaken or gaps had been made in their formation, the cataphracts charged home.

BYZANTINE CATAPHRACT, AD 300
The Byzantine cataphract was perhaps the ultimate development of armoured cavalry. Equipped with bow, lance and sword, cataphracts could deal with almost any situation, bringing formidable fighting power to bear using the mobility of their horses.

ENDNOTES: TRANSITION TO THE MEDIEVAL PERIOD

At the beginning of the Migration Period, military power rested with infantry in most areas. Not always the well-drilled chequerboard infantry of the Roman legions, but competent footsoldiers all the same. As a general rule, most states and tribes had a military class, which included the smaller ruling class.

Members of the military class provided professional soldiers and the nobles who led them in battle. This force was then augmented by troops levied or otherwise raised for the duration of the crisis. These men were not professionals, but might have some experience and even some training if their rulers thought it useful.

Over time, the military class in most regions began to make increasing use of horses. At first perhaps as transport to and from the battlefield, but soon the élite were fighting from horseback. This offered many advantages besides the obvious one; a man on a horse has the advantage of height over a soldier on foot. Horsemen could wear heavier armour without becoming excessively burdened by it, and were more mobile than infantry. Their appearance was intimidating, especially to ill-trained tribal militiamen. A blow delivered from above, or a spear charged home from a galloping horse, had a greater effect than a blow struck with strength of arm alone. Thus there was a gradual move towards a mounted élite, sometimes backed up by lesser mounted troops. However, the system did not greatly change. The military class still formed a small segment of society yet provided most of that society's fighting power.

A heavily armoured horseman was an expensive investment but represented a formidable concentration of combat capability, to the point where masses of infantry became increasingly irrelevant on the battlefield. Or at least, many societies thought so. There were additional advantages in concentrating military capability in a small ruling class. Any rebellion by the lower orders was far less likely to succeed if the common folk lacked military experience and effective weapons.

Thus the move from noble-led infantry forces to a military system based around a small élite mounted and armoured at great expense was a logical one. It did, however, result in a move away from an organized military system of professional soldiers and back to one of individual warriors.

This move was not entirely complete. Most states deployed some skilled infantry – often archers or other missile troops – in addition to their cavalry, and rounded out their force with a levy of cheaply equipped spearmen or similar infantry. For sieges and garrison work, infantry were also necessary and in some cases, well trained and equipped. Nor was the move from barbarian infantry to armoured cavalry either universal or simultaneous.

However, as the medieval period continued, the military systems of most states were based upon noble heavy cavalry who were warriors rather than soldiers. The drill and discipline needed to maintain the cohesion of a legion or a phalanx in action was replaced by individual fighting prowess and courage in battle.

In some ways this was a retrograde step; the hunter-gatherer-turned-warrior had become a soldier and evolved his art to a high pitch, only to return once more to being an individual among a group of warriors capable of only the most basic unit evolutions. Yet the cycle continues as the needs of society change.

Today's armed forces are made up of soldiers rather than warriors, led by professional officers rather than socially appointed nobles or heroic leaders. Yet there are times when a soldier must also be a warrior, fighting as part of a loose warband of his peers or even alone. Special forces raiding parties, small patrols, squads manning checkpoints, sniper teams and other small units, often operating far from support, must function as both disciplined soldiers and individual warriors.

It would seem that the line between warrior and soldier has always been, and remains, a fine one.

BIBLIOIGRAPHY

Adcock, Frank E. *The Greek and Macedonian Art of War.* Berkeley, University of California Press, 1957.

Anderson, J.K. *Military Theory and Practice in the Age of Xenophon.* Berkeley, University of California Press.

Banks, A. *A World Atlas of Military History.* London, Seeley Service & Co, 1973.

Barker, P. *Armies and Enemies of Imperial Rome.* Worthing, Wargames Research Group, 1981.

Caesar, Julius. *Commentaries.* (Ed. and trans. John Warrington), London, 1953.

Campbell, Duncan B. *Greek and Roman Artillery, 399BC– AD363.* Oxford, Osprey Publishing, 2003.

Carter, John M. *The Battle of Actium.* London, Hamish Hamilton, 1970.

Casson, Lionel. *The Ancient Mariners, Seafarers and Sea Fighters of the Mediterranean in Ancient Times.* 2nd ed., Princeton, Princeton University Press, 1991.

Connolly, P. *Greece and Rome at War.* London, Macdonald Phoebus, 1981; American ed. Englewood Cliffs, Prentice-Hall Incorporated, 1981.

Ducrey, Pierre. *Warfare in Ancient Greece.* (Trans. Janet Lloyd). New York, Schocken Books, 1986.

Ellis, John. *Cavalry: The History of Mounted Warfare.* New York, G. P. Putnam's Sons, 1978.

Ferrill, Arther. *The Origins of War: from the Stone Age to Alexander the Great.* New York, Thames and Hudson, 1985.

Fields, Nic. *The Hun.* Oxford, Osprey Publishing, 2006.

Fuller, J.F.C. *The Generalship of Alexander the Great.* Wordsworth Military Library, Cambridge, 1998.

Gardiner, Robert (ed). *The Age of the Galley.* London, Conway Maritime Press, 1995.

Garlan, Yvon. *War in the Ancient World.* (trans. Janet Lloyd), London, Chatto & Windus, 1975.

Gibbon, Edward. *The Decline and Fall of the Roman Empire,* two vols., Everyman's Library Series, New York, Knopf, 1993.

Gilliver, C. M. *The Roman Art of War.* Stroud,Gloucestershire, Tempus, 1999.

Goldsworthy, Adrian. *Roman Warfare.* London, Cassell, 2000.

Goldsworthy, Adrian. *The Punic Wars.* London, Cassell, 2000.

Goodfellow, D., ed. *Atlas of Military History.* London, Collins, 2004.

Grant, M. *Romans.* Edinburgh, Thomas Nelson & Sons Ltd, 1960.

Grayson, A.K. 'Assyrian Civilisation' in J. Boardman et al. (eds). *Cambridge Ancient History.* Cambridge, Cambridge University Press, 1991, p.194–228.

Green, Peter. *The Year of Salamis, 480–479 BC.* London, Weidenfeld and Nicolson, 1970.

Green, Peter. *The Greco–Persian Wars.* Berkeley, University of California Press, 1996.

Gurval, Robert A. *Actium and Augustus.* Ann Arbor, University of Michigan Press, 1995.

Hackett, J. ed. *Warfare in the Ancient World.* London, Sidgwick and Jackson, 1989.

Hanson, Victor Davis (ed). *Hoplites: the Classical Greek Battle Experience.* London, Routledge, 1991.

Hanson, Victor Davis. *The Wars of the Ancient Greeks.* London, Cassell, 1999.

Head D. *Armies of the Macedonian and Punic Wars, 359BC–146BC.* Worthing, Wargames Research Group, 1982.

Healy, Mark. *The Ancient Assyrians.* Oxford, Osprey Publishing, 1991.

Heather, Peter J. *The Fall of the Roman Empire: A New History of Rome and the Barbarians.* New York, Oxford University Press, 2006.

Holmes, R. *The World Atlas of Warfare*. London, Mitchell Beazley, 1988.

Humble, Richard. *Warfare in the Ancient World*. London, Cassell, 1980.

Hyland, Ann. *Equus: The Horse in the Roman World*. London and New Haven, Yale University Press, 1990.

Josephus. *The Jewish War*. London, Penguin Classics, 1981.

Keegan, John. *A History of Warfare*. London, Hutchinson, 1993.

Kern, P.B. *Ancient Siege Warfare*. London, Souvenir, 1999.

Lazenby, J. F. *The First Punic War*. Stanford, Stanford University Press, 1996.

Leach, John. *Pompey the Great*. London, Croom Helm, 1978.

Livy. *History of Rome*. (trans. B. O. Foster, E. T. Sage, and A. C.Schlesinger), Loeb Series. 14 vols. Cambridge, Mass., 1919–1957.

Livy. *The War with Hannibal*. London, Penguin Classics, 1970.

Marsden, E.W. *Greek and Roman Artillery*. Oxford, Clarendon Press, 1971.

May, Elmer C. *Gerald P. Stadler, and John F.Votaw. Ancient and Medieval Warfare*. The West Point Military History series, Wayne, N.J., Avery Pub. Group, 1984.

McCartney, Eugene S. *Warfare by Land and Sea*. New York, Cooper Square Publishers, 1963.

Morrison, J.S., J.F. Coates and N.B. Rankov. *The Athenian Trireme*. 2nd ed., Cambridge, Cambridge University Press, 2000.

Perrett, B. *The Battle Book*. London, Arms and Armour Press, 1992.

Plutarch. *The Fall of the Roman Republic*. London, Penguin Classics, 2005.

Plutarch. *Lives*. New York, Penguin, 1987.

Pritchett, W.K. *Ancient Greek Military Practices. Part I*, University of California Publications, Classical Studies, vol. 7, Berkeley, University of California Press, 1971.

Pritchett, W.K. *The Greek State at War. Part II*, Berkeley, University of California Press, 1974.

Richmond, I.A. 'The Roman Siege-works at Masàda, Israel', *Journal of Roman Studies*, 1962, p.142–155.

Rodgers, William Ledyard. *Greek and Roman Naval Warfare*. Annapolis, US Naval Institute, 1964.

Sage, Michael M. *Warfare in Ancient Greece: a Sourcebook*. London, Routledge, 1996.

Shipley, G. *The Greek World after Alexander, 323–30BC*. London, Routledge.

Simkins, Michael. *The Roman Army from Caesar to Trajan*. Osprey Publishing, 1992.

Stark, F. *Rome on the Euphrates*. London, John Murray, 1966.

Starr, Chester G. *The Influence of Sea Power on Ancient History*. New York, Oxford University Press, 1989.

Tacitus. *The Histories*. London, Penguin Classics, 1975.

Thucydides. *History of the Peloponnesian War*. London, 1954.

Warry, John G. *Warfare in the Classical World: An Illustrated Encyclopedia of Weapons, Warriors, and Warfare in the Ancient Civilisations of Greece and Rome*. Norman, University of Oklahoma Press, 1995.

Webster, G. *The Roman Imperial Army*. London, Adam and Charles Black, 1974.

Whitby, Michael. *Rome at War, AD 293–696*. Oxford, Osprey, 2002.

Vegetius. 'The Military Institutions of the Romans' in T. R. Phillips (ed.) *Roots of Strategy*. Harrisburg, 1940.

Yadin, Y. *The Art of Warfare in Biblical Lands*. London, McGraw Hill, 1963.

Yadin, Y. *Masada, Herod's Fortress and the Zealot's Last Stand*. London, Weidenfeld and Nicolson, 1966.

INDEX